When I V

By Edythe Nelson C...

Psalm 91

Edythe Nelson

Recognitions

A very special thanks to my cousin Marna Benion, who was my adviser, and editor. She spent day and weeks editing my book, only to have some of it "fly away" off my computer. I then rewrote areas, changed, added and deleted until I no longer had the courage to ask her to "redo" any more editing. So, where there are mistakes...they are mine and mine alone. And besides her hours of editing, she also referred me to Rhonda Kay Edwards.

To Kay Edwards, a published author, I thank you over and over. I have never met you, but your time and patience on instructing me with getting the book published, doing the formatting, picking out book covers, and doing the final procedures, exemplifies a true Christian in giving of one's self.

Lastly to my husband, Jerry. He has eaten fast food often, did laundry, cleaned, been patient over the many times he heard me say, "oh no", when I accidentally deleted something, and on and on. Thank you dear for your encouragement, love and long suffering.

I wrote this as "I remembered things" as accurately as possible. All my siblings have passed on and an unable to verify my stories. But like many siblings, their view point may have been. "no siree, I was the one that did so and so and you were the one that didn't". Be that as it may, I hope you will enjoy reading my childhood journey as much as I did reliving it.

Introduction

The youngest of ten children, I was born at home. My siblings did not know my mother was pregnant until the day I was delivered. It was not common to speak of being pregnant in the 1930's. Expectant mothers wore loose fitting clothing to disguise the pregnancy, which is a stark contrast with today's world where tight-fitting tee shirts are the norm for displaying the pregnancy. Why things had to be so secretive, I don't know. Most pregnant women were married back then, and so it wasn't a matter of legality. My two oldest brothers were twins and only lived to be a couple of days old, and so basically our family consisted of eight children and Mom and Pop.

The closest sibling to me in age was my brother Carl. He was eight years older than me. After Carl was my sister Bee, ten years older, and my sister Wanda, twelve years older. The next four were brothers. They were old enough to be my father, and believe me they assumed that position. I recall being spanked by most of them; however, having parent aged brothers came with some perks. This will be revealed later.

Apparently, my mother waited to give birth, until my siblings were conveniently in school for the day. Whew...how did she managed that? When Wanda, Bee, and Carl returned home after school that day, Mom asked Carl to go get a hankie out of the clothes basket for her. Our clothes basket was oval in shape and served many purposes including cradling a newborn. As the story goes, Carl ran into the bedroom and all but had me standing on my head as he searched for a handkerchief for Mom. He kept digging and digging around and finally came back to the living room where Mom and Pop were waiting, exclaiming that he couldn't find a hankie. Mom told him to go back again and look carefully at the top of the basket. He did so, and hollered that there was a baby in the basket. Upon hearing that, my sisters came running to see the baby, too. What a surprise that must have been!

When I was born my four oldest brothers had graduated from high school. Two were still on the farm helping and two had left home. My brother Cecil said it was quite a shock when he received a letter from home stating that Mom had given birth to a little girl.

This book then tells the stories of where and how we lived as I remember them. All the way from South Dakota to Iowa. Hopefully it will give you an insight of how farm life was then, compared to farm life now. What it was like to be raised by siblings and how life carried on without a mother.

Chapter One

The Johnny Place

When I was a child, I thought like a child, I reasoned like a child. I Corinthians 13:11.

My parents were renters and moved quite often. I don't know the reasoning behind the moves unless the grass looked greener on the other side. To distinguish between the different places we rented, we gave each place a name. This chapter is devoted to the Johnny Place which contains my earliest memories. I will try to give you a full picture of our neighborhood, town, events, and what our house was like.

We lived in a farming community with friendly neighbors, and therefore, exchanged lots of visits. When I was three years old, I decided that I wanted to visit our nearest neighbors, the Gundersons. This turned out to be a not so good idea. It was a nice sunny day and I asked my mom if it would be alright if I visited them. She said, "No not today." So, if mama says no, what do you do? Well, you ask Papa. I found him out by the barnyard fence, and he said that I could visit the neighbors. I must have thought if a person is bent on sinning, do it up big. Now my sisters each had a large doll. I was three, and the dolls were as tall as me. I had to drag them as they were too large to carry. In my parents' bedroom, was a slanted ceiling storage closet that covered the full length of the bedroom and that's where the dolls were stored. My sisters hadn't played with dolls in quite a while; after all they had real live me. I was forbidden to play with those dolls unless of course, my sisters were there to protect them.

I must have been a very strong-willed child because after my dad had given me permission to visit the neighbors, I sneaked into the house and got one of the big dolls. I dragged it outside and put it in Carl's Red Flyer wagon. Then off I went in the direction of the neighbors. Now the sound of a metal wagon on a gravel road is hard to conceal. Whether it was that noise or my mother just deciding to check on me certainly curtailed my attempted visit. Whatever the case, I heard my mother calling my name and she was on a fast trot after me. I can still see her in her white dress as she approached. She was gaining ground, so I dropped the tongue of the wagon realizing I couldn't win and climbed into the wagon and began to cry even before I was disciplined. Don't tell Children and Family Services, but during my childhood I was disciplined with switches, belts, and razor straps. I did every kind of dance known to man, even though our family felt dances were worldly and not allowed.

Mom turned the wagon around and pulled me back to the side yard. She picked up a switch and remember the forbidden dance? Never mind. I did the two step with absolutely no training! We often kept a washtub of water under the tree for the men to rinse off when they came in from the field or barnyard. Since it was a very hot day, and the welts were bright red, I got to climb in the tub and cool off. That was one day, I didn't like the color red. My father got the story from my mother, and the lesson he taught me was that, "YOU NEVER NEVER ASK ME FOR SOMETHING IF YOU'VE ALREADY ASKED MOM. DO YOU UNDERSTAND?"

My brother Rex often treated me as if I were his child. Whenever he went to town, he would take me with him in our new 1936 gray Ford that Pop just bought. Rex would make it a point to stop at Woolworth's 5 and 10 after he had run his errands. I LOVED licorice candy and it could be purchased for a nickel or dime. At the front of the store was a candy counter with glass bins of candy about eye level. A clerk would scoop up the candy of choice and weigh it. I usually chose jelly beans which had a lot of licorice in the mixture of different colors and flavors. Rex would tell the clerk that I especially liked licorice, and the clerk would patiently take the candy scoop and try to get as much licorice in the mix as possible. She then would deposit the candy into a little white paper sack. Candy corn was my second choice and my third choice was also Pops favorite...orange slices.

There was no need to tell Mom when I had eaten licorice candy because it was usually all over my hands, face, and clothes. On those trips into town, I stood up in the front seat, usually by the driver. There were no child car seats then, and there were consequences. Once Rex had to slam on the brakes, and my head crashed into the windshield. Of course, I cried a lot so we went back to Woolworth's where Rex purchased a red patent leather purse for me. Red was my favorite color and that purse went with me everywhere. However, that purse met its fate as one day Rex put me in the car, and somehow my purse got slammed in the door. Patent leather cracks and my purse was badly cracked. Again, we stopped at Woolworth's, but alas they were out of red children's purses. They did have a white one that Rex bought for me, but it did not replace the red one and therefore I never carried it around as much.

Our house had a large dining room with a dinner table that seated about twelve people. Drop in dinner guests were not uncommon. Adults, young people, relatives, church friends, and neighbors were often seated around that table. Other dining room furnishings consisted of a large rocker, a buffet (which my Dad called the sideboard), a floor console radio, and a potbelly stove that was put up in the winter and taken down in the summer to make more room. My dad's boxes of chocolates were kept on the buffet. I guess I got my love of candy from him. For his birthday (which was in

August) and or for Christmas, he got BIG five-pound boxes of an assortment of chocolates and one or more, three-pound sizes of chocolate covered cherries. (Who ever heard of a pound or twelve-ounce size?)   I had been told not to ask for his candy. So, when he came in the house I would ask him, if he would like a piece of candy, naturally hoping for a piece. Sometimes that worked, other times it didn't.

Breakfast was a big meal, the noon meal was called dinner, and the night meal was supper. (I still call them that unless we are having a sandwich and then that is lunch).   Breakfast was served after the men did the morning chores. Dinner time was when the men needed a break in the heat of the day. We ate supper after the night chores were done. We all waited to eat together matter how late. In the summer, the men would work in the fields until almost dark, then do the chores, and after that eat. Eight or nine p.m. was not out of the ordinary for supper. I would sometimes get so hungry waiting for supper I would feel sick, and Mom would tell me to eat some crackers which usually helped. After supper the ladies, except for me, washed the dishes. I stayed in the dining room with the men who crowded around our radio. We would listen to Fibber Magee and Mollie, Lum and Abner, Amos and Andy and other programs. If music would come on...either my Dad or my brothers would stand me on their knees and hold me tight by my ankles. I would then twirl from side to side and sing "Ooh la la, Ooh la" and clap my hands.

I think our home furnishings were average with the exception of our refrigerator which was run by kerosene. Upon opening the door, a small light bulb gave light by the ice maker as we had electricity at the Johnny Place. In the top section of the refrigerator was a freezer that held ice cube trays, we had three aluminum trays, each fitting in its own shelf. They didn't have the release handles that came with the later models. Removing the ice from the trays was sometimes a challenge. We often resorted to a variety of ways to get the cubes out. Sometimes a dinner knife would work, but that could result in punching a hole through the thin aluminum trays. If this happened, my father would then take a nut and bolt to fill the puncture. We didn't buy new things back then...we fixed them.

To the side of the kitchen was a pantry. Rex would pick me up and we would go into the pantry. It was off limits to me ordinarily. My sister Wanda would yell, "Rex and Edythe are in the pantry", and my mother would feign a look that said we were in trouble! We had a huge bread box in there that sat on the floor. (Gordon had made that in shop class at school and it was intended to hold wood for the stove but we used it for a bread box). I suppose there was bread inside, but what I remember are brown sugar packages. We could reach in and get a huge lump of brown sugar. On the pantry shelf, we could reach for delicious shredded coconut, marshmallows, dried apricots, prunes, dates, and raisins. There was a huge glass jar with a tin lid on the side filled with salted peanut cookies. (The jar was kept from when my parents owned a grocery store and perhaps was used for the sale of cookies or candy). This room was a child's wonderland, and we frequented it often.

Our living room at the Johnny place was furnished with a blue-green sofa and an upholstered chair, a piano which held all the children's graduation pictures on its top, a wooden rocker, the library table, and a pot-bellied stove in the corner during the winter.

Mom and Pop's bedroom was just off the living room. It held their bed, a dresser, my crib and a sewing rocker (a rocker with no arms on either side). Mom could sit there and patch clothes or knit with her arms extended. My brother Gordon made a duplicate of that rocker which I now have in my home. Other than the lights, the only electrical item that I can remember us owning back then was an electric heating pad. My family would use it to warm the crib before bedtime. For safety reasons, they would not allow it to be left in my crib for the night.

The rocking chair in the living room only had one arm, it was not always so. There was a group of ladies from church, called the Women's Missionary Society. I don't recall everything that they did, but they made quilts for one thing. They would take turns meeting in one another homes. The men would usually come that day and help chop wood or help in the field. This was a family event that included children. At noon, a large meal was served for all.

One rather large young lady came to our house on one missionary meeting day. She asked my mother which one of her sons she liked the best. My mother politely replied that she liked them all the same. "Oh," she responded, "surely you like Rex the best, I do." That love fantasy, was short- lived for as she sat in our wooden rocker she somehow wedged herself in it, and couldn't get out. A group of ladies were standing in the kitchen silently laughing with tears running down their cheeks. I didn't know they were laughing tears, as one woman was leaning on the refrigerator by the air vent making her hair blow. As a child, I somehow thought this lady's hair was caught in the refrigerator and was hurt. Others were in the living room, but no one could get the young girl out of the chair. They had to call the men in from outside; one being my brother Rex. They sawed off one arm of the rocker to free her. That was the last time I remember her coming to our house. We had that one-armed chair all the years I lived at home. It did generate a lot of conversation as to why the rocker only had one arm. My Dad would simply say, they had to saw one side off.

On the back side of the kitchen was a stairwell that led to the bedrooms upstairs. For some reason, I was never allowed up there; but that didn't mean I didn't try. I would get as far as the top steps where there was a large landing. It also served as Gordon's bedroom. In that area, he had a desk with pigeon holes in it, and in one of the pigeon-holes, was a toy machine gun small enough to fit in your hand. It was camouflage color and had a small crank on the side. When you turned the handle, sparks would fly out of the end of it to look like it was being fired. He also had a musical instrument, called a sweet potato. It was tan in color and shaped like a fat gun. You blew into it and placed your fingers over the holes like you do a clarinet. On the window in the landing, Gordon had a wire connected to something he called a ham radio. He would let me see him in operation, but it was a quick look because I never got any farther than the landing. It was well worth the spanking though. Looking back, I have often wondered about the other bedrooms and what they were like.

Chapter Two

How I Found Out About the Woodshed

I had lots of fun playing with other kids at the church ladies' meetings. At Aunt Sadie's (not our aunt but our friend's aunt), we made mud pies. She had empty oval cans from smoked oysters that we filled with a dirt and water mixture. After setting in the sun for a while, they would dry out, and we could turn them out and make lovely shaped pies. I was even convinced by older children that this was the real thing, hence my first taste of mud pies. I think some of the ladies' missionary meetings were often prayer meetings too. With kids doing all kinds of things, we were probably first on the list of prayer requests.

One of the things I learned while at one house was, we could lock some of the other kids in the toilet. These toilets were not indoors, but shanties with two and three holes. While I didn't participate in that particular activity when we were at the ladies' missionary meetings, I did try a similar idea at home.

My dad's mother, Grandma Nelson, would come to our house occasionally and spend a few weeks. Her husband had passed away, so she no longer kept her home but took turns staying with her married children

.

I think our home was Grandma's least favorite place to stay, for one reason...ME. She would often have the responsibility of watching me while my siblings were in school and my Mother was about doing all the things a mother does. My mom was not only active in church, but she also was on the school board. In addition, she would also go to various homes as needed to care for the sick. She tended a huge garden, did ironing for her large household, and on and on.

I found out I could get away with lots of stuff with Grandma. Grandma realized the brother that had the greatest influence on me was my brother Rex. So, whenever I would act out, she would step outside and call for Rex. When he came in, I would always be sitting nicely on a chair or doing some quiet activity. He thought Grandma imagined things until...Grandma went to the outhouse. As I was coming out, she needed to go in. So, when she stepped in, I asked her if she would like me to lock the door. In no uncertain terms she yelled, "NO". Most outhouses had a lock on the outside to keep animals from pushing it open and making a home there. I immediately locked the door leaving her screaming. Rex just happened to be walking through the grape arbor just then and heard her. I got a tremendous spanking from him and of course had to unlock the door. This is when I also found out about the woodshed.

No doubt the toilet incident was relayed to Pop. Because when he came inside from his farm work, he got my attention when he said to me, "DO I NEED TO TAKE YOU TO THE WOODSHED?" Now I didn't know what the woodshed was, but the tone of his voice made me think it wasn't a place I wanted to go. When I started to cry, it became all the worse...for then the statement came. "• stop your crying, or I'll give you something to cry about• ." So, for me, the woodshed was a dreaded place to avoid.

While on the subject of Grandma; Carl had a rubber knife. The blade was painted silver so I suppose it looked real. I would grab that knife and tell Grandma I was going to stab myself. She would yell, "No, no, " and try to grab it from me. Most of the time she was sitting in the rocker by the pot belly stove and I could easily out run her.

I would stand on chairs and jump off and make a lot of noise when we were alone. I did all kinds of things to aggravate her. When I got older and visited her, I think her memories of me as a young child giving her a rough time, never faded. She didn't seem to enjoy my visits much.

Evidently, Grandma didn't like dolls. When we would go visit Grandma in Iowa, I would want to take my newest doll to show her and Pop would say "• Leave your doll in the car, Edythe." Years later, he told me the reason why. He said Grandma thought they were like idols. It was he that persuaded Ma to let his younger twin sisters have a doll when they were little girls. (My father and his siblings called their parents Ma and Pa.)

One of the pieces of furniture I was allowed to stand on, was the library table and only when I was lifted and placed there. When someone stood me on the library table, it was to sing. Apparently, I learned to sing quite a few songs at a young age. My sister-in-law Bea told me the first time she came to visit, Rex stood me on the library table, and I sang "School Days." Evidently standing on the library table was practice for standing on a stage. My parents entered me into a kids' talent show on the radio. I remember going to the radio studio where there were lots of kids. I didn't have any nice anklets...so a lady Evangelist by the name of Sis Batherm, stood me on a table and put new anklets on my feet. The anklets didn't make me sing any better because a twelve-year-old boy won. Even though I didn't win, it launched me into a singing career that lasted until I was about fourteen. But from time to time I sang on church programs on the radio station WNAX, which aired out of Yankton, South Dakota and Sioux City,

Iowa.

Chapter Three

The Town of Meckling and the Tabernacle

Our church was called the Tabernacle. It was the Assemblies of God Church in Meckling, South Dakota. I thought it was called the Tabernacle because the building was a sheet metal Quonset hut. Two other churches in town were the Congregational Church and a Lutheran church which had the traditional type church buildings. Until I was nearly five, the Tabernacle was the only church I knew. In fact, I later learned that my mother was with a group of five ladies that prayed for an Assemblies of God church to be birthed there and it became the first Assemblies of God church in the state of South Dakota. Church was a great place and the friendships were so close it seemed as though we were related when in fact none were our relatives.

The church had electricity, but there was no running water, and we used an outhouse. It didn't even belong to the church, but was owned by a neighbor. In the winter, sometimes if we needed the facility we could walk over to the parsonage which was just around the corner and use their indoor one.

The Tabernacle floors were made of sawdust. I sat between Mom and Pop. Sometimes on Pop's lap. But I was taught to be very quiet during church. No toys were allowed from home. My mom showed me how to make twin dolls with a handkerchief, or occasionally I could have paper and pencil for scribbling. The most fun was to take my shoes and make roads in the sawdust. No matter if I played with my shoes in the sawdust or not, everyone including me, had to empty their shoes before going in the house after a church service.

On the back of the church was a picture of a cradle. It was called the cradle roll. From it hung ribbons with pictures of the babies from the church. The pictures were mounted on a piece of cardboard and hung diagonally. Someone would carry me back there and show me my picture. I still have my cradle roll picture. Children were on the cradle roll until age three, after which you had a Sunday School class to attend. Nurseries were not heard of. I remember the little children's red painted chairs in our class. We were given picture cards of a story from the Bible that we got to bring home each Sunday. My dad would give me a penny to put in the offering. The penny would be tied to the corner of my child size handkerchief. The teacher would then undo the penny and put it in an offering plate. Don't ask me why, but children would often chew on the corner of their hankies. And if the knot was tied hard and it was wet, it was almost impossible to remove. Yukky! All I can say is, I'm glad things have changed in that area.

My father was one of the deacons, and I was to be an example of good behavior. If I was not, I got thumped on the head or had my ear pulled as a signal to shape up. We sat up near the front of the church, in the pews. Behind the rows of pews were wooden folding chairs if needed, to accommodate a larger crowd.

One of my dad's jobs was serving communion. Evidently, the deacons were assigned different isles. So, when the time came for my Dad to fulfill that service, I would get off his lap and sit right next to the aisle. The reason was a Bro. Hollingsworth also served communion. When he passed our pew, he would always reach over and pat me on the head. At communion time, I remember him singing, "At the Cross, At the Cross"• as he passed by. Children can't remember how they are treated. I did, and it was a wonderful feeling to be acknowledged and treated so special; even if it was just a pat on the head.

Because we had such a big family, we would have to make two trips with the car to church. I think I was usually in the last load. One Sunday evening we were late and as I said my parents sat near the front of the church. They tell me that as my dad carried me walking towards the front of the church trying to be inconspicuous, I proceeded to yell out, "Hi folks" as we passed all the pews.

My mother had terrible headaches. I suspect due to high blood pressure. On one particular Sunday evening, it was so severe she had to leave the church; but not before she saw my sister Wanda acting the part of an angel from the balcony. Immediately afterward she had to leave. I ran after her because sitting quietly was not fun. She had already told me to stay, but about the time I got to the door, I saw some children doing their part in the program and wanted to run back. Since I had already disobeyed I had to go home, and I missed out on the rest of the program.

Sometimes during the summer, we would have dinner on the grounds at the Tabernacle. The only thing I really remember about that, was in front of the church was a large tree stump and a girl four or five years older than me, was standing on it twirling around in her yellow taffeta dress. She was eating something I had never seen before, and so I asked her what it was. She said, "It's an olive, and you can't have any because you are too little."• After that I couldn't wait to taste an olive. I never had one until I was in my early teens, but I knew immediately when I tasted it, I was going to like it! I also learned that the tables that held the food were nothing but saw horses with pieces of lumber placed on them and covered with table cloths. Folding chairs were brought outside from the church and blankets were placed on the ground for the children.

Evening church didn't start until eight p.m. since most of the congregation were from a farming community. It certainly wasn't uncommon for services to last very late at night. There was a prayer room right behind the platform. It had wood floors, and I suspect served as a Sunday School classroom on Sunday mornings. Nonetheless, after every service, people moved to the prayer room. It had long benches, the full length of the platform, secured to the wall on each side of the room. Had it been out front, it may have been called an altar. But we didn't have an altar probably because of the sawdust. Anyway, people would pray until the wee hours of the night. Lots of stories of answered prayer came from those times. People obviously enjoyed talking to God longer then than we do now.

Every adult in our church had a title. It was always Brother and Sister, and the last name accompanied that. Our Pastors were Brother and Sister Gottwald and I believe their favorite hymn was, "Look to the Lamb of God". It seemed like we sang it every service. The ones that started the church were Brother and Sister George, and were lifelong friends.

We had lots of traveling preachers come through, and many stayed at our house. People miss out a lot today by not having missionaries and evangelists stay in their homes. Such interesting stories and lessons were learned from them. The following is a list of people that I remember either speaking at our church or staying in our home: Sister Batherm, The Lundstrom's, the Lindquist's, The Webb's, The George's. The Argues', and C.T. Beem. Brother Webb would always ask me if he could pick me up by my ears. He would place his hands on either side of my head over my ears and lift me up. I can remember being scared, but always running to him when he came.

CT Beem later became well-known when he became a radio announcer on the Revival-time radio program, but to me, he was like a relative. My brother Marvin, or MC. as we called him and CT went to North Central Bible College together. I believe CT was in the first graduating class and my brother MC the second class. Since CT was from our church, Pop hired him and my brother MC to work in the fields in the summer to earn money for their fall semester. I heard about this story later on in life which was: MC figured out a way to cut the weeds out of the corn rows quicker than hoeing them out. If they took their hoes and scraped them across the top...it would get the weeds out to ground level. Then they could take a nap in between the corn rows. My father seemed not to be the wiser. But CT couldn't stand it. He came to my Father wanting to give the money back. My Father told him he had been satisfied with the work and refused the money. So, CT felt forgiven. I can't imagine my brother doing such a thing as he was always like "Honest Abe".

Some of the Women's Missionary Meetings were held at the Parsonage and we kids would have a wonderful time. Across from the Parsonage lived a lady by the name of Sis. Dunbar who must have been a widow. She had an older son who talked us younger kids into going to Mr. Young's grocery store one day. He said if we went there we could get candy. None of us had any money, but a group of us kids went into Mr. Young's grocery store and asked him for candy. I remember what I got, which was a BB bat sucker. I still picture Mr. Young as he often stood outside the grocery store in his white apron. I remember him especially well that day! Somehow, my parents found out about the candy, and my dad marched me inside the store to tell him, that my father said I had to pay for my candy. I don't believe I got a spanking that day as Wanda was always my intercessor. She stated that one of the older boys told me I could get it for free, and I had believed him.

Kitty corner across from the grocery store was Overton's gas station. The Overton's had a daughter Peggy, who was my brother Gordon's age. We had huge soap bars from Proctor and Gamble that was stamped, "P and G" in big letters. We teased Gordon and said those letters stood for Peggy and Gordon so they must be going to get married. In the gas station window, was a set of Peggy's doll dishes. One day when we went to get gas, they gave me those dishes. It had plates, cups and saucers, and a teapot. My sister Bee had play dishes that she kept perfect in their original box and her set had tiny spoons, knives, and forks. Occasionally, she would play house with me, and we would use her play set.

Next to the highway was Mr. Gil's Garage. It was an open sided building that you could look in when passing by. It was always very dirty with oil and grease everywhere, and Mr. Gil was always covered with dirt and grease. They didn't have the equipment that they do now, and I believe they had to lay on the ground to get under the cars to work on them.

The church would often have Cottage Prayer Meetings and Brush Arbor Meetings. I think that a Brush Arbor meeting was like a Revival meeting held outdoors under a brush arbor. I remember attending at least one. We walked over a stubble field to get to the brush arbor. I have a picture of myself about three years old walking across that field with a parasol. Mine parasol was child size and was used for shade. (Ladies used parasols in the summer for outdoor events). It must have been on a Sunday as farmers couldn't have attended otherwise.

Chapter Four

The School and the Neighborhood

With eight children, both of my parents had a keen interest in our school. Pop was on the school board while my mom was president of the PTA. She also belonged to a book club that I believe was related to the school. All my siblings went to the Meckling School except me. I was too young to attend, but could visit the school with one of them. Visiting children could go and sit in the seat with their brother or sister, as I usually did with Wanda. I would often attend when there was a party or something special. People celebrated birthdays back then at school, and homemade foods were allowed. Can you imagine?

One day, someone, passed out bubble gum at school. We seldom had gum at home. Our gum consisted of paraffin or wax from off the sealed jelly jars. The jelly gave it a flavor for a while. But if you did get gum, you chewed it, and then you saved it for several days. Wanda happened to have saved hers on the metal strip of her notebook. She came home from school and lay on the couch as she was prone to "sick headaches". While she was on the couch, I spied the gum, took it and got it all over myself. They used kerosene to get it off me and it burned as they scrubbed. A song came out once titled, "Does the Chewing Gum Lose Its Flavor on the Bedpost over Night". Yes, it did, but we would save our gum on the bedpost if we had any. I do recall that Bazooka bubble gum came with a comic strip inside the wrapper and you were sure to lick the wrapper to get all the flavor.

Bee would help with the morning chores and not take the school bus. Mostly because the chores took a long time. As soon as she finished her chores she would run the mile and a half to school and often outrun the bus, I've been told. She was warned never to get in a car with a stranger. So, if one offered, she would stand on the running board.

Our neighbors the Whittaker's had a daughter considerably older than me, and if we ever visited there I got to play with her doll house. It was equipped with all handheld furniture. I never saw anyone else with anything like it during my entire childhood.

We visited the Browns in Vermillion. Their house had burned down, and I believe my family took something to them for their new place. They had a child about my age, whose name I forget, but I do recall that the house had almost no furniture in it. Not even any chairs. That was really strange to me. On the enclosed back porch were some barrels that contained food. One was macaroni. So, the little girl and I took handfuls of macaroni and ate it raw. I remember the crunching sound as we ate. We also used it to play with somehow. How could anyone ever get rid of a barrel of macaroni?

I learned the usual Nursery rhymes and children's songs and was always asked to "perform" by singing or quoting poems and rhymes. Did you ever wonder whoever thought up those nursery rhymes? Whoever Jack was, must have been ADHD. jumping over a candlestick!! I sympathized with poor little Jack Horner sitting in a corner on Christmas Day eating his Christmas pie. Today the parents would have been contacted by CFA. Maybe he was the same Jack that jumped over the candlestick and was getting punished. Well, it is food for thought. Yes, I get a little wacky at times.

One Christmas, I remember getting a toy paddle with a small rubber ball and rubber band attached to it. I would bounce it up and down with the rubber band. However, the rubber band soon snapped - so one of my siblings put it back with a straight pin. Well, that didn't last long, but I saw how it was done. I held a pin in my mouth to fix it and promptly swallowed it. That was checked daily for several days, and I will spare you the details of how it was checked, but it was never found. However, for years, I would feel something sharp stick around my middle area and would let out a scream. My parents mentioned once they thought it was the pin had lodged in my system. Indeed, that feeling lasted until I was in my twenties.

Our friends the Steele's lived in a basement house. I think someone may have started to build a house but somehow only got the basement finished. Across the back was the roof for it, and it was covered with black tar paper. You could walk on the roof, as it was ground level. It had an outdoor cubby hole and in one of those cubby holes was a doll stroller. One day they gave it to me. I have a picture with my doll in it. There was also a small house on the property where I believe their housekeeper named Ethel and her daughter Gwendolyn lived. Gwendolyn was raised with the Steeles' two daughters, as Mrs. Steele had passed away at a young age.

We had a bunk house on our property. That was where hired men slept. Many of the farms had bunk houses. It was a two-story building similar to a garage or a place to store machinery at the ground level. An enclosed stairway led to sleeping quarters over the garage. We girls were never allowed there. It was for men only.

The Hollingsworth's were also lifelong friends. Rhoda Kay was a couple of years younger than me, but I remember playing with her a lot. Cecil worked for them and stayed in their bunk house. Wanda worked as a housekeeper for them as also did my cousin Elinor who came from Iowa to live with us for a while.

The Moore's had a goat named Rex and he did not like me. He ran loose around the yard and when we went to visit them, he would run after me. I was so afraid of him.   Safely inside, Mrs. Moore and her daughter would be making all kinds of crafts and needlework. For one craft, they cut pictures from calendars or magazines, glued them to cardboard pieces, varnished them, and put them together with yarn to make waste baskets.   I had never heard of a waste basket as we use the coal bucket for trash at our house.

There was a train that would go past our house at certain times of the day.   Out front of the house, was a deep ditch and the railroad tracks were elevated about head level. When I heard the train, if MC was at home, he would stand me on his shoulders by the ditch so I could wave at the man in the caboose. It seemed wherever a train was, the man at the caboose had the job of waving. They probably still hold that position.

Mom cut Carl's hair in the dining room. I remember one day looking at the cape she had on him while cutting his hair...and it was my yellow dress. I guess it was just the right size for a cape.

Seemingly one of our neighbors gave us a canary to babysit, which eventually was deserted by its owner. I remember feeding the canary in its cage and Mom would enjoy listening to it singing. So, the punch line is, I don't recall anyone else during my years of growing up, having a bird in its cage in the house. We were special!

Chapter Five

Stories I Heard from my Siblings and Others from my Dad

These things all happened either before I was born, or I was too young to remember the events.

This incident happened when my family lived at the North Place. The folks were at church, and the kids were left at home and in bed for the night. Suddenly they heard someone come in the house. They didn't have electricity then, just kerosene lamps. The lamps were of course, blown out for the night. Cecil grabbed the lamp chimney and stood over the landing of the stairs. It was pitch black, and the man came up the stairs very slowly. The steps creaked each step he took, and when he got to about the top step, he must have heard Cecil breathing, for he turned and went back down the stairs and out of the house. That man almost met his demise there.

Another time the older children sent Gordon out to empty a jar of spoiled canned food. It was night, and they ganged up on him and came around a corner and scared him. It scared him so bad he couldn't let go of the jar. The folks were home that night, and they had to pry his clamped hands loose.

One day the family went to church, and the second load came home and left Wanda at church not knowing which load she was in. When they went back to pick her up...she simply said in her toddler voice..."you got for me"

Gordon and Rex were playing in the barn, and for some reason, the horse in the stall got scared and pinned Rex against the stall. He hit the wall so hard that it broke his finger and the bone was sticking out. Gordon ran to the house and told the folks. They brought him in the house, gathered around and prayed, and it went back in. Pop offered to take him to the doctor, but Rex wanted to believe he was healed. So, it was decided they would wait until morning. When Rex awakened in the morning, even though it looked good, he agreed to go to the Doctor. When the Doctor looked at it he said, "who set your finger?" The answer was "no one". He said, "Well, it's set perfectly, you can go home."

Cecil was with the folks one time when they had a car accident. He nearly bit his tongue in two. They said it was hanging on by a thread. Of course, they rushed him to the doctor – there were no ER's then. Doctors' offices must have been like clinics. I can't ever remember anyone going to the hospital. Everything was taken care of by the doctor and or by prayer. The doctor said he couldn't sew it, so he learned to let it heal by itself and with prayer

.

All of my brothers played a musical instrument. Marvin and Cecil played the trombone. Which Marvin kept up throughout his life time. The other three boys played the trumpet. Rex played throughout most of his lifetime. Wanda, Bee and (me eventually) played the piano. One day Cecil was in a music store in Yankton owned by Lawrence Welk. Cecil was looking over the different instruments and trying out trombones and trumpets. Mr. Welk stepped from behind the counter and immediately offered Cecil a job with his orchestra. Cecil didn't feel the job would go along with his Christian beliefs and declined the offer. Obviously, he was very good though to be invited to play in Welk's orchestra.

My father as a young man worked in a Clothier. In fact, the man's name that owned the store was Swan Nelson, but no relation. Pop learned how to be a sharp dresser and always wanted his family to look well-dressed. If we were in a church program, new clothes were usually sported. In one particular case, Bee was doing a recitation. But before she spoke, she said to the audience, "see my new shoes?"

Sometimes my dad would joke around with people's last names. A neighbor's last name was Heater, but he called the lady Mrs. Furnace when speaking of her to our mom. One day, young Cecil was with his dad at the Heater home. As children, we always addressed an adult with Mr. or Mrs. and never by their first name. I think my Dad must have greeted Mrs. Heater as such, but Cecil spoke up and said, "Yeah, but my dad always calls you Mrs. Furnace". Oops.

Cecil had another story to tell. He had taken his girlfriend to some event in Vermilion, and Pop cautioned him to be aware of the upcoming snowfall, and not stay out too late. Nonetheless, by the time they started home, there were snowdrifts across the road so deep they couldn't go forward or backward. There was nothing to do but to walk to a nearby house where Cecil barely knew the people by name. The man invited Cecil and his friend in the house. Since the family was already in bed, he wasn't too friendly, but he did tell them they could sit by the stove and keep it fueled all night. He said, "When we get up in the morning, then you can go to bed". So that's exactly what happened. His girlfriend took the parent's bed, and Cecil took their children's bed. He said this continued with this uncomfortable situation for three nights. His biggest fear was facing Pop. However, when he got home, Pop didn't say anything, and he didn't either. It was never brought up.

I saw the house where my dad was raised, and even visited there once when I was a teenager. I was impressed with how nice it was. Anyway, my dad said they used to have lots of young folks over for parties. His parents owned a pedal organ which most of his sisters learned to play, and my dad played the harmonica. One night after the guests had left from the party, the kids were sitting around reviewing the night while waiting for the fire to die down. One of the young men at the party was prone to seizures and had asked to play my dad's harmonica, which was granted. His brother Bernie said, "Virdie, (my dad's name) you should never have allowed him to play your harmonica. Now you will have seizures". My dad had been sitting on his leg trying to get warm and apparently it had gone to sleep. When he stood up to go to bed, he fell on the floor. He was sure Bernie was right.

Another story that my dad told was about the night it was pouring down rain, and he was returning home from a date. Since the horses knew their way home, he could wrap the reigns around the buggy knob, and duck down under the overhang and stay fairly dry and go to sleep. When the horses turned into the barn, and my dad started to undo the harness, a voice from the hay mow said, "Hey, your folks said I could sleep in your barn tonight." Being pitch black in there, it scared my dad and he said, "Well you better watch out because I'm pitching my harness over that way."

Grandma was known to feed the hobos and there supposedly was a man's handkerchief tied around the pole by their house which would indicate to other hobos that this was a friendly place. Pop said she usually didn't invite them in, but would fix a plate of food for them to eat on the back porch.

Pops older brother Bernie, and Pop were born on the same day, but Bernie was six years older. Bernie thought at first that Pop was his birthday gift. Pop told me Bernie was quite the dapper young man.

Pop's father, my grandfather, who passed away before I was born, limped. He was bitten by a poisonous snake as a young boy and his muscle atrophied. I asked how they cured it, and was told they packed it in mud.

My dad said at Christmas time the custom was to go to church for a program and often receive some Christmas presents. Usually, the presents were tied to the Christmas tree branches. One year he got a pocket watch. He suspected it was from his Uncle Orley. (His Uncle Orley died not long thereafter when he was riding on the field drag and it flipped up and killed him). On another occasion, Pop saw in a catalog where you could order a watch, fob, and chain. He sent off for it. When it arrived, it was only the fob and chain. He reported it back to the company, but they said, "sorry, the comma was in the wrong place. It should have said watch fob, and chain". So, he lost his money.

Once when my dad was visiting one of his aunts, they were chatting after supper. Someone said, "I milked Blackie" and as they did the door knob rattled. So, someone else said, "I bet I can say I milked Blackie without the door knob rattling." And it rattled again. At that point, they jumped up and blew the lamp out. Apparently, nothing ever came of it...but they didn't throw caution to the wind.

When I was a young child, they didn't always dig post holes and set posts for fences. They would sometimes plant a hedgerow. I got to see the hedgerow my Dad planted as a young man still in use.

My parents owned a grocery store one time in Mt. Zion, Iowa. They gave out calendar plates to their customers at Christmas time, which I have one. The men that sat outside the store on barrels were considered part of the spit and whittle club. Anyway, one snowy day an elderly man who lived alone, died. The doctor needed to be called to verify his death and it was going to be a difficult trip for the old doctor to get there through the snow. A couple of the guys that were loafing decided that they would go out to the deceased man's house, prop him to a sitting position and put a cigar in his mouth as though he was still alive. When the Doc arrived, I guess he nearly had a heart attack.

The usual trick at Halloween was to knock over an outhouse. One year some young folks wanted to tip over a neighbor's outhouse, but the owner had taken a lantern and sat inside to ward off any offenders. The lantern gave off enough light for them to see the old gentleman had fallen asleep. So, they tipped the outhouse over, door down. Pop said you can guess the only way he had to get out.

Another time Pop, his mother and his Uncle Orley went to a night church service. When Uncle Orley took off his top coat, he knocked off the man's wig in the row ahead of them. The man quickly tried to recoup, while Grandma laughed uncontrollably. She had a way of laughing with no smile on her face and no sound, but Pop said her stomach was bouncing up and down. My sister Wanda laughed the same way.

Chapter Six

The Westerville Place

It was customary if farmers were going to move, they would do so in the month of March. The winter crops were out, and the moving was done before the spring planting. I don't remember anything about moving to the Westerville Place. My birthday is in April, and so the move would have been one month before my fourth birthday. The only memory I have other than Pop saying that he had found the perfect place for my swing is just being there. It seemed every time we moved, he would always say there was a perfect place for a swing. Perhaps that was his way of giving me something to look forward to, in case I had any trepidations about moving to a new place.

Lots of changes were in store at the Westerville Place. Bee, Wanda, and Carl finished the school year in Meckling. It was about seven miles away. Close to the end of the school year, Mom had a stroke. Pop and Mom's bedroom was downstairs, but they moved Mom upstairs evidently to a quieter zone. Mom's sister, Aunt Sadie came from Iowa and stayed with us until school was out. I remember liking her very much. I don't have much time frame for things that went on during that period, so things may be out of consecutive order.

My sister Wanda had a little walking cane, that had a furry stuffed monkey attached to it. She got it from the Amusement Park in Sioux City. After Aunt Sadie left, Pop moved upstairs with Mom. Bee, and I took the folks bedroom downstairs. When Mom was in her upstairs room, she would tap on the floor with that cane, and it was my job to see what she wanted. Many times, she would just want me to sing to her. One song I remember singing was "Sing and Smile and Pray." I often sing it yet.

Gordon was in a car with a group of young men when they spied a hub cab lying in the road. That would be worth money! Gordon jumped out of the car to get it, but another car ran over Gordon before he could escape. His back was broken! He spent quite some time in the house healing. Even though Mom was not well enough to do much, she could crochet and knit. I was told that it was therapy for her to get her hands moving. She taught Gordon those crafts while they both recuperated. I especially remember one wine and gray puff rug they made. Together they also crocheted a beautiful bedspread. Incidentally, Gordon kept up that practice most of his life...crocheting and making rugs. I suppose that might seem quite unusual for a man, but not really, I guess. God was a tailor making Adam and Eve's clothes.

Gordon would do light work around the farm, and paid quite a bit of attention to me. When he came in at night from milking, he would sit in the living room. I would crawl on his lap and comb his hair. He would also play hide the thimble with me, (that's exactly what the game was) and he taught me not to lie. Once I tore up pieces of paper and put in his mouth. I told him it was candy, so he swallowed it. I said with wide eyes, "Did you swallow that?" He said, "yes, you told me it was candy." I said, "but it was paper." He said, "well you mustn't tell me that if it isn't candy". I was scared he would get sick or something. As kids were prone to do, they would chew on paper sometimes. My folks told me not to do that, as parts of the paper contained rags which indeed you could often see rag fragments. Well the rags I knew about were very dirty, so believe me, I never ate paper.

I would often talk Carl into telling me a children's fable at night. My favorite one for him to tell was, "Jack and the Beanstalk". He dramatized it so well. Hmm. I wonder if this Jack was any relation to the one that sat in the corner or jumped over the Candle stick. Come to think of it a very nice boy in my first grade was named Jack., so maybe Jack was better than he was made out to be. I told you I get wacky at times.

A road grader would smooth the gravel road that passed by our house which was located quite near the road. I would run out to the road and wave at the operator. He hollered something to me one day, and this is what I thought he said, "Bye run oleon". So, whenever I heard the road grader coming, my family would say, "here comes the Bye run oleon". I would quickly run to the road and wave. Since that was a long-standing joke I asked my sister in later years, what he said. She told me he said, "Hello little girl, how are ya?". Well with the roar of the machine it didn't translate well, I guess. One day, he asked me if I would like to ride in the road grader. (That was back in the days when you could trust everyone). So, he stopped the road grader and helped me up inside. There was a seat, but I remember you could look down and see the ground underneath. There were no floorboards-just the clutches etc. So, of course, that was quite an experience for a little girl.

The barn there was overrun with mice, and the cats couldn't keep up with their control job. So, Pop hired someone much like a traveling salesman that had ferrets. I didn't know much about them, except this man came and showed me what looked like white rats. They were long and skinny. He kept them in a wooden box that had a round hole at the top. I wasn't allowed to watch the "kill", but the ferrets chased after rats and mice. The man stayed and visited awhile, as farm people took time to do that. I meandered out to the barn, and he gave me a couple of pennies. As I said before, you could buy suckers or licorice sticks with a penny, so I didn't forget that.

We had a cistern at the Westerville place. It was located over the mouth of the well and wasn't anchored down. It was sort of a square pump and a handle that you turned around instead of up and down. If you pumped a certain way, it would move off the foundation and you could see the water. That's exactly what happened one day. I went out to pump water into our tin cup (all households kept one hanging by a wire for everyone's use). MC was home upstairs studying. I cranked the pump handle, and it slid over. When it did, I fell to the side of the well hole with my feet dangling down. I could have turned around and crawled away, but instead, I sat with my feet dangling over the hole, screaming. Well, MC heard me screaming and thought I had fallen in as my cries echoed down the well. He came running down the stairs and fell several steps. Yes, he hurt his back, but he came out any way to get me. After that, I wasn't allowed to pump the water.

While living at Westerville Place, I got "pink eye". It was a severe case, and it was awful. I would wake up in the morning, and this must have occurred before Bee, and I moved downstairs because I can remember trying to come downstairs with my eyes matted shut. If they heard me, they would come and help me down since I couldn't see. Someone would get a rag and soak it in warm water and place it over my eyelids until I could open them. Again, the WM's (Women's Missionary) met at our house as we still lived close enough to attend the Tabernacle. But at one of those meetings, I still had the pink eye. I wasn't able to play with the kids and had to stay upstairs the whole time. Bummer. Ooh the wonderful treat served that day. Bee made red jello, and after it had set, she used real whipped cream and whipped it together. It was a lovely pink. She brought me a dish upstairs so that I could have some. I tell you I had great siblings.

When the new school year began, Carl went to school nearby. He was in seventh grade, and that was his first country school. Wanda stayed at Hollingsworth's as a housekeeper and finished her junior year in Meckling. Bee was actually ahead with her schooling for her age, so it was decided she should stay home and take care of Mom and me. She was a grade ahead for her age and graduated right with her age group, even though she sat out the one-year taking care of the household.

Carl's school was very close to the house, and even I could walk there. In fact, Mom and I walked there one day to some party. What I remember was, the teacher hid peanuts in the shell, and we all had a chance to look for them. My mom pointed to a decorative round hole in the library table, where one was hidden. Funny what a person remembers. Carl's birthday was in February, and they had a birthday party for him at our house, with the school kids being invited. One of the games they played was this: They took a table leaf and placed it over a chair and made it kind of a teeter-totter. They would blindfold someone and have them stand on the table leaf in the low position. Then they would take the blindfolded person and place their hands on the shoulders of the person guiding them. The guiding person would move their bodies up and down to make the blindfolded person think they were teetering up and down and then tell them to jump. In actuality, they hadn't moved, but the blindfolded person would think they were up high and when they jumped they would feel so silly because they might only be a few inches off the floor.

The Christmas tree at the Westerville place stood in the corner. That year, my four oldest brothers were all now working in Rapid City. They mailed home a big box of Christmas presents. It came a few days before Christmas, and on the outside, it read, "Do not open before Christmas". It had all kinds of Christmas stickers all over the outside of the box. Christmas morning when the box was opened, inside was a big, big, round red and yellow ball. I was so excited because I knew it was mine. However, there was no name on it, so Pop made me wait until all the designated wrapped gifts were passed out. There at the bottom of the box, was a sticker that had fallen off the ball with my name on it. I had also heard that large balls had a small hard ball inside to make it bounce. So, after it was sort of beat up and lost its color, I took a knife to check that out. Wrong! No small ball inside. Also, I received a doll from my parents that year that I named Verla. She had hair and her eyes opened and closed. She wore a lovely white apron over her clothes.

There is a story as to why the doll was named Verla. When I was born, my parents tried to find a name, which had the same initials as my dad's. His was V.A. and most people called him by his initials. (Funny how so many people went by their initials back then.) My dad was V.A. Three of my brothers went by their initials; M.C., C.M., and H.R. And one of their friends were C.T. Anyway, they couldn't think of any name that they liked that started with a V. So, I was named Edythe. I hated it as a child and still do. The only redeeming factor to me was that it had a little bit of flare with the different spelling. My grandmother sent a letter saying, "I thought of Verla for a first name". They all liked it, but it was too late. It was already registered at the court house. That story was told to me, and so I named my doll Verla, wishing that had been my name.

One of the things that was fun for me when my folks would go to Vermillion shopping was to leave me off at CT Beem's place. He was married and had a daughter Darlene almost my age. They lived in a white house on a corner of the block, and their house had stained glass windows over the top of the regular windows. Ruth would make a paste with flour and water, and give us old magazines that we could cut out pictures and make scrap books. On one particular day, it was Darlene's job to pick up any trash from the yard. The yard was neatly mowed and so different from our yard that was mowed with field equipment.

Another playmate memory coincided with Mom's stroke as I was dropped off at different homes to receive care. I loved going to the Hollingsworth's to play with Rhoda Kay. We were outside making mud pies and for whatever reason that day, I took my spoon and conked her on the head. So, she hit me back. Well, I went in to tell her mama. Her mom said, "Yes, I saw her, but I was looking out the kitchen window, and I saw you hit her first." So, I got busted.

I had to take naps every afternoon. One day I came out of the bedroom and I said, "Do I have to take naps anymore?". Bee answered, "No". Just one simple word. So, I thought there had to be more to it than that, so I repeated my question, and her answer came back, "I said, No". So that was the end of my taking naps.

One day a little girl was at my house, and I told her I sang on the radio. Our radio console floor model was sitting nearby, and she said, "well get behind there and sing". I can see where a child would imagine that was how it was done.

Here are two more stories from Westerville. One is a very exciting one. We had a wood kitchen cook stove and a huge teakettle made from hammered aluminum that always set on the stove. Many people commented on the size of that teakettle as it held a gallon. Every night we would fill it with water so we could have at least warm water to wash our face with when we awakened.

Bee and I were lying in bed, (now remember I was only four) and Bee woke me up and whispered in my ear that someone had just come in the house - meaning - a thief. I whispered back., "I want to go upstairs with Mom and Pop," and she put her hand over my mouth and whispered, "no". We laid very still because about then, someone opened the top dresser drawer which was only inches away from our bed since it was a very small bedroom. Now as silly as it seems, most men would take their pocket watch off at night and put it in their top dresser drawers along with their billfold and/or money. I mean in nearly every household that happened. HOWEVER, since my Dad was upstairs, there was nothing there. Then this man proceeded to go out to the kitchen and empty the teakettle. Not sure what he needed the water for, but he took it outside and then came back in and put the empty teakettle back on the stove. (Nice of him). We lay there until morning. I guess I went back to sleep, but Bee did not. As soon as Pop came down the stairs in the morning, Bee told him the story. He, of course, was skeptical until he checked out the water in the teakettle, which made a believer out of him. He surmised the guy must have needed the water for his car radiator and while getting the water, decided to check for cash.

Well, it was March and we had only lived at the Westerville house a year. But the grass was greener near Yankton...so this time I remember the move. One truck load of furniture was taken to the new place. My folks had kept the refrigerator crate box and Bee and Mom was left to pack it. In that box went our feather tick mattress folded over our framed door size mirror to protect it from breaking. Other light things were packed on top of that. In case you don't know what a feather tick mattress is, it is much like a pillow made with blue denim striped ticking and stuffed with cleaned chicken feathers. It fit the size of the bed, and from time to time one of the quills of the feathers could stick through and prick you. Making a bed to look nice, wasn't like throwing the covers over the bed today. The feathers would all bunch up under you or in one spot as you slept, and would take quite a time in the morning to get the feathers smoothed out to look like a solid mattress.

Anyway, when they arrived at the new place with one cattle truck load full of furniture, it was discovered the people hadn't moved out yet and we had to stay in the Westerville house for the night. The guys unloaded that one load of furniture in the barn and came back. Bee and I had no bed to sleep in, so they partially unloaded the refrigerator box, and we slept there. Refrigerators were pretty narrow then and we barely had enough room to sleep on our sides. I do remember thinking, "What if the mirror breaks underneath the feather tick, and we will both get cut".

The next day we finished the move.

Chapter Seven

The March Place

We moved in March to the "March Place". That is kind of funny when you think about it. We arrived with our last load of belongings, and the people were still there. The house had an add-on kitchen and enclosed porch, a huge bedroom with a black cupboard in it, that people called a sideboard which went from ceiling to floor. Evidently this room had been the kitchen at one time. There was a closet with cupboards in it off the bedroom. (A pantry at one time). As the people were still moving out, and we were waiting to move in, a very kind lady came to me. She said." Come with me; I have something for you". She went to the bedroom closet formerly the pantry and pulled out a beautiful Easter basket. Such beautiful pastel colors I had never seen. I think Easter was soon after we moved in and I kept reminding Mom and Bee about my Easter basket. We certainly had never had anything like that in our family so I wasn't sure what to expect.

The kitchen was large enough to support the cook stove, cupboards, our kitchen table and chairs, and Mom's sewing rocker. Also, there was room for the washing machine to be pulled inside when it was winter. On the back of the kitchen door was our hand towel. It was on rollers, and it covered nearly the full length of the door with a complete loop of toweling. You rolled it around to a dry spot when you wanted to dry your hands. The kitchen sink was merely a cabinet in which you set two wash pans so two men could wash at the same time. The water bucket was placed at the end of the sink When they finished washing, they would throw the water out the back door.

As Bee and Mom sat in the kitchen sewing one day, I began to inquire about the Easter Basket. Those two concocted a story about the Easter bunny coming and that he would put stuff in my basket. I asked how he would get in? Well, there was a long narrow window in the kitchen that had a sliver of glass missing and Bee said." that might be a spot he could get in". I swallowed that hook line and sinker. Then what to do with my basket? Well, it was to go at the end of my crib.

Before you wonder about me in a crib...children were expected to sleep in a crib until they were at least seven years old. You could purchase either a six or seven-year crib. Mine was wrought iron, and I believe it was the crib all my siblings had slept in at some time. Obviously not all my siblings could sleep in it as long as I, because most were only two years apart in age. So, I'm sure they had to move out for the next kid. Anyway, there were sharp narrow posts around it for decorations and for sure that would keep a kid from crawling out. However, at my age, the front side of my crib was lowered to mattress level so that I could crawl in and out easily.

On Easter morning, I woke up to find that indeed the Easter bunny had come and left me something in that basket. It was a red child's size shovel filled with candy and wrapped with cellophane. Can you beat that? That shovel gave hours of fun as around one side of the house were long dirt-filled boxes for flowers. But for me...It was a place to dig with that shovel.

One sad thing about moving to the March Place was that we had to leave the Tabernacle because of distance. Our new church was in Yankton. It too had sawdust floors. The congregation was not nearly large as that of the Tabernacle. Nonetheless, it was fun. Two ladies were the pastors there. Sister Blick and Sister Horton. I will discuss things about the church later.

Carl had to finish out the few months of seventh- grade at Slowly Country school before he went to eighth-grade the next fall. It was two miles away, and sometimes he would ride Ribbon our pony there. The school had an open sided barn stall for the purpose of student's riding horses to school. Carl would take a gunny sack full of hay with him and dump in the manger for her.

Our school didn't have kindergarten, only town schools did. So, I didn't start to school until I was six, which was first grade. Wanda moved back home before school started the next fall. She had gone all her school years to Meckling but now had to go to Irene to school for her last year. Bee started back to school that fall as Mom seemed to be strong enough to stay alone. I wanted to go to school like my siblings so Mom decided she should teach me how to read and write. She had a book that was hers from her first year of reading, and she taught me from that. It was very old and fragile. She used flash cards to teach me the alphabet and the phonics method to read. After that how to print. (Little did she know God's plan for that early teaching).

Sometime that year, I got whooping cough. They prayed and tried every home remedy they knew, but nothing worked. Our neighbors the Voll's were Norwegian, and they said if you mixed whiskey with honey, and a little pineapple juice that would help. So, Mom decided to try it, borrowing some whiskey from them. Sure enough, it worked. Later on, Wanda told me what the concoction was and laughed as she said I sure begged for that cough medicine. The girls were warned not to tell Pop about the whiskey. We were tea teetotalers, and I doubt he would have approved it. They say it took about six months for me to get entirely over the whooping cough.

Aunt Erma and Uncle Frankie came to visit. They visited more than Pop's other siblings as they had a dual purpose. My dad was Aunt Erma's brother, and the Steele's that lived in Meckling were Uncle Frankie's brothers. Aunt Erma would gather a bunch of the older children and go to Sioux City, Iowa to the Amusement Park. I never got to go, but she brought me back a stuffed monkey. It had a flexible covered tail, and it could be twisted around to do all sorts of things. We named the monkey "Abie". I think it must have arrived about the time I was getting over my whooping cough because Pop made up something that I could give the monkey. It was a silly little routine when I would say that Abie was sick. Pop would say, "well give him a dose of syrup a sipe a cinnamon". So, for years when anyone got sick we would use that phrase.

One time when we went to Iowa, we went to see the Keokuk Dam. Aunt Erma bought me a china elephant. It was a dark purple color with "Keokuk" inscribed on the side. That was a start of my collection of what people called "what nots".

Chapter Eight

Winter Time at the March Place

We only had two stoves to heat the whole house at the March Place. The cook stove heated the kitchen, and our pot belly stove heated the dining room. Downstairs was our eat in kitchen, our parent's bedroom, dining room and a parlor with French doors that was closed off during the winters. Upstairs were three bedrooms. Some people would probably call our dining room a "great room" in today's world. It had a huge dining room table that would seat twelve, a buffet, a couple of stuffed chairs and the stove.

The upstairs was completely unheated and probably one reason I still slept in a crib in Mom and Pops room. When it was really cold, I was allowed to go upstairs and sleep between Wanda and Bee. We had three or four homemade wool pieced quilts that were piled on our beds. They were so heavy we could hardly turn over. We didn't have night clothes, so I slept in my undershirt and long stockings with a garter belt on, plus the flannel rag wrapped around my chest when I caught a cold. Mmm.

Do I need to explain the flannel rag? Well, if we had a cold, we would get our chest rubbed down with Vicks or Mentholatum before going to bed. My dad and I preferred the Mentholatum as it didn't have near the strong smell. However, after trial and error, Vicks seemed to work better. It would be stuffed up our nose and even at times a pea size amount put in our mouth to swallow. Anyway, a flannel cloth was then wrapped around our chest to hold the heat of the medication on your chest.

We had what they called soap stones, and we would put them in the cook stove oven to heat during the day. Also, there were a couple of flat irons that sat on the back corner of the stove. At night, we would wrap several layers of old newspapers around them and take them to bed to keep our feet warm. As they cooled off during the night, we could remove a layer of newspaper to get closer to the soapstone. I used that old standby until I graduated from high school.

If you were sleeping upstairs, you took a glass of water with you in case you wanted a drink in the night. You kept it within arm's reach of the bed, and you had to drink it before morning, or it might be frozen solid and break the glass. Worse, if you had to go to the outhouse in the middle of the night, you had two choices. Using a slop jar that contained the elimination from several people and smelling that terrible smell when you took the lid off; or getting completely dressed and going to the outhouse. If you used the slop jar (it always seemed to have a lid that never fit) you might be the one to empty it the next day. And if it was three fourths full, carrying it down the stairs and to the outhouse without slopping any on you was a real feat. I guess that's why they called it the "slop jar".

We kept wood in the wood shed to fuel the stove, but two things I remember about the wood shed that year. Pop decided to sell seed corn on the side. It was kept in the woodshed, and when people came to buy seed corn, he would give them a free pencil that had "Turner Seed Corn, V.A. Nelson, Yankton, S.D" printed on it. But my dad wasn't always out there selling seed corn. I found out he liked to wrestle. I heard him tell my mother, that so and so was coming over because he thought he could take him on. So, whether it was selling seed corn or wrestling, I was not allowed in the wood shed. Of course, he didn't call it wrestling, he just said I think I can take so and so on.

Probably the grossest thing I can remember was something that seemingly all families had for people with colds. Yes, it was the "snot rag". It was tied on the back of the door handle. Of course, we didn't want to use our nice clean handkerchiefs that we carried in our purse, which in our case was old torn up sheets, and they were slick. The whole family would use the snot rag and try to find a clean spot when we blew our nose. Well, need I say more?

Pop was always the faithful father getting up first and starting the fire as it usually would go out at night. Then he would holler for us kids to get up. Some had chores outside and some had breakfast duty before getting ready for school.

One thing I remember about our winter attire at that age was long stockings. I hated them. I wore brown during the week, and on Sundays I wore white. Sometimes I wore anklets over the top of my white stockings. The garter belt was a very complicated thing to manage for a young person, but I learned. My mother couldn't find the right size stockings for me, as I had long legs. So, she cut the toes off them and sewed them straight across. They were very uncomfortable. My Dad wore spats on Sundays. They were a cuff like a thing that fit over his ankles with hooks for fasteners, and it was my job to fasten his spats. I had a white fur hand muff and a long coat for dress. My snow suit was for every day outdoor wear with mittens that were attached with a crocheted string and strung through the coat sleeves. That way they never got lost.

At Christmas, our tree was always cut from the property. It too set in the dining room. A few of the decorations on the tree stand out to me. We had red velvet ropes that we wound in and out of the branches. We also had silver twisted metal pieces painted different colors on each twist and it seemed they were constantly in motion. There were icicles made out of glass, and yes if dropped they broke. We had silver tinsel like we have today and real candles, about the size of what we put on a birthday cake. After Christmas, all were taken down and stored for the next year. The silver tinsel was also picked off and reused perhaps missing a few strands on the tree. The tree was cut into small pieces for the heating stove and it made a very hot fire as the branches burned quickly. Christmas paper was not ripped apart as one might do now, but carefully unwrapped and stored to be ironed and reused. I don't ever remember ribbons, but we had lots of stickers on the paper. I remember one year I asked Pop if we could light the candles. He said, "yes for a few minutes while we are in the room". The lamp light was blown out, and we oohed, and aah-ed, and then the candles were snuffed out.

Our table was given to my mom for Christmas from the four oldest boys who were working/ pastoring in Rapid City. They also gave her a table service of China that served six. I believe my Dad paid for a good portion of the table and getting it delivered. It lasted us through all the years I lived at home and we kept it extended with the table leaves in it. The next Christmas they gave her the remaining china service of six. I now have those dishes. Some, of course, were broken over the years leaving me with a service for ten.

As a rule, the gifts were usually wrapped and put under the tree sometimes as late as Christmas Eve. The last doll I received, was when we lived at the March place. It was fashioned after one of the Dionne Quintuplets. Mine had the name of Cecilia attached to it.

For as long as I was at home we always received bags of candy for Christmas. They magically appeared on Christmas morning and had our names written on the sacks in pencil. The bags would make an outer circle around the tree. My dad would buy tons of candy and nuts, and spend Christmas eve filling the bags. We would start saving our brown bags several weeks before Christmas. On Christmas morning we had candy, nuts, and an apple in our sack.

Ribbon Candy was one of my favorites. Hard candy had designs in the center of each piece. There was a shiny white square piece of candy that was filled with tiny chopped nuts. Another favorite was hard taffy that looked like white and pink snowdrifts. They were huge pieces that you had to try and break to get a piece small enough to fit in your mouth. Orange slices, peanut brittle, coconut flakes, cream filled chocolates that looked like fat church steeples, wintergreen candy and all kinds of nuts. English Walnuts, pecans, hazelnuts, almonds, Brazil nuts and peanuts filled our bags. My favorite nut was the Hazel nut. A large delicious apple would top off the sack. I believe those candy sacks took the place of Christmas stockings that many children received. My parents tried hard to teach us the real meaning of Christmas, and Santa Claus was downplayed. Then on New Year's, we might get another sack full of the same kinds of candies and nuts, if it had been a prosperous year. New Year's candy bags were always white.

Christmas cards were received and I'm sure were sent from our home too, although I don't remember that part. We not only received Christmas cards, but New Year's cards also. Most of us can't even get Christmas cards sent off, much less a week later have New Year's cards. To think they were all hand written, not typed and one hundred duplicate letters made to include in the card. I don't remember when New Year's cards dropped off the scene, but how did everyone do it all? We lived a half mile off the paved highway on a gravel road. Our mailbox was at the corner of the paved and gravel road and we looked forward to finding cards there after our walk to and from.

Christmas day breakfast was served before chores, as normally we did chores then breakfast. In this way, we could get the dishes done while the men were still outside. In case you don't think it took a long time to do dishes -I'll explain. Two dishpans of water were set on the stove to get hot. That is after you have pumped two water buckets full. Once the water was hot and it might take a while, you got the soap ready to put in the dish water. Oh yes, it was homemade soap, and it didn't make much suds. We used a cabbage cutter to shave off bits of soap, for both homemade or purchased kind. (The purchased bars of soap were real hard, and since we purchased them in huge quantities, I could use them to play with like building bricks). We used cloth salt bags for our dishcloths. We would put the shavings of soap inside the bag, and twist it around and around until the water became milky.

The dishes were washed in a certain order. The less soiled ones first. Glasses, plates, silverware, then pans, and lastly the skillets. The iron skillets were always black on the bottom, so we would pat them dry with the dishcloth. Then set them back on the stove to dry out before setting them in the warming oven. We had a second pan with water to rinse the dishes. As it cooled down more water would be added from the teakettle, although sometimes we would leave the dishpans setting on the cook stove while we washed the dishes. If the water got too hot while washing the dishes, someone would have to move it to the sideboard. They were huge dishpans, and with the water in them, were extremely heavy.

The dishes, of course, were hand dried with a towel. Behind the stove was a rack on the wall that would swing out to hold three or four dishtowels to dry. Our dishtowels always had an embroidered design on them. When the dishes were done, the dish water was poured in the slop pail, that sat on the back porch and that was given to the hogs. The rinse water was given a big sling out the back door. The dishpans were hung on a wall on the back porch. The linoleum was mopped on our hands and knees, and clean newspapers put on the floor for the men to step on when they came in from the barn. If company came, the newspapers were quickly removed and voila a nice clean floor.

The milk would be brought in and put through the cream separator. For many years it had to be hand cranked, (but later on when I was in high school we got an electric one).   There was a strainer that set on the top. Inside the strainer was a milk pad that was put in clean for morning and night. Somehow the milk separated from the cream and when the last bit went through, we watched and poured a can of water in the separator to clean it out. The skim milk was brought in for our cooking and drinking. If we didn't drink it all that day, it was given to the hogs, and the next morning we started over. Oh yes, we did keep the cool milk until the warm milk cooled.

NOW, after all of the chores, we were able to open our presents. We could also eat as much candy as we wanted, whenever we wanted, all day. That was the rule, and no one ever got sick. But that's why we were ready for another sack one week later on New Year's. It also provided a stall for a late afternoon Christmas dinner. I don't remember what we usually served, except for four things. We had cooked cranberries that we served in a special dish, Jessie salad (we named our recipes after the person we got them from) celery that could be dipped in our salt dishes and candied sweet potatoes.

Chapter Nine

The Yankton Church

We lived about twenty miles outside of Yankton, which had the closest church of our denomination. The memories of that church also are still vividly imprinted in my mind.

A blind lady and her two daughters came to our church. I had never been around anyone blind before, and I discovered a lot about blind people. Sis. Jones's daughter Bernice, would guide her to her pew before going to be with her friends. I visited their house occasionally when my parents went shopping. Her daughter, Connie, was about six years older than me, but still not too old to play. Their house was sparse with furniture, so Sis. Jones didn't bump or trip into things. I also saw how Sis. Jones swept the floor. She would feel all over the floor with her hands to make sure it was clean, then take a piece of newspaper and sweep the dirt up on the paper. We had a dustpan with a waist-high handle on the back of it that we could step on a spring to hold the lid open. So, sweeping on a newspaper to gather the dirt was new to me. I also learned that everything had to be kept in the exact place. For example, the milk was in a certain spot in the refrigerator, butter on a certain shelf and so on. One day she had fixed lunch to have ready when my parents came back from shopping. She made gravy, but unfortunately, the girls had returned the chocolate milk to the spot where the regular milk was supposed to be. I don't know what all she served, but one thing was gravy, and they all knew the problem when they tasted the sweet gravy. Fingers were put to the lips not to say anything. So, the gravy was served without an incident.

My mother was my Sunday School teacher. Every Saturday night, she and Bee would do cut outs of printed Bible stories characters to be placed on a flannel board. That was not as easy as now. Each of the characters or objects had to be cut out and colored. I would ask if I could color the pictures, but wasn't allowed. After they had been colored, they had to cut pieces of flannel the right size to glue to the back. Each piece then had to be laid separately on the table to dry otherwise, they would stick together. At church, a flannel board was propped up on something so my Mother could illustrate the story. Most of the time, we students were allowed to retell the story using those pictures. The last Christmas my Mother taught me, she gave little story books to her students. The outside cover had a picture of the nativity.

Although lady evangelists were common, this was the first I could remember having two ladies for pastors. Their names were Sis. Blick and Sis. Horton. Often one of the lady preachers would find a song for me to sing that would fit in with their Sunday sermons. Two songs I remember singing were, "Dare to Be a Daniel" and "Your Roses May Have Thorns".

We got new song books (hymnals) at church, and I was so looking forward to seeing one...until the pastors announced that you had to be of school age to use the new books. The tears begin to softly roll down my face, and one of the Pastors saw those tears and quickly added, but if you can read, you can use the new book. I think that she knew my mom had taught me to read. I was so glad to hold a new book in my hands.

A couple of funny things that happened at church. In the summer, the windows of the church were open to let the breeze in. Unchurched teens liked to stand outside and make noises trying to disrupt the services. Sometimes they would throw rocks, or eggs, or holler and make noise in general. One evening two boys kept up the heckling outside the windows. They hadn't reckoned with the speed of my cow chasing father. My dad got up from his pew and went outside. The boys took off at high speed and my dad in full chase. He caught both boys, grabbed them by the back of the shirt collar and brought them into the church. He plopped them down in the back row and returned to his seat. After the boys sat there for a while, they decided they could sneak out, but never did they or anyone else bother disrupting the service again.

My brother Carl met up with a boy about his age there in town and invited him to church. He lived several blocks from the church, so we would go there on a Sunday morning and give him a ride. One Sunday the boy didn't come out when we honked, so Carl went to the door. Apparently, his mother was a bit wacky. She invited Carl in and told him, "I have Jesus locked up in my cedar chest, do you want to see him?" Suddenly Carl came flying out the door and in the car with no evidence of his friend. He was so out of breath he could hardly relay the message. But after waiting awhile, the boy never came out. In fact, the boy never returned to church.

MC was one of the speakers at church   He was always one to use illustrations for his sermons as a way for people to remember them. In fact, not too long ago, I met someone who had heard one of his sermons, and they remembered the illustrations he used. So, one Sunday MC used a pair of scales that he had made from things at the house. His sermon was... "You Are Weighed in the Balance and Found Wanting." He enlisted the help of my dad, and they took an old scale and rigged it up. Although I was only five years old, I still remember it.

Speaking of MC, he was holding a revival meeting in a town nearby. He had rented some rooms over the top of a store. He posted announcements everywhere announcing the revival and borrowed the piano from our home. I went with them to deliver it. Mr. and Mrs. Chapman from our church had a pickup and it was loaded in the pickup and transported to the building. Unfortunately, there were many, many steps to get to the top. If you look at some old store buildings, you will see what I mean. I remember the struggle trying to get the piano up those narrow stairs. There wasn't room for anyone on the side of the piano, so a couple of people got in front of the piano and several behind pushing and lifting and shoving, taking a very long time to get it to the top. I am surprised it survived. On the way home, it was very late, and several were crowded in that pickup cab. I was sitting on Mrs. Chapman's lap when she looked out the truck window and exclaimed, "Oh, there is the big dipper, I wished I had a drink from it!" I had never heard that about stars before, so I assumed she saw one laying along side the road. I couldn't imagine how she could see it in the dark. As I later learned about the stars, I remembered Mrs. Chapman and knew that was what she was talking about.

Saturday was hair washing day. The wash pan was filled with warm water, and my hair dipped up and down in it and then shampooed. "Well" water was what they called hard water. If you could catch water in a rain barrel, it was soft water. Hard water made your hair feel gummy no matter how much it was rinsed. My hair was fine, and it tangled easily and produced much crying as they tried to comb the tangles from my hair. Sometimes they would put vinegar in the water to "break" the water. I learned the feel if enough vinegar was in it to "break it".

After my hair was dried with a towel, it would be wrapped around long strips of rags and the rags tied with a knot to keep them from falling out during the night. Yes, we slept like that all night, to allow them to dry. In the morning when the rags were released, voila, you would have long curls.

Sunday was a day we would almost certainly have dinner guests. Often, they were speakers from church, the pastor, or friends. The meal was not prepared before we went to church, so it took a couple of hours before things were ready. They did make the desserts on Saturday as that was always baking day. Pies were the usual pick. Saturday my Mom would make an extra crust for supper and a soft- filling for it, custard or lemon and they became known as Saturday pie. Left over pie dough was cut in strips, sugared and sprinkled with cinnamon, baked and eaten immediately for a treat.

While the food was being prepared after morning church, I would often wait in the car and look at my Sunday School papers. In the spring when we had removed the heating stoves, it would often be cool in the house until the late sun warmed up the rooms, but the sun in the glass windows of a car warmed up nicely and quickly. So, I would wait in the car until dinner was called. (I still like to sit in a sun-warmed car in the cool of the year). But one particular Sunday, there was a young man at our house for dinner. His name was Eugene and was attracted to my sister Bee. Our family was one for great jokes and fun in general. Bee was making coleslaw, and when she stepped into the other room for something, Eugene took the coleslaw and hid it by the piano in the parlor. Bee looked and looked all around for the dish of coleslaw to put the dressing on it. Dinner was ready all but that. Not knowing the circumstances, I came running in the house and went to get an extra chair from the parlor. All of a sudden, I burst out saying, "I smell coleslaw". Everyone laughed because the coleslaw had been found. A side note about cole-slaw. Eating the core of the cabbage was akin to eating the heart of a watermelon. Whoever could win the favor of getting the cabbage core was indeed favored, and they had a salt shaker in hand.

After dinner, I remember the young folks sitting on the porch outside and saying that certain words sounded funny. One was the word "much". They would repeat that over and over and laugh and laugh. I couldn't think how that struck them so funny, but obviously it did. For a while we did get a Sunday paper, but Pop made us wait until Monday to read the funnies.

As stated earlier, Sunday evening church was eight P.M. This allowed farmers time needed to do chores and get ready for church. Getting ready for Sunday night church, my mother would take a curling iron and reset my curls as during the day my curls would go limp. The curling iron looked similar to a pair of scissors or tongs. My mother would light a lamp and stick the tongs down the lamp chimney to heat them up. The handle would hold it in place in the chimney.

Since Sunday dinner was later, we didn't have to have supper until we came home after church. So, figuring church out at perhaps ten P.M. and a forty- five-minute ride home, it was always late when we ate. Our speed limits were generally thirty-five to forty-five miles per hour. My Father didn't want any of us to have to cook a meal that late, so Sunday night popcorn was our tradition. We would pop a dishpan full, and nearly all of it would get eaten, except the old maids. (that was the corn that didn't pop but would perhaps burn) and Wanda liked those. We also had dinner leftovers if there were any such as cold fried chicken, pie or jello. No excuses were used to stay home for Sunday night church because the kids had school the next day.

One fourth of July, lots of church people came to our farm, and someone had an accordion. They sat outside on the porch, and we sang songs until dark. They had me do the choruses as I could flow from one to another naturally. I felt proud as I heard the adults talking about it. It's so important to include all ages involving anything at church. No wonder even children loved church.

I remember CT Beem and his wife and daughter Darlene would come and preach at church. As I said earlier after the service ended we would go to the back of the church to the prayer room. I would come to the prayer room with my parents, but Darlene got to stay at the back of the church and color in a coloring book. I couldn't figure out why she got to color and I couldn't. But, as preachers, her parents would be busy praying with people, so they used that method to occupy her.

One year I was to sing for the Christmas program, and I needed a new dress. The program was at least one day before Christmas because I had a package under the tree. After some discussion, they told me I could unwrap a certain gift and in it was a royal blue pleated skirt with straps that held it up, plus a white blouse. Someone suggested I needed a light blue sweater to wear with it, but they couldn't find any, so they got me a red sweater. When I sang at the program, the Pastor said I looked like the flag with the red, white and blue. In the meantime, my outfit was re-wrapped, so I would have a package to open Christmas day. Eventually, they found me a light blue sweater to wear.

On many days, I would go in the parlor and play church. The parlor had French doors and was closed off during the winter as there was no heating stove in there. I would still go in there and wear a coat. We had a pedestal that was supposed to be for plants, but most of the time it was empty. It was rather tall, but I could stand on a chair, and use the pedestal for a pulpit. Of course, I would bang away on the piano too for that part of my play church service. One Sunday though, I came home from church and picked out a song on the piano. Because I had banged on the piano for so many months, no one paid any attention to me when I tried to tell them I could play a song. When MC came home for a visit, I told him I could play a song. He came into the parlor and said, "Yes, that's Rock of Ages". Since he played the trombone, I figured he knew how to play the piano also. So, I asked him to teach me. He said, "if the song reaches high notes, you go up the scale, if it goes down low, you go down the scale". And that's how I learned to play the piano. I took off after that with many songs. I only could figure out my right hand though. I knew that didn't sound quite right, so I simply played the same notes with my right and left hand, which added a little bass.

Chapter Ten

Rapid City, South Dakota: The Interim

We made several trips back and forth to Rapid City over the short time I lived in South Dakota. It seems we would always get behind diesel buses on those trips, and I would get deathly car sick. With no air conditioning, our car windows were always wide open. Many stops were made for me to upchuck along the way. The trees were always a blue-green with a foggy haze around them, probably due to the fumes from the buses. I've hated blue-green ever since. I can't even wear sunglasses with the blue-green tint! They tried everything to alleviate the suffering of my car sickness...front seat, back seat, lying down, sitting up, and even resorting to buying Dentyne chewing gum. That would work sometimes and sometimes even if I wasn't nauseated I was sure it might be coming on so that I could get that gum. It was always kept in the glove box. By the way, do you know why it was called a glove box? You got it right. You kept gloves in there for winter when the steering wheel was so cold you could hardly hang on to it with bare hands.

One day when Mom and I were home alone, she needed to use the outhouse. She was washing dishes, and I was just learning how to help by drying the silverware, and I didn't like doing that. Before Mom left for the outhouse, she suggested I see how much of the silverware I could get dried before she got back.   In my young mind, I knew what she was trying to do. I can even remember telling myself that "she just wants to get the silverware dried". So, I pouted for a few minutes. Then I felt really bad, and tried to get as many dried and put away before she got back in. Our silverware tray in the drawer was made from wooden cheese boxes. There was one for each type of silverware.

Mom came back in the house, and a few seconds later Pop came inside. He said something to her and as he did, she slowly started to bend down and not say a word.   Pop immediately recognized it as a stroke and carried her to bed. He told me to bring a kitchen chair. I suppose I had to drag it. He tipped the chair backwards with the back of the chair over the bed. He then grabbed a pillow and put it over the legs of the chair and more or less used that as a prop to set Mom up. For some reason, I guess he thought she shouldn't lie down. I remember him calling out to God in a loud voice. Praying wasn't unusual in our house. It was something that was done all the time, so it wasn't strange or unnatural to hear him pray, except his prayer was like he was calling for help.

Again I don't remember the sequence of things, except she wasn't able to talk right for a while.   She could talk, but something had gone wrong. She wasn't able to read or write, so my dad now taught her how to do that.

He taught her the alphabet all over, just like she had taught me. Some things came back to her quickly, but she might say...A, B, and then forget. So, he'd say a couple of letters and then she could pick up. Wrong names were given for different things. For example, she called me Shebem. Again, as a child, it didn't anger or upset me, I knew she wanted me and I would answer the call. As I got older, I wondered if that word or name had a spiritual meaning, but have never been able to discover it.

One of the lady preachers suggested Mom come and stay in the parsonage for a while in Yankton and she took care of her there. It had an indoor bathroom and also a furnace so there was heat throughout the house. I remember Pop saying." they have cotton sheets on their bed for her and use them year-round". Well, at our house with little or no heat in the bedrooms, we had to have flannel sheets, plus three or four other blankets on top of that to keep warm. I couldn't imagine sheets in the winter. I believe she stayed at the parsonage for two weeks.

My brother MC was pastoring his first church in Rapid City, S. D. He was the second Pastor of that Assembly of God church there. He was single and lived in the Parsonage and it was decided that Mom and I should move in with MC since she needed a modern place for recovery. It was a long drive, but worth it as the parsonage had electricity, a furnace, running water and indoor bathroom. The work was so much lighter there and Mom was a big help to the young single Pastor.

Staying at the parsonage was really fun for me, for several reasons. For one thing, my brother was the preacher. For another, my brother Cecil rented out one of the rooms of the parsonage. He ran a wrecker service and had a phone in his room. I was told not to bother him as he might have been up all night making service calls, but it sure was hard not to do so. The parsonage had a phone, and we didn't have any on the farm. So, I would try to talk MC or Mom into letting me answer the phone. I had to answer it properly and say, "Hello, this is the Parsonage." But since Cecil had a phone in his room, he would sometimes call and play tricks on me. He would make up some serious story, and I would think it was for real. Later on, he'd quiz me about the phone calls, until one day he let me know it was him.

The parsonage had a path to the church side door, and MC would go over there and study. He also had a secretary whose name was Saverna. She could cut through a couple of back yards from where she rented a room and be at work. She often would take me back to her room for a visit. The people that rented her a room had two full-size poodles. Now I'd never seen poodles before, much less any kind of dog in a house. I couldn't get over it. We always had dogs. All of our neighbors did, but they were outside.

(Incidentally, when you moved to a new farm, the old dog stayed behind, because at your new place it was naturally assumed the dog went with the property). I nearly got in trouble over assuming Saverna was MC's girlfriend. In fact, we were invited out to MC's actual girlfriend's parents' home for dinner. They were people in his church. Evidently, MC had asked Hazel Brunner to marry him, and this was an opportunity for her parents to get acquainted with my mom and vice versa. They had several daughters. One at least five years older than I and one two years younger, so I had someone to play with. In the course of our playing, I revealed to those girls, that MC had a girlfriend and her name was Saverna. Well, that got relayed to Hazel and her parents, and it nearly caused a falling out.

One of the parishioners in the church was an Indian girl by the name of Rose. She invited us to eat at a restaurant where she worked, and paid for the meal. I didn't ever remember eating at a restaurant. That was pure excitement for me.

Since it was customary to have guest evangelists and speakers quite frequently at church back then, we got to enjoy visiting with them. It was always the Pastors job to host them as putting them up in a hotel was unheard of. MC took advantage of having several lady speakers while Mom was there, so there would be no impropriety. In fact, there were guest rooms in the basement where two lady speakers stayed while we were there.

Now Cecil was quite the comedian, so one night while a couple of lady speakers were there for supper, Cecil took a thin strip of paper, wove it back and forth fan style and stuck it up his nose. They were unaware of that, so in the middle of eating, he made the pretense that something was wrong with his nose and began slowly to pull out this long strip of paper. One of the ladies began to gag and had to leave the table. He did things like short sheet their beds while they were gone for the day etc. So, they tried their best to get back on him and hid his socks in the teakettle. I doubt he owned over three pairs of socks, so he was at quite a loss. Such were the days of laughter and fun.

Cecil began dating a lady from another town. She was a widow with three children. Her husband had been killed in the gold mines, and one son was a year younger than me. So, in the course of meeting her, I had someone to play with again. Indeed, he did marry her and together they had a daughter, Linda and so I became an aunt later, at the age of eight.

I had some glass beads that someone had given me. They were called "sun beads". MC had a sprinkler out on the lawn. When I would wear those beads and stand out by the sprinkler, they made a rainbow color. It was there in that neighborhood that I met a girl much older than I. Her name was Edith also and she would stop by and talk to me if I was out in the yard.

My favorite toy was a whirly gig. I think they are called pin wheels now days. If the wind wasn't strong enough to blow it, I would take it with me in the car when we went for a ride and hold it by the side window and let it blow. Didn't take much to entertain children then. MC would take us on trips up to Dinosaur Park, Pigtail Curve, Skyline Drive, Mt. Rushmore and other places. He made things fun for Mom and I.

The doorbell often rang at the parsonage. Sometimes it would be a drunk wanting money. Other times it would be a couple wanting the Parson to marry them. At one such time, they asked MC to perform the marriage, but they had no one to be a witness...so Mom and I got to be in the wedding. There was an elderly lady that roomed at the parsonage also. In fact, they gave her the living room which had French doors that closed it off. The parsonage had a kitchen and a huge dining room that could serve as our living room. There was a bedroom for MC, and one for Mom and I and that was all we needed.

Alas, spring had come in Rapid City, and it would now be warm enough back at the farm house so Mom wouldn't have to carry in wood to keep a fire going. So back to the farm we went.

Chapter Eleven

Back at the March Place

We returned from Rapid City in time for Wanda's graduation in 1941, and we more or less traded places. Wanda then moved to Rapid City and stayed with Marvin. A prominent doctor by the name of Doctor Dolly soon employed her. She served his household as the nanny and cook. She helped MC by being the church pianist and keeping up the parsonage. In fact, Wanda usually served as church pianist wherever she lived.

It was time to plant the garden on the farm. Mom's complexion was always milk white, winter and summer. She never tanned, and neither do I. However, I am not white like she was. She had to wear a hat outdoors as she didn't really sweat and she needed the shade. I also had a straw hat, child size. That was always fun to pick out a summer hat. It had a string through the sides and a slip knot that went under my chin. I worked in the garden also. After all I was big enough to be going to school the next year. But that wasn't the only reason I did garden work. I was saving money to buy sparklers for the Fourth of July! So, I pulled weeds in the garden. We would often put tin cans over a stick to mark the end of a row of vegetables to identify what we had planted.

My mother had warned me to be careful of snakes when I was outside. Even though I had never seen one, when I did I knew immediately what it was and went screaming in the house. One day I went to the garden, and the can have fallen over. I went to pick it up, and it had a snake in it. I told my father, and he headed toward the garden. He said, "Now if you are lying to me, we are going to the woodshed." Wanda heard him say that and she said she prayed the snake would still be there. It was! A few days later as I went into the parlor, there was another one stretched out by the door on our parlor rug. Bee came in and killed that one. On one particular day, my father killed twenty-seven snakes. One had a beautiful skin, and he wanted to skin it and take it somewhere to make a belt. Thankfully he didn't do it. Wearing a snake around your waist repulsed me.

July 4th was a holiday except for the chores. We went to the bluffs that night to watch fireworks and then came back to Yankton and had ice cream. The ice cream was packed in a pint size carton with the flaps up! The cost was five cents. I would usually get butter brickle. (Sometimes in the summer after church Pop would go to the ice cream store and we could get ice cream then too.) After arriving at home, we did our fireworks. That was the first time I'd ever been able to do sparklers. We had stopped at a little roadside stand a few days before the Fourth and bought our fireworks. I don't remember what the others got, but I remember mine. I earned ten cents to spend for pulling weeds. So that was one time, weeds were a welcome sight.

A band of gypsies had put their tents up on the James River right across from our property. That was not a problem until the baby chicks arrived. Mom had ordered lots of baby chicks from the catalog. I think around five hundred. The chickens would arrive in boxes with round holes cut in the side for them to breathe. We were given a certain date to pick them up from the store such as Penny's, Sears or Monkey Wards. You could always count on some being DOA, so extra chickens were always included. It was a pleasant sound to hear the loud cheeping in the back seat of the car as we were bringing them home.

I loved to go in the brooder house where the chicks were. It was always nice and warm in there in the early spring. Sacks of feed were kept there and made a nice place to sit. The feeders looked somewhat like the top shelf of a long tool box and were cleaned and filled each day. Quart jars with a special lid let the water leak out slowly so the baby chicks could sip their water. They two were cleaned and filled sometimes several times a day. As the chicks got bigger, we would use gallon jars for their water. A thermometer was kept in the brooder to make sure the temperature was stable. There was a heated stove actually called the brooder in the middle of the brooder house. It had a rounded hood that sat close to the ground. The chicks would gather under there to keep warm like a hen's wings so to speak. A thin layer of straw was spread over the wood floor.

Each day we would count the chicks, which was a trick as they kept moving around. We would get estimates as we wanted to make sure they weren't dying from coccidiosis or some other disease.

One morning Mom came in from the brooder house and said, "Well, I think I have about fifty chickens missing". So, my dad didn't say anything. Then the next morning, she said. "Wow there's at least a hundred chickens missing." About that time some of the neighbors begin to say they had different animals missing.

I happened to be outside one afternoon when a big truck passed by. It was stacked high with furniture, and on the back, a calf was tied with ropes. I ran to find my father, and he and some of the neighbors got in their cars and went to the gypsy's camp and found many of their animals. I don't know what took place, but they soon left the area, nor do I know if everyone got their stolen items back.

Not only did we have chickens, but we had turkeys. I don't remember how many or what we did with them, but there was one Tom turkey that was huge. He was about my size, and whenever I came outside, he would try and flog me. So, my dad got a stick and placed it just outside the door that not only I but others used. That was one mean turkey.

On one particular day, I was met with big Tom Gobbler. I grabbed the stick and hit him. It did not deter him. So, my dad yelled at me to hit him harder. No results. He said, "Hit him hard". Well, a five-year-old doesn't have a lot of strength, but I hit him hard enough on the head, that it made him dizzy and he spun around and around. In a little bit he got up and walked away, but that was the talk at the supper table that night.

Another time when I was an evening subject was after Carl came home from school with some important information he had learned. He learned that your stomach was the size of your two fists placed together. We had a rather large lady in our neighborhood by the name of Mrs. Gunderson. A lovely lady, but quite large. So, I promptly said, "well I bet Mrs. Gunderson's stomach is much bigger than that", assuming a stomach was what you saw on the outside of a person.

We didn't do birthday gifts at our house unless you counted choosing your favorite cake to be baked. Mine was always chocolate with a special white frosting that Wanda made. I remember Bee's was marble cake and Carl's was yellow with chocolate frosting. Pops was white cake with hickory nuts. Certain things might count as a present though. On my birthday Pop came in and announced "twin colts were born today, right on your birthday. Let's name them Sophie and Samantha, how does that sound?"

Just like we had our favorite cakes, we also had our favorite hymns. Pops was "Home Sweet Home". Carl's was "Love Divine", especially the verse that said, "here I'll raise my Ebeneezer', Rex's was "Constantly Abiding", Bee's was "Some Golden Daybreak" and Wanda's was "Jesus Opened Up the Way".

One Easter, Pop started a tradition. About a week before Easter, he hid about a dozen eggs in a box. Then I was encouraged to hide some. If he found mine, he could add mine to his box and vice versa. At the dinner table, he would give hints as to where they could be found. "Up high" said Pop. I looked in a tree. I looked in the hay mow. But "up high" turned out to be on top of the outhouse. Of course, I usually ended up having the most. We hid eggs like that each Easter until I was in high school.

A group of trees down by the barn would blossom in the spring I don't know for sure but I think they were apple blossoms, and were just beautiful. Things that were natural or God created were always of great interest to us. Rainbows were a source of great exclamation as well as beautiful rocks. Iowa has the prettiest rainbows and South Dakota has some of the prettiest rocks anywhere. As a child, I loved pretty rocks and still do. I would bring them home, wash and keep them. Wanda gave me a white denim bag once for keeping the rocks. We had culverts near the house that were big enough that I could bend slightly and walk in. That was often a great place to find washed out rocks. The rocks there would sparkle like crystal and diamonds.

One year the James (Jim) River flooded our fields. It came up close to the barnyard. Our house sat on a knoll so we were OK. Haystacks in the fields were left floating. City people brought their boats from Yankton. They would knock on the door and ask if they could park in our driveway and unload their boats. Occasionally someone would offer us a fish or two of their catch for the use of our fields.

We ate a lot of wild game. When my dad would come in for the noon dinner he would often bring in pheasants or squirrel, and yes, fish. So, we would clean them and have them at suppertime. In fact, we had fried fish a lot. Most all the meats we consumed were fried. My dad would clean the fish and skin the squirrel, but everything else was left to the women. I would watch my Dad clean the fish, and he would hand me the gills to play with. They were like small balloons. Smelled, but fun.

The dog that came with the March place was called Mugsy. After meals, my job was to scrape the plates. Because the food was plentiful at our house, any left overs were taken outside and given to the dog. This included chicken bones, pork chop bones, potatoes, gravy, etc. One night, when we had fish, I took the fish bones out and gave them to the dog. Well, suddenly we heard the dog coughing, and Pop said, "Edythe what did you do with the fish bones?". When he found out I had given them to the dog, he asked my mother for all the dried bread we had and quickly gave it to Muggsy. Fortunately, Muggsy was OK, but I understood not to give the dog fish bones. In fact, many times I myself would get a bone caught in my throat, and dry bread was used.

South Dakota was known for having lots of pheasants, and relatives from Iowa would come and stay with us so they could go hunting. One time when Uncle Ray came from Iowa to visit, he shot a very colorful pheasant. He took it to a taxidermy in town as it was so outstanding in color and size. It was to be ready just before he left to go back home. On the day he went to pick it up, the man told him he was sorry, but he had ruined it. My uncle asked for it back, but he said he had to throw it away. No one believed the man, but of course, there was no proof.

We had a narrow road up the hill to one of our fields. It was washed out with the rains and if you didn't stay on the track perfectly when driving a car, it would drop off in a deep rut and knock the muffler off. On one particular day, my mom wanted to take a snack to the men in the field at the top of the hill. She decided to drive the car up there, even though it was tricky. Sure enough, one place wasn't wide enough for the tire and we slipped into the deep rut. I think that was the first time I ever saw my mother cry. We got out and walked the rest of the way up the hill to where the men were and they came and retrieved the car. No damage was done.

Speaking of crying. I had problems with my heart. Some of the doctors said it was a heart murmur, others through the years would say it was pleurisy pains. All I know is, I would get these piercing pains in my chest and cry. The more I cried, the more the pains shot through my chest. My dad would call me, and I would sit on his lap. He would put his hand over my heart and pray for the pain to go away, and it usually did, but I also knew it was a way to get attention.

One day I went to the top of our hill that was a pasture. Some would even call it a small mountain. About half way up, there was this huge rock that we would often sit on to rest before going to the top. On this particular day, I was alone and decided I would see if I could move that rock. It probably had rained to soften the ground, because I worked and worked until I got it loose and gave it a push. It began to thunder down the mountain gathering speed as it went. The problem was there were cattle lying down at the base and it was headed for them. I remember gazing at those cows and thinking I was in BIG trouble as it would surely kill them. Because animals are sensitive to ground trembles, they got up and moved before it hit them. Sometime soon thereafter, I overheard my dad talking and he said, "you know that big rock that was half way up the hill? It's now down at the bottom of the hill. I can't imagine whatever jarred it loose". I never said one word.

I guess parents have a way of testing their children for truthfulness. Since the enclosed back porch was an add on, there was a window by the kitchen wash basin that overlooked the porch. My dad kept his razor in the window sill nearby. I was looking out the window watching him use the milk separator and accidentally knocked off his razor. No problem. I just picked it up and placed it back on the sill. I continued to watch him and when he was finished he brought the milk in the house. As I ran to greet him, he said, "Say. Did you knock my razor off the window sill?" To which I quickly replied, "No". Right then I had a woodshed experience in the kitchen except it was with the razor strap. I remember pondering what could be wrong with knocking off a razor. Ohhh testing time.

The razor strap hung very near the window, and many times the razor strap took precedence over the wood shed. Also, my sisters used the fly swatter on my legs. The fly swatters then were metal, and they could sting. They were like a metal screen with bias tape over the edges. Speaking of fly swatters that was one way of killing flies, but we also had fly stickers. It was a small spool that when you pulled on the lid opening, a swirl of sticky stuff on paper was released. The flies would be drawn to it and stick to it and die. The stickers usually hung down from the ceiling and if you accidentally walked too close to it, you could get your hair stuck in it. Many people had that experience.

Pop had pulled the washing machine in the house one day for Mom to do the wash. At this point I wasn't aware of all it took to do the laundry, so I'll explain that when I come to the age of "wash day knowledge". After starting the washer Pop left and went into town. My dad was quite an expert on guessing clothes sizes for our family and on this particular day when he came back from town he had brought our mother a pink dress with blue polka dots, as a surprise. She said, "Oh Virdie, you shouldn't have". And he replied, "Well it's just a wash dress," meaning it could be washed in the machine. But I took it to mean it was something for her to wear when you washed clothes. I thought, well, that is nice enough to wear to church. A side note to our Maytag washing machine. One hymn we sang at church was..." Like a Mighty Sea". Before I could read, I thought they were singing "Maytag washing machine".

On the porch was a drain where you could let the water out of the wash machines, and it would run under the porch and out a little hill. Well, that little hill was a source of money finding. Evidently the people that lived there before never took the change out of their pockets before doing the laundry. So, every time it rained, it would uncover a coin or two. That to me was akin to the gold rush.

My dad owned a combine and would hire out to other farmers. He would haul his combine to their place and then use their horses or tractor. We grew wheat ourselves and sometimes I could ride in the wagon that brought in the wheat. If I stood in the back, I could grab a hand full and chew it like gum. Yes, that was fun.

We had Mennonite neighbors about a mile and a half from us. One day Pop took us for a ride to their place and we were invited to tour the Mennonite living quarters. A little girl was standing by the side of the house eating the cake crock. (an explanation here about cake crock. When Mom or one of the girls would bake a cake, they would like to know if I wanted to come and lick the cake crock. I thought that the batter was called cake crock, not knowing it was the batter that was mixed in a crock. But from that time on, all the family called the batter - cake crock). We toured their sleeping quarters, which was a huge dormitory. Their dining room, was a long, long room with lots of tables, much like picnic tables.

My father used something they called the buck fork. It was a fork rigged to a front part of an old car, no top, no sides, but a seat. They had to crank it to get it started but it worked wonders. After the hay was mowed, they could take the buck fork and gather up lots of hay and carry it to a pile to make a haystack. The hay was then used to feed the animals in the winter.

Muggsy was able to bring the cows in at night. I'm not sure what command they used, but she would go round up the cows from the pasture by barking at the heels and keep running from one side of the herd to the other. Other times someone would ride our horse Ribbon to bring in the cows.

Once the cows were in the stalls and the men were milking, I would often go to the barn and watch the cats play. I had no idea that later in life I would hear of people keeping cats in the house? My dad would rig up some kind of a ball to hang down from the doorway, and we would watch the cats scramble after it swinging back and forth. He would often let me milk and shoot a stream up in the air for the cats to scramble after. Well, the cats weren't the only ones that got squirted with milk. The men would try to squirt milk in my mouth. If they missed and hit my dress, it would leave a stiff residue, and a soured smell.

One of the silly things I remember was some boys out shooting pigeons in the barn, and a young boy of about eight came running in the house crying. Somehow, he had become the target of one of the BB guns ammo and got hit in the hip. A group of women were at our house for a WM meeting, so they removed it with a needle, and that was that. There was no doctor, no ER, just good old home remedy.

My mother was very faithful with her prayer life. I couldn't tell time then, but one of my sisters told me that Mom prayed every day except Sunday from eleven A.M. until twelve noon. If it was warm enough, she knelt by the couch in the parlor on our beautiful tan rug with the Indian designs on it. I was sent out to play. But either I would forget, or I would have a question and would come in to speak with her. In doing so, she would reach her arm around me and pull me down to her side to pray. She would tell me to pray that the boys wouldn't have to go to war. (meaning my brothers of course). I then asked her, "What's war?" She replied with, "it's something awful". I just couldn't envision the meaning of war.

Chapter Twelve

School Days, School Days

Finally, I was old enough to start school. I knew exactly what I wanted to start school with. My first wish was for a dinner bucket like I saw Pop use once. He was working on a farm for someone and they had fixed a snack and taken to him. I guess we drove him to this place in the morning so we could have the car, because at night when he came in from the field, he had this dinner bucket that was the most amazing thing I'd ever seen. He opened it up to show me that there was a place for a thermos with hot coffee and a place for food in the lower part of the bucket. It was interesting to me because my siblings used empty Karo buckets for their lunches. The bucket was much like you see construction workers using today. So that was our first purchase for starting to school.

One of my brothers gave me a huge green ever-sharp pencil filled with lead refills stored inside the pencil. I had to unscrew the cap to get the extra lead. Another brother gave me a pencil box. In preparation for school, let me tell you the most important things were one, a lunch bucket. Two a pencil box and three a box of crayons. My pencil box was green. It had a snap cover over the top. On the top shelf was a place for pencils, erasers, and crayons. The bottom drawer had a protractor and a compass. I don't know what the protractor was for, but my brother Carl showed me how that I could spin the compass around and make beautiful flowers. My ever-sharp pencil had to be left at home as well as the indelible pencil. The indelible pencil looked like any other pencil, except when you wrote it was purple. But if you spit on the lead or stuck it on your tongue and wrote with it, it would be a bright purple and could not be erased. So, a lot of transactions were done with indelible pencils. I suppose a lot of spit was used too.

Now the sad part about the crayons were that Pop thought a box of eight was plenty big enough for me. The ones in our Sunday School class were usually just stubs with no paper around then. But when I got to school and saw some that had twelve, sixteen and even twenty-four crayons, I was a bit disappointed. I was also disappointed when I saw that my big Red Chief tablet wasn't as pretty as those with pictures on the tablet cover. My dad wanted more bang for the buck, so that's what I got. It held a lot more paper than the ones with the picture cover on it. Also, the paper was yellow, which was supposed to be easier on the eyes. You would think that clothes would have been an important part, but I don't ever remember that being an interest until perhaps fourth grade.

As stated before, my mother had taught me the alphabet, how to read and print before I started to school. So, when school started, I already knew how to sound out the letters of the alphabet. Our school also taught phonics, so it was pretty easy for me to read my first book, "Run Dick run. See Spot. See Spot run." Phonics were taught by pulling down a big paper roll on the wall. Each section had a letter of the alphabet on it with a picture, and you had to make a sound. The one I remember most is the letter "S" It had a picture of a teakettle on it with steam coming out, and we were to make an SSSSS sound for the steam. Today I believe it's a snake for the letter S as many children wouldn't know anything about a teakettle.

Because I could read immediately, the school teacher, whose name was Miss Chance, had a little chat with my parents and wanted to have me skip first grade and go into second grade. But after talking with each other, they concluded that would not be a good idea. So consequently, I was bored. I'm sure you are all familiar with these signals when in school, but I'll review them just in case: You raised your hand if you had a question. If you needed to go to the toilet, (that was the universal word back then) you held up one finger. If you wanted a drink of water, you raised two fingers. Unless you were in class session, you couldn't talk or whisper. If you were caught whispering or some other infringement of the law such as chewing gum, (wax in our case) or throwing paper wads, the teacher would keep a list. At the end of the day, your name would be put on the blackboard, and if it was, you would have to stay after school for anywhere from five to ten minutes.

Being bored, I guess I whispered a lot. The strange part was I never knew I was whispering. I was always truly shocked if my name was on the blackboard. Sometimes my parents would pick me up from school, as it was two miles one way to our house. One and a half mile on pavement, and half a mile on gravel road. IF my name was on the board, I would always pray that my parents would be late picking me up, because if they were on time, I would have a lot of explaining to do and sometimes a trip to the woodshed.

My first year in school, enrollment was twenty-seven, and that was for all eight grades. My brother Carl was a freshman. My sister Bee was a Junior. Since it was eighteen miles to Irene High School, they rode the school bus. I believe the folks always drove me to school, but it was coming home I had to walk. The problem was, there were three brothers I had to walk with the first mile and a half. The youngest was Ronnie and he was in my grade. As we walked along he would use filthy sexually explicit language that I had never heard, but knew it was wrong as it made me feel terrible. As I look back on it, Ronnie had quite a speech impediment and he probably was trying to make up for that somehow. Tattle telling was forbidden at school and I didn't tell my parents either. The two older boys would just laugh and egg him on. One girl Juliette sometimes walked about half mile with us before she turned off on her road, but that was rare.

The school bus would often pass me as I walked along and Bee and Carl said it just made them feel awful to see me walking while they rode. As it got closer to winter, Bee asked the bus driver if he would stop and pick me up. He said, "no, it's against the law for me to stop on the highway, much less take anyone who is not on my route. When he saw how cold it was, he had a change of heart and told them if I would be at his last bus stop right across from my school when he let Ordell off, I could get on. However, that didn't work out very often, due to timing. Sometimes when school was out, I would go to that bus stop and wait and wait, only to find out that the bus had already gone. One time in particular I thought my parents were going to pick me up. The teacher had finished her work for the day and as I was still waiting she asked me what I was going to do. So, I said "I guess you'll have to take me home". She did, but I found out at home that was not something I was supposed to do.

Book learning I don't remember much about...just the fun things in school. This was the only elementary school I attended that had a basement. The furnace was down there and it made a lovely place to play on rainy or snowy days. All holiday parties were down stairs and in addition it served as a community room. My Dad would help count the votes at the school during election, and since all was hand counted and checked it would be long after midnight before they finished.

We only had a merry go round for play equipment and I soon found out it was not for me. We would eat lunch and head for the merry go round. Poor teacher, I wasn't the only one she cleaned up after. Since no one rode horses the years I attended, we girls used the stable for a play house. One girl even brought curtains to put over the window to make it homier.

Halloween was my first school holiday, and was held at night with everyone's families attending. Our family made our masks with paper sacks, drawing on faces, cutting out holes for eyes, nose and mouth. Bee was very artistic. She even cut on ears and glued on the side of her mask, and made slashes along the bottom to represent a beard. A prize was given for the one who could fool the people as to their identity. We bobbed for apples, and had popcorn balls to eat. Several days before the party we would hand cut confetti that was used to sneak up behind someone and throw on them.

Grandma Nelson's birthday was December fourth. We made an annual trip to Iowa for that. I don't remember if we alternated staying with family members or how that worked out, but this particular year, we stayed with my Mom's sister Sadie.

Cars then had only a small heater box that hung down underneath the center of dashboard, and gave very little heat. We still wrapped up in out winter coats, boots, gloves and covered ourselves with Indian blankets. On this particular trip I remember being thirsty the whole way. Mom and Pop had borrowed my thermos and filled it with coffee, but we had no water. So, they gave me a sip of coffee. That did not satisfy, so when we arrived at Aunt Sadie's I had some water, but that didn't quench my thirst either. So, she sent someone to the cave to get some homemade apple cider. It was cold and I drank glass after glass.   Apparently, no one paid attention as to how much of it I was consuming while Aunt Sadie was cooking up a patch of fried potatoes.   Let me tell you apple cider on an empty stomach had long lasting results. I missed two weeks of school before I was well enough to return.

The interesting thing the year before when we went to Iowa, they left Carl at home to take care of the chores. He was only in eighth-grade. I can't even picture leaving an eighth grader home now days to run the farm. Care included horses, cows, chickens and hogs. However, they did ask Peter Voll to come and spend the night with him for protection from tramps, or thieves. Still mornings he had to start a small fire in the cook stove, make his breakfast, fix his school lunch, do the chores and get ready for school. After school, fix a fire, do the chores and make his supper. No small feat for someone that young. He probably had to walk to and from school unless he rode Ribbon.

Back to school, preparations were being made for Christmas. We made wonderful things out of construction paper such as wreaths, Christmas trees, bells, etc. to hang in each of the school windows plus prepare for our school program. I had a part in the play. The play had something to do with a little boy getting hit by a car. I played the part of the boy and of all things I had to borrow Ronnie's striped overalls! They tucked my hair under a boy's cap and Ronnie's brother was the Dad who picked me up, supposedly being hit by a car. My line was. "I, I's alright" waking up from being knocked unconscious.

Now the party! Back then it was assumed that the teacher would buy gifts for all the students. We all bought her gifts too. I don't remember what I gave, but I remember what I got from my teacher. It was a NECKLACE. Clear colored marble like beads that was held together by gold catches. It was sooo pretty. And Santa Clause came. He handed out the gifts and had nice things to say about each child. I was so intrigued by him. I was shocked to find out many years later it was our dad who played Santa, since we didn't do Santa stuff at our house. My sister told me he went to great lengths to find out from the teacher about each student and their parents' names. I always liked to do acting throughout my life and apparently my dad did also as he was asked to be Santa the next year by popular demand.

My school lunches were always so much fun. While it was warm weather my mother would often put a penny in my lunch bucket and a note to the teacher that would allow me to cross the street to the gas station. They had quite a candy selection there. My favorite was licorice. The problem was sometimes the only licorice they had was shaped like a pipe. A no no in our family. Some kids would buy candy cigarettes, but that didn't interest me as they weren't licorice. I resolved the dilemma about the pipe by quickly chewing of the bowl part. The stem looked like a regular piece of licorice then. Not only was it fun to get candy at the gas station, but out front was a cage with a couple of chipmunks. There was a wheel in the cage and you could watch the chipmunks make that wheel spin around and around. Beside the penny, my favorite school lunch was sugar sandwiches. Bread, and butter sprinkled with sugar. In the winter I had soup in my thermos. Oh wow, the aroma when I opened that thermos was the envy of many. If my thermos had soup in it, Mom would put milk in a pint jar and many of we school kids would put the milk out on the cold, snowy window ledge. By noon it would have an icy crust across the top.

Next was Valentine's Day. I found out each of us had to make our own valentine boxes for class mates to drop their cards in. They were set out about a week before and could only be opened on the fourteenth. Bee showed me how to cover a shoe box and decorate it. I also made cards for everyone living at home and hid them in the cupboard in the bedroom, but for school I gave cards we purchased. I watched as others would put cards in some of the boxes that had a sucker inserted in it, or a stick of gum taped to the back. I was so in hopes I would get one like that. You didn't have to give a card to everyone, but my family made sure I did. Basically, the cards were reruns. You could tell because a name had been erased off the back and your name written over it. That was just common. There were only a few that got a valentine with a sucker or gum. I wasn't one of them.

Meanwhile TRAGEDY STRUCK AT HOME.

Carl and Bee were at the Irene high school and met each other in the hall, with these words. "something is wrong at home". They felt so strongly about it they convinced someone to drive them the eighteen miles home. That in itself was no small feat. When they went in the house they found our mother on the bedroom floor by the bed with the feather tick mattress pulled over on her. She evidently fell before she could get in bed and struggled to pull herself up.

Their ride had left, so one of them stayed at the house while the other ran the half mile to Voll's. They got Norbertha to stay with Mom while

Peter drove them to the gas station which was the closet place with a telephone. Talk about miracles, first to convince someone to drive them home because they FELT something was wrong. Second, they happened to know where our dad was working that day and knew those people had a telephone. Of course, the information was relayed to our dad, who immediately left for home. I guess Bee and Carl were scared since they both came to the gas station. Then they walked across to the school and knocked on the door. That's how visitors entered in those days. I watched as Miss Chance went to the door, then turned to me and told me to get my coat and things because I was going to be dismissed early.

We all three were in the back of Peter's car and Bee and Carl were whispering, but no one explained what was going on. I have little recollection about arriving home or what things immediately took place. However, Dr. Stansbury from Vermillion came and gave her some medicine. She was asleep or in a coma for five days. When he came back to check on her, he asked for a pencil. He took her eyelid and rolled it over the pencil, checking her eyes. I'm not sure what he told Pop but several people from both the Tabernacle and Yankton church soon came as well as several pastors. Many stood around in the bedroom while some of us sat. Wanda had come from Rapid City and was holding me on her lap in the sewing rocker. Bee was sitting on the crib mattress. A lady was soothing Mom's brow and saying, "yes, Sister Nelson". She said my Mom was quoting scripture. All of a sudden Wanda said, "Oh, she has stopped breathing". I said, "let me tell Bee". She said, "Bee knows", then I saw her weeping. We were there for a period of time and then ushered out of the room.

As was done in those days, the ladies went in the room, made the bed neatly, combed Mom's hair and made the body presentable. I didn't know much about death or funerals, but about a month or two before, my mother took me to a funeral of a little boy perhaps five years old. She explained a lot of things to me then. He was dressed in a suit and had his hands folded with a flower in them. So, for quite some time after, I would sleep on my back with my hands folded in case I died, so I could look nice.

Soon we were invited back in to the room. Pop immediately picked me up and held me. We stood at the foot of the bed by the dresser. One of the small dresser drawers contained my children's hankies. So, I asked my dad to turn around so I could get a hanky as I noticed people were crying, and I wanted to do what they were doing.

We left the room after a while. I don't remember the body leaving the house. I suppose someone contacted a coroner. I do remember it being late at night and I heard a terrible wailing outside. I opened the porch door and saw that all my brothers were there. All five boys and my dad made a circle with their arms around each other's shoulders weeping loudly. I remember hearing my dad say between sobs… "our home is gone". Now to a six-year-old, I thought that meant we didn't have a place to live, and that was scary for a while.

Chapter Thirteen

The Funeral and Final Days on the March Place

Yes, it's a miracle that God in His great providence had my mother take me to a funeral of someone that was not a relative and explain a few things. Now it was the day of Mom's funeral and the church was packed. I don't know how much longer it was from the time of her death until the funeral, but it was enough time for my Aunt Erma and Uncle Frankie from Iowa to come, and what a big help they were.

I remember exactly who the singers were and what they sang. It was CT and Ruth Beem. They sang, "Good Morning Up There." It was confirmed to me less than five years ago when Darlene, sent me some of her dad's notes she had found where he listed the song that they sang.

Then came the processional. It was raining and cold since it was February. As is still the custom in some places, people stood outside on either side of the exit to honor the casket and family as they left the church. But my father had all he could do to stand. Everyone but Pop and I, Aunt Erma and Uncle Frankie were outside. They whirled a chair around and sat my dad on it. He couldn't stop weeping and wailing. After what seemed a long time to me, his sister Erma said, "Virdie, it's raining, and the people are all standing outside; we need to go". (I don't think my siblings would have felt comfortable telling my dad what to do) At that point, he picked me up and carried me over to the casket so I could have one last look.

On the way to the cemetery, we had a flat tire. There was nothing to do but change it. It had stopped raining but was very muddy. We only had gravel roads. So, the men got out of the car, rolled up their pants legs and changed the tire. On we went to the cemetery. Most of the people were already there when we arrived. It was too muddy to drive the car back where the burial was. I remember Wanda saying to Pop, "Edythe doesn't have a winter coat, and it's too cold for her to walk back there". So, it was agreed that I stay in the car. It seemed forever for the people to come trickling back. The first two ladies that came back looked up and saw me in the car. I waved, but since they didn't wave back I thought, "Well maybe that's not what you are supposed to do at funerals". So, I didn't wave at anyone else.

They didn't have fellowship halls in the churches back then...so a large group of people came back to our house. I remember neighbors and church folks already there who had prepared and brought in lots of food as well as kept the fires going.

Different family members began to leave at some point in time, but things were not back to normal. Wanda came home to live and to be the lady of the house. It was a bad winter, and I didn't attend much school. In fact, at one point I was taken back to school to collect all my things from my desk. I remember all the school kids were very quiet and just stared at me. I didn't attend school anymore that year. We only had eight-month schools back then, so school was out in April. What a wonderful thing that God had impressed upon my parents not to promote me to second grade. I would have missed out on so much training.

I suddenly remembered the Valentines I had made for my family, and I told Pop, that Mom's Valentine's card was in the cupboard. He very gently said, "Well go get it, I will have to look at it for her".

Easter came, and I think I must have had preferential treatment. My dad took me somewhere just before Easter, and on the store shelf, I saw this great big chocolate Kewpie doll. I think it was about twelve inches high. It cost fifty cents. I remarked about that doll, but knew not to ask. Somehow, I was distracted in the store and did not know he purchased it until we got home. I had imagined that candy doll would last forever, but to my surprise when taking my first bite, I found out it was hollow.

Mother's Day arrived and the custom was for people to wear a boutonniere to church. You wore a red flower if your Mother was living. A white flower indicated your mother was deceased. It tore my father up to see his four children riding to church with him that Sunday wearing white flowers, while he wore a red one. I'm not sure when then custom faded out, but I don't see that much anymore.

Father's Day came. Wanda took me into town and bought Pop a belt. It was of clear plastic, with a tiny red stripe on it. I didn't know about Father's Day, or that this was a gift. On the way to church Pop said, "Boy, I need a new belt really bad". I said "well, why don't you wear the belt that Wanda got you?". She said, "shh" and my Father said nothing. I loved going to Yankton shopping, especially to J.C. Penny's. When you bought something and needed to get change back, the clerk would reach overhead and unscrew a cup that was connected to something that looked like a telephone line. She would put the money in the cup and pull a chain, and it would send it up to the balcony business office. They would make the change and send it back down the wires. Depending on the business there might be several of those cups going up and down the track. Pop thought our shoes should be purchased at Penny's. Open toed shoes were in style for the ladies, but Christians felt that was too worldly and we were forbidden to wear them. All ladies wore dresses, never slacks, and the dresses had to have long sleeves and full collars. Wanda, Bee and Mom all had long enough hair to sit on. Pop wondered if the long hair wrapped around Mom's head might have been the reason for her headaches which led to strokes. Not long thereafter Wanda cut her hair.

One of the things I liked my dad to do in the spring was to make whistles. He would take a small green branch and cut it off to I suppose about 6 inches. He would then take his pocket knife and tap around the green part. It would slide off in one piece, and he would make a notch in the inner part, put the green part back on and I could blow on it and whistle. That would last until it dried out. I remember him doing that for me for several years.

Summer came, and Gordon came home. He stayed at home and worked all the summer waiting for his "call" from Uncle Sam. I remember him helping Carl make sling shots. They found a tree branch that was shaped like a "y". Then took some old patching rubber from something and made a fine strip to stretch across it. The center of the rubber strip was a little bit wider and you would put a rock there, pull out the rubber band and let it fly. It was great fun that I even got to try.

The rope on the tree branch near our front door was beginning to rot. One day, Carl decided to show me how high he could swing. When he got up pretty high, the rope broke, and he had a hard fall. Keeping the swing board notched out to fit the swing was also quite a trick. It could become wider when the rope wore the wood away, and a new board might have to be found and notched.

One scary and at the same time funny thing happened. I was out playing and looked up and saw a tramp coming down the road. Wanda, Carl, and Bee were in the house. I ran into the house and told them. They looked out the window and saw him coming down our driveway. He had a long stick over his shoulder with a pack on the back of it. Muggsy began barking furiously. Carl and Bee ran in the pantry and Carl grabbed a ball bat. Everyone knew that the first thing a tramp wanted was food and would head for a pantry. We had no locks on our doors then except a hook over the front door. The tramp was so tired he walked across the porch and couldn't get in the front door so headed around to the back. Wanda had hidden in the closet in Pop's bedroom, which had a window in it. Just as the tramp passed by the window where Wanda was peering out, she saw that it was Gordon and yelled to Carl and Bee that it was their brother. In the meantime, no one had told me where they were hiding, and I was running around the house trying to find someone. Fortunately, we found out it was Gordon before he was way laid., because he did head for the pantry. A piece of equipment had broken down on his machinery, which he removed and started walking home with it. It was hot, and he put his coat over the end of it, making him look like a tramp. Tramps were common and I knew what one looked like.

I don't remember when Gordon was inducted into the army, but he left me his silver bank shaped like a cruise ship   Bee bought his big Bible from him that he had recently purchased. Before he left for the service, the custom was for soldiers to make a tour of their relatives to say goodbye. So, Carl and Gordon went to visit our Iowa relatives. They stopped at my Mom's sister's house. When they knocked at the door, they greeted her with "Hello, Aunt Molly" and she replied with "Aunt Molly? Who are you". So that became a saying if we didn't recognize someone, we would say, "Aunt Molly, who are you?"

When the time came for Gordon to leave, we took him to Yankton to leave on a bus. Lots of families were milling around waiting for their sons to depart on the bus. I remember sitting in the car while Pop and Gordon were standing outside by the bumper. Pop prayed for Gordon and I heard the bus call. Just then I saw a girl crying as she and her boyfriend kissed on the lips. We didn't kiss in our house, and it made me feel very uncomfortable. Funny what stays with you.   We sat there and waited until the bus left. My Mother's prayers weren't answered as far as her boys not going to war, but she didn't have to witness it. And those prewar prayers are no doubt one of the things that brought all three of my brother's home from the war with no injuries.

Gordon was in the war; my mother was buried and if that wasn't adjustment enough in itself...along came war rationing. Again, as a child, there were changes, but for me, life went on. Did I miss my Mother? Of course. But thankfully I was surrounded by my siblings and church family to help fill the void.

Gasoline, sugar, coffee, aluminum, shoes and rubber were some of the things that I recall being rationed. Since I could read, I remember so clearly the sticker that was on the passenger side of the windshield that said, "Is this trip necessary?". Since we needed sugar to do our canning, we adjusted our sugar consumption by using honey on our oatmeal and salt on our grapefruit. Instead of lots and lots of desserts, we learned to have "Brown Betty". Brown Betty was graham crackers with canned apples or something like that dumped over cracker pieces and whipped cream on the top. We didn't have to travel to work, so gasoline was basically used for the hay buck, shopping and going to church. My dad would get up in the night when he would hear cars pulling out of our driveway knowing they had stolen gas because the ground was wet under the gas barrel. I heard people talk about gas being siphoned from their car tank as they shopped or went to church.

Speaking of cars, in spite of the war, there were things we could buy to spruce them up. We purchased a little fan with rubber blades that were affixed to the steering wheel stock. That would help keep the frost off the windshield in the winter; because at times we would have to stop and scrape the windshield, drive a little farther and scrape some more. However, in the summer, that little fan could be used to cool the driver. (except in the heat the rubber blades would often rot). Also, the side windows helped direct the breeze on a person. Every "cool" car had to have a fancy spinner knob on the steering wheel and a fancy knob on the gear shift. Our knobs had pictures with pheasants on them. The hood ornament made a car really stand out too. In the summer, a canvas bag could be purchased to hook over the hood ornament and hang down over the radiator. The bag was filled with water, and it would somehow cool as you drove. When needed, you could pour yourself a drink in a collapsible aluminum cup. That was very important for travel in South Dakota as there were miles and miles of flat lands with no place to get water. It was about then that Wall Drug Store in Wall, South Dakota begin to advertise they had free cold ice water. Someone even carried one of their signs over to Germany as my brothers saw when they were in the war.

My family were rarely coffee drinkers, so that wasn't a problem during the war. Sometimes they might drink Sanka and Postum. We had ration books. Each member of the family was allotted a book with so many stamps in it, and it was to serve for a certain period. There were red ration books I think for gasoline, and blue ones for sugar.

Aluminum was at a premium. People would find discarded gum wrappers and peel the foil off them. Each stick of gum came in foil over wax paper. Carl especially would look out for discarded gum wrappers along the sidewalk after church and peel off the foil on the way home. Even tobacco bag linings and tin cans, made a collection to be saved and taken to the receiving place.

We walked a lot doing farm work, and the soles of our shoes would have holes where the greatest wear occurred. We learned how to cut out cardboard and stick inside our shoes to help preserve our stockings. Bee could cut hers out to fit perfectly inside her shoe. Mine was not so neat. Metal heel taps were pounded in our shoes to keep our heels from wearing down. You could buy two heel taps for a quarter. If your shoes still fit you and the sole was worn out, you might have a half sole replaced or at the shoe shop a full sole. Otherwise the repairs were done at home.

We missed making fudge, but one of our neighbors found something called "junket," and it was a pretty good imitation. One kind of Christmas hard candy was replaced with a jelly type filling. It tasted horrible in my estimation. Now it has become a permanent candy choice. Jello was at a premium, and we usually ate lots of jello, so that was a bit of sacrifice. We previously made lots of lemonade, but that was replaced with nectar. We got it from the Watkins man. He would make periodic rounds and if we bought spices or something he would always give a gift of some kind. I remember the combs were made out of hard rubber until the war when Watkins came out with a tin like comb. The Watkins man would demonstrate it by dropping it on the floor so you could hear the sound.

Rubber tires were another thing at a premium. I can still see my dad patching the tubing for the tires. The tires back then had a rubber inner tubing. So, changing a tire was a dual thing. You had to take out the tubing and get the patching can out of the car. You first would use a piece of metal to rough up the spot around the hole on the inner tube, smear this very strong-smelling glue around the area and cut another piece of rubber a bit bigger than the hole and it would somehow adhere quite well. Next you had to pump air in the inner tube and place it in the right spot in the outside tire.   Pop patched our rubber boots too.

I don't know if this had anything to do with the war or not, but my neighbors, the Voll's, had something they called Oleo. It wasn't colored like it is today when you purchase it. The oleo came in a bag, and a tube of yellow coloring came with it. You could dump the coloring in the bag and knead it around until it came out yellow colored. We churned our butter and never used this stuff called oleo. But the Voll's didn't want to bother coloring the oleo, so they spread this white stuff on their bread. From time to time I would stop at the Voll's house after school. They were the nearest neighbors to us, and today they would have called this babysitting. Then? They were just doing the neighborly thing when no one was at home to stay with me. They would watch for me, and one of them would stick their head out the door and say, "you are supposed to stay with us". Going inside, they would then cut me off a slice of thick bread and spread it with lard. Well, it was uncolored oleo, but to me it was lard! I wouldn't eat it until they found out why. Then they would take a small portion of the oleo and squeeze a little color in it for me.

I did enjoy stopping there though. Sundays, we didn't cook oatmeal because we were hurrying to get ready for church, but had cold cereal like Nabisco Shredded Wheat or Post Grape Nuts. The Voll's had Post Tens and each of these little boxes had cut outs on them, in the shape of stores and houses. So, they saved those for me to cut out and play with.

One of the things that just blew my dad's mind was sunflower seeds. One of the dreaded weeds that got in the fields were sunflowers, and they were forever trying to eradicate them. Of all things Carl happened to see and buy, was a package of salted sunflower seeds. We were all sampling them. Tasting and spitting, but it didn't tempt my father one bit. He couldn't believe someone was making money off things we whacked down.

War bonds were also for sale. We had savings bonds books. You could ask for a book I think at the Post office, and stamps to fill the book were 10 cents each. Once the book was filled, you could turn it in for eighteen dollars and seventy-five cents or wait until it matured ten years and it would be worth twenty-five dollars.

Well, now that I explained about rationing and the changes that happened that year, I will bring you up to fall. The school year was about to start. Wanda had good experience in being a substitute mother hiring out as what we now call a nanny. She noted the big heavy lunch bucket I carried my first year to school was too heavy for me and it would bang my leg as I walked, causing a huge bruise. So, she talked Pop into letting me get a smaller lunch bucket. I don't remember the figures on it, but it was a red square box style and yet had the thermos in it. It was much easier to carry. I was going into second grade. Bee was now a senior; Carl was a sophomore. The bad thing about getting my crayons with the war rationing was that they were now a lightly tinted wax and would often melt or easily bend in your hand. Some kids even chewed them. So, getting my crayons wasn't as much fun.

Apparently, we went to Iowa for Grandma's birthday party again. We stayed at Aunt Lori's house. She was surprised that I didn't have any night clothes but offered me one of Lorna Jean's nightgowns. It was white with lace at the neckline and across the bottom. Lorna Jean was their daughter who was five years older than me and had polio. She stayed in a hospital bed situated between the parlor and dining room. Of all the terrible things, they put a metal brace between her legs, (quite close to her ankles). It was used to lift her. I could talk to her, but that was about it. She was totally helpless. Back then they thought polio was caused from eating unpeeled peaches. They were sure it was the peach fuzz, so everyone made sure to peel their peaches.

During that visit for Grandma's party at Aunt Euma and Uncle Carl's, plans must have been made to move back to Iowa. I was not involved in the planning, but that's the only idea that I can come up with in my latter years. So, we headed back to South Dakota. (Aunt Lori let me take that beautiful nightgown home because Lorna Jean had outgrown it). Was that ever nice!!!

On the way back from Grandma's birthday celebration in December,

Pop decided to take us through Des Moines, Iowa. By the time we got there, it was dark and the stores were closed. No doubt this was planned because he stopped the car and we got out and walked up and down the streets to look at the wonderful store window decorations. Animated figures were in many of the stores, and it was like a dream come true for a child to look at those things. I believe the emptiness of not having a mother/wife, made him want to add a little cheer to the season. Wow, that was a winter wonderland. I probably slept under the horse blanket the rest of the way home with visions of sugar plums dancing in my head.

Christmas was different that year, but Wanda let me in on an adult thing. She made all kinds of candy and cookies to ship to Gordon, Rex, and MC overseas. Rex and MC were married by then. Sister Chapman came out and helped her pack the things in a box. They had a few more things to add as Pop was in town buying our Christmas candy. He came home with the candy and nuts. When they got them, all situated in the box, and while Pop was outside, Wanda called me from the dining room and let me see inside the box. I thought I'd never seen anything so wonderful. She quickly sealed up the box, and it was taken to town for mailing. I heard years later, the box arrived long after Christmas, with nearly every piece of candy and cookies broken, but they and their buddies gobbled up the crumbs anyway.

The arrangements were made for Carl and Bee to move to Rapid City to stay with Marvin and finish their school year there when we moved to Iowa. For Bee, it was a move for the rest of her senior year. I know it was a great transition for her, leaving a high school of perhaps fifty students to her senior class of several hundred. For some reason, Pop didn't want them to finish their year out in Iowa.

So now Bee and Carl were gone, and it was just Pop, Wanda and I. Well, I was excited about going to be by my aunts and uncles, so it didn't seem too much of a disappointment to me to move.

I continued with my second-grade schooling until the day Pop picked me up from school to close out my desk. It had been a rough year as I had missed so much school in my first grade, that going everyday was hard, and I had to learn Arithmetic. I hated it. I couldn't understand it. Subtraction was particularly difficult. The problems were like "eleven, then a question mark underneath it and underneath the line would be twenty-two". I was supposed to fill in where the question mark was. It was horrible. Not only that it seemed every kid in school had an Aunt Mary. Don't ask me why, but that made me cry. It sounded like such a lovely name to me. When Wanda found out why I was crying, she eased the pain by telling me our Aunt Mollie's name was actually Mary.

Most likely we moved around March so we could arrive in time for crop preparation. I just remember Uncle Vern pulling up in his big old cattle truck. Our furniture was piled high in the truck with its sideboards up. We must have looked like the Beverly Hill Billies. I went running up to the truck saying they had forgotten my rocks. I was trying to drag the bag they were in, but was told there was absolutely no room to haul them. I'm sure no one knew how important that was to me, or they would have somehow found a spot. I also had to leave my scrapbook. Mine was a catalog that had pictures glued over the top of each page. I used flour and water glue to make such a lovely book. Those were my two most cherished possessions, and they were left behind. I didn't know my scrapbook was gone until later. Muggsy was left behind for the next tenant. We stayed with friends that night; Uncle Vern went on, and we started another journey.

Chapter Fourteen

Iowa Bound to Uncle Carl and Aunt Euma's

Pop purchased Rex's Chrysler since Rex was going into the service. On our way to Iowa, the car broke down. I don't remember what town we stayed in, but we stayed in a hotel for over a week. The car garage didn't have the parts, and they had to send off for them. Every day my dad would walk down to the garage and stay all day, I suspect to get on the nerves of the people so they would speed up getting the parts. I don't remember much about our room, but we were on the second floor, and it had long winding stairs from the lobby. There were no elevators. The male clerk was too friendly with Wanda in my opinion. With her missing out on doing things with young people her age, because of being a surrogate mother, she may have enjoyed the attention.

Where we ate doesn't ring a bell, or what we did to occupy our time is lost in space, but I do remember Wanda telling Pop I needed a new dress. I guess we only had a few changes with us, so we walked downtown to a store, and she bought me a dress. The only one she could find to fit me in that small town was my hated color. It was a blue green one with a white ruffle down the bodice. But at least it was a new dress.

After many days, we arrived at Uncle Carl and Aunt Euma's home. Arrangements had been made for us to live in the corner house that they owned. It was very small with only four rooms. An eat in kitchen, living Room, back porch and two bedrooms upstairs. There was also a fruit cellar just outside the back door. It was a cave with a door on it, as many farmers had. Fruits and vegetables were kept in the dark cave, and they would last a long time. The house either hadn't been lived in for a while, or the last tenant hadn't taken good care of it, so we lived at Aunt Euma's while Pop and Wanda worked on the house. Pop was Uncle Carl's hired hand, so he could only work on it at night. They wallpapered, painted old cupboards and put new linoleum on the floor.

Wallpapering was not a two-hour job. Some people would just paper over the other wallpaper until it would build up with several layers. Pop did everything right though. The old wallpaper had to be scraped and peeled off to the bare walls. The new wallpaper had to be measured and cut. Two saw horses with lumber boards over the top, provided the work tables. The wallpaper paste had to be mixed and prepared. Then a special brush was used to slap on the paste. Next it had to be lined up with the pattern on the piece that was already on the wall. Sometimes for whatever reason, the piece might slide down the wall, and it would have to be re-pasted and lined up again. My dad was a hard worker. If there was any free time between planting and reaping the crops, he would hire out for different jobs. He painted barns, houses inside and out and was well known for his excellent wallpapering skills.

We stayed at Aunt Euma's a long time while our little house was getting renovated. Fortunately, Aunt Euma's had a big house. There was an upstairs with four bedrooms, plus a finished walk up attic. Pop had his own room, Wanda and I shared a room, and the school teacher had another bedroom. Aunt Euma boarded school teachers for the nearby country school. Uncle Carl and Aunt Euma had a bedroom downstairs, and Grandma's bed was in the parlor. They had a furnace in the basement, electricity AND an indoor bathroom.

My teacher just happened to be Miss Webb, my father's first cousin. She was so nice, and I suspect I may have received special treatment. She stayed at Aunt Euma's during the week but would go home on week-ends.

Here is a description of Aunt Euma's house. Between the dining room and parlor hung a curtain of beads. Everyone always remarked about those beads. In the parlor, she had a player piano. Oh, what fun that was for us to play those piano rolls. She also had a Victrola. She even had a couple of little records for children. One played "Mary had a little Lamb, " and the other played "Little Bo Peep." You had to crank the Victrola, so at first some of the songs might be a little high speed, but as it began to wind down, it would drag. Aunt Euma was very particular about her records and it was OK for me to play them as long as I asked. However, one day, I broke one of the kid's records. I hate to say it, but Wanda and I just put the broken record back in with the rest of the records without saying a word, and she never mentioned it. Oh dear, your sins will come back to haunt you even if you know the Lord has forgiven you.

Aunt Euma's bathroom was painted in purple and lavender. They didn't have such paint colors back then, but she figured out how to mix some paint and come up with that color. She had tile pieces on her floor that was shaped like a baby's foot. People always commented on her purple bathroom.

Next to the bathroom was where the water heater was located. It was kind of a little closet with just a curtain over it. She called it the "hot" room. If she washed her hair, and Wanda pin curled it for her, she would sit in the little hot room, and it would help dry her hair. Wanda knew how to finger wave too, so Aunt Euma would ask her to fix her hair.

There was also a wash house. I'm not sure how it was heated, but Aunt Euma did her canning and laundry there. Outside the wash house was a grape arbor over a sidewalk that led to a water pump. Next to that was a fish pond with several kinds of gold fish that grew to about 12 inches. In the center of the fish pond was a bird bath, with lily pads growing around it. Aunt Euma kept several goldfish in the house in a regular gold fish bowl. In the spring she would transfer those to the fish pond and those little bitty fish would grow quite big. I found out the size of the gold fish is determined by the size of the space they have to swim in. In the winter she would transfer those from the fish pond to a big horse tank in the barn, and they would get even bigger. Then she would start all over again in the winter with the small fish in the fish bowl.

One of the other fun things I did, was to change her pictures. She had an oval picture frame on the wall by the clock. Magazines and calendars would carry full-size pictures without advertising on them, and she kept a stack of those. I could go through the stack and choose what picture to put in the frame. The same picture had to stay in there for at least two weeks.

Aunt Euma and Uncle Carl also had a floor console radio, a wall telephone and subscribed to a newspaper. We would gather around the radio in the evening and listen to Dr. I. Q. It was a quiz program, and if you were the first to answer the question by calling in, you could get a box of Mars candy bars. We never won. Since my brothers knew they had a telephone, they would try to call us from the army post, but with it being a party line, it was often difficult to hear what they were saying. The daily newspaper, had a little puzzle in the back called "The Wishing Well". We were to cross out certain letters that Aunt Euma helped me with, to give us our wish.

The house had highly polished stairs steps and a banister on the side. One of the things I liked to do was sit at the top of the stairs and bump bump on my bottom all the way down. I found out it drove Grandma nuts. I wouldn't do it when Aunt Euma was in the house, but waited until it was just Grandma and me, and I would bump down the stairs.

About the last thing I remember is that there was always a square of honeycomb in the center of the table. Aunt Euma kept her salt and pepper, butter, jam and honeycomb on her kitchen table all the time. At the end of the meal, it was covered with a small table cloth and ready for use the next time.

Let me tell you about Indiana School which was my second school. Slowy School was my first and this school building was considerably smaller than Slowy school. Slowy school even had room for a stage. Even though it was small, Indiana was acceptable. For one thing, it was only three-fourths of a mile to school, and I always walked to and from. Not only that I often had nice kids with whom to walk. One family, the Braden's, lived to the east of us, and they had an older girl Johanna, and two brothers, William and Robert. The Johnson's to the west of us had four children. Wanda, Beverly, Doris, and Melvin. I liked them with the one exception.

One-day Johanna and I were walking to school, and we saw some wildflowers. We stopped and picked a big bunch to take to the teacher. The Johnson kids were ahead of us and just before we got to the school, one of the girls turned around and said, "what do you have in your hand?" We said, "flowers for Miss Webb". I suspect since she knew we might get special favor, and she didn't have anything for the teacher she quickly retorted, "Oh those are snake flowers. I wouldn't be caught dead giving those to the teacher". Well, we didn't want to give something awful to the teacher, so we threw them down.

Our Superintendent at that school's name was Miss Lyons. Her job was to make periodic visits to all the country schools and unannounced, I might add. She didn't want to touch the door knob with her hands, so she would put her handkerchief over the doorknob to enter and exit. She would check to see if the water pail was full, the washbasin clean, and observe while the teacher taught a few classes.

The teachers used their own money for such things as "Old Dutch Cleanser", soap and toilet paper. Miss Webb would bring a small amount of Old Dutch Cleanser in one of her empty moisture jars. Those jars had such pretty colored lids such as pink, purple, and rose, that we school girls would request to have the jar when it was empty. So, she had to keep a list of requests. When it came to me she said: "Surely Wanda has jars like this that you can have". But the only jars Wanda had, was Noxzema that came in a large navy-blue jar.

I learned things in that neighborhood that I had no idea existed. One day soon after we moved in, I was walking to school and came to the very first house. A man was in the yard that I thought was Uncle Carl. I called to him and waved. He just turned around and didn't respond. When I got home from school that day, I told Pop about it. He said, "Well that man's name is Bernie and its Uncle Carl's brother. They don't speak to each other and since we are staying at Uncle Carl's that makes him not like us too". I couldn't imagine brother's not speaking! Our family was and is very, very, close, but we were not the hugging, and kissing kind. It was the same way with all my aunts, uncles and cousins. We looked after one another, and were always excited to see one another, so this was foreign to me.

While staying at Aunt Euma's, she taught me how to tell time. Unlike today where all the clocks are digital, the clocks then were Roman numerals. Why, I don't know. So, she taught me how to count by fives and read Roman numerals so I could tell time.

One day after school when I arrived at Aunt Euma's, my temporary home, she told me that I was to go to the corner house. It would have been about a block away. I went in the house and looked around as I had not been in there before. Aunt Euma's home had all the modern conveniences, and now we were back to the outhouse, and no electricity. Wanda had neatly fixed the kitchen up with a tablecloth kitty corner over the table. I had not seen that done before; it looked kind of classy to me.

Now and then Joanna and I would stop by Aunt Euma's on the way home from school and say "hi" to Grandma. Grandma would tell us stories about her childhood and always wanted to quiz us on our spelling. The Des Moines Register came out with a one- hundred-word spelling list once a year to prepare students for a spelling bee. Apparently, spelling was one of Grandma's gifts so she would drill us on those words. Grandma told me when she was in school; she was made fun of one day when the teacher asked her to read a word. It was pigeon, but she pronounced it pig on. An older boy in the back of the room, went Ho, Ho, Ho. And the teacher said, "Now Willard, she is just learning to read". Willard was about twenty-one years old, as students worked so much on the farm, they could only catch snatches of school.

Occasionally Aunt Euma would ask me to stay in the house with "Ma" while she went to town. If Grandma had a "spell", I was to switch the pole light on and off a few times, and Uncle Carl would come in and diagnose the problem. One night I was there, and both Uncle Carl and Aunt Euma were gone. Grandma and I were mighty hungry. I had kept the kitchen range going (even though they had a furnace they still used the range cook stove). Grandma said, "get out the skillet, and put some lard in it and we can have fried mush". I didn't know how to fry mush, so she came out and said she could do it. Well, I'd never seen Grandma in the kitchen before; she usually just sat in her rocker. So, she came out and began to fry mush. Her skin was almost transparent it was so thin, so when the grease popped on her, she had big blisters. But I will have to say; she made the best mush I thought I'd ever tasted.

Aunt Euma decided I needed to learn to iron. I guess I was about eight years old. So, she had me iron Uncle Carl's cotton shorts. She always starched and ironed them. I could only imagine how that must have felt. Road rage. Undershorts rash. I think I would have grouped them together. I also learned to iron the men's handkerchiefs, too.

Even though Aunt Euma and Uncle Carl seemed to have the best of everything, they worked for it. That summer she had me come and pick up walnuts under her tree and bag them, while she dressed chickens. We headed to Airfield where she would drive up to a neighborhood. I would run up and knock on a door and ask them if they would like to buy fresh cleaned chickens or walnuts. I remember knocking on the door of one house, and a male voice kept yelling out, "Just a minute," So I waited and waited. Pretty soon a man came to the door and apologized because he was in the bathtub, had to dry and get dressed. I can only imagine his disgust when he found out it was a sales pitch. Needless to say, he didn't buy anything.

With jello being hard to buy during the war, Aunt Euma made it known to people getting groceries, to bring her some if "jello had come in" Usually people could find a box or two to bring to her and consequently she had one whole cupboard full of jello. She would often have Wanda come and clean house for her, taking a whole day to clean. At the end of the day, she would give Wanda a couple of boxes of jello, or if she fixed Aunt Euma's hair, she would give her a couple of gold fish. Wanda got to pick out the ones she liked, but had to leave them because we didn't have a goldfish bowl. Not a complaint was verbally mentioned to Aunt Euma. Why did I mention this? While it may seem that we were taken advantage of at times, but learning to keep quiet usually pays off. At the end of her life, Aunt Euma left all of us something. God has a way of making things up to us.

Aunt Euma and Uncle Carl always kept their houses and barns well painted They had a painter that came, and his name was China Baker. As he would paint the outside of the house, I loved to watch him because he always talked to himself. I would stand by the window on the inside and watch his lips move up and down, as I had never seen anyone talking to themselves.

Another person in the neighborhood had the name, Fatty Davis. He was thin as a skeleton and lived in a railroad box car. I asked my dad why they called him that when he was so thin. He said..." Well, he used to be fat, and people made so much fun of him, that he lost weight". A lesson on how words can hurt.

The Braden's and our family were good friends. With our parents' permission, we children often walked to each other's place to play. On one particular day, I was at the Braden's home, and we climbed up on a fence and then on to a roof of a shed. It was a slanted roof, and William and I somehow dared one another to jump. This was in the hog lot, and there were lots of corncobs below which could have been added danger. I was the first to jump. I landed OK, so now it was William's turn. He suddenly declared he heard his Mother calling even though no one else did, and scampered down the safe way and ran into the house.

Bogus was the nick name for the town of Abingdon, our closest town. My dad explained to me where the name came from. He pointed to an old two-story unpainted building where supposedly bogus money was churned out. I recently talked to an Iowan and told them I lived near Abingdon at one time. They had no idea where I was talking about, and then I said, Bogus. They knew exactly of which I spoke and were shocked to hear that was a nickname. The town had one gas station, where the proprietor would come out to fill our gas tank. The top of the gas pump was clear glass and had marks of one, five, ten etc. on the side. He would pull a lever back and forth on the side of the tank and it would pull the gas up to the level on the glass top that indicated your requested amount of gallons.

We attended the Christian church in Abingdon and it was much different than the churches we attended in South Dakota. It was very formal and served communion every Sunday. But no one came by our pew and patted me on the head as at the Tabernacle. They were without a piano player, so Wanda filled that position immediately. My Aunt Euma went to church there. Before we moved from that area, my father led his nephew Merle and his wife Arlene to the Lord. God obviously had a purpose in our being there. One other good thing happened at that church. I was sitting by my father and apparently did something that could have taken me to the woodshed. When we got home after evening church, he spoke rather sternly to me about my behavior. He said, you are eight years old now, and you will never receive any more spankings; but he laid out some rules nice and clear. Indeed, I never received any more spankings after that.

While we lived at the Cline house, we received notice that Cecil and Irene had a girl and they named her Linda. Me, an aunt at the age of eight? I was a wee bit jealous though when my dad went to see her at some point in time. He brought back a picture of her with a stuffed rabbit that he got for his first grandchild. (He never gave me a stuffed toy!)

Chapter Fifteen

Fruit Basket Upset

As was aforementioned, Bee and Carl had finished school in Rapid City and had worked most of their summer there before coming to Iowa. Our little two-bedroom house was a little more crowded, so Wanda went to South Dakota I suppose for a much-needed break from being an early surrogate mother. She visited her old friends there and soon found a very profitable job.

She became employed by an attorney in Vermillion as their nanny. Dr. and Mrs. Collins and family liked Wanda right away. One day she fixed one of their meals, and they couldn't believe what a good cook she was. They loved her as a nanny, and they loved her as a cook. But the cost of her room and board was eating up her salary, so the Collins's made her an apartment on their third floor. They obviously knew a good thing when they had it.

The family began entertaining a lot with such a good cook. The complete care of the home was too much for one person, so they hired a school girl to come and help Wanda. Wanda's salary was $100 a month plus her room and board! That was very, very good. She had weekends off to go to church and was allowed to entertain guests in her apartment evenings and week-ends. I believe God was rewarding her, for having to skip her young years of being a substitute mother. She bought herself a very nice gabardine coat. Quite classy! She also bought me clothes and mailed home to me. In the meantime, she met a nice young man, and they became engaged.

As I said, Bee and Carl were now home, and Wanda was gone. Fruit basket upset. Carl started to high school in Packwood. He was a Junior that year and had to walk three miles before catching a bus for the last four miles. A young lady from our church in Bogus walked two more miles than he did. For some reason they never liked walking together so Carl would either try to get ahead of her or lag behind.

Miss Webb had resigned from Indiana school to get married, and Miss Buch was now my third-grade teacher, and she was just as nice. My first three teachers were wonderful. Miss Buch introduced us to "old Maid" cards that we girls could play at recess in the winter when we couldn't go outside. However, that was short-lived for me. My father did not allow card playing, and when he heard about that activity, I was forbidden to play.

I don't remember much about school there except that is where I learned my multiplication or" times table" as we called it. I had a terrible time learning my "times" so I had to bring my flash cards home to practice in the evenings. My father was a very smart man, even though he didn't go beyond eighth grade. He simply couldn't understand why I couldn't get it. I would stand at the kitchen table evenings (which is where we spent evenings) while he sat and drilled me. I would try to keep the tears from rolling down my face, and my eyes would become so blurred I couldn't see the cards. Crying for that reason, was not allowed.

Our Christmas there at that house happened to fall on a Sunday that year. I remember it, because we did open our presents before we went to church. Carl got something for him to keep warm walking to school; a mackinaw jacket, ear muffs, a corduroy hat and two pairs of corduroy trousers...one wine colored and one turquoise. Miss Buch gave me a play set of dishes. The plates and the cups were green with white saucers. Someone gave me my very first pair of pajamas! They were red flannel with yellow animal designs and even had a pocket. I wore them around before we went to church that morning. I remember the pocket because.... I had stuck some of my Christmas candy in there. I also received matching red house slippers. I had never had those before either. We always, I mean always had a Sunday afternoon nap. After dinner I put my pajamas on for my nap and guess what? The candy that was in my pajama pocket was now all covered with fuzz; but I ate it anyway.

Another thing that stands out at that house was when C.T Beem came by and spent the night. I think some of us went down to Uncle Carl and Aunt Euma's so he could have a bed. Our Aunt Erma was also his aunt by marriage, and she lived just outside of Packwood. But how honored we were that he came by for a visit and stayed at our humble home when he could have stayed at Aunt Erma's nice big home. His stay stands out to me, because I had never had a children's book of my own. Before he left, he opened his suitcase, and I saw that he had two books inside. He hesitated a minute before handing me one of those books. I know he must have gotten them for his daughter Darlene, but he sacrificially gave me one of those.

Aunt Erma, my dad's sister was Aunt Euma's twin sister. She and Uncle Frankie had a fun place to visit. They lived on a farm near Packwood. It was a huge house. Unpainted on the outside. But so nice on the inside. There was a huge eat in kitchen with a pitcher pump at the end of the sink. Her kitchen was always neat as a pin because she had a prep pantry attached to the kitchen. It was a place to mix, cut and chop without messing up the kitchen. When finished she could shut her pantry door and leave the mess behind.

The dining room, held a huge table and several comfortable chairs there and was separated from the kitchen by an archway. Another archway led to the parlor, which had   lovely furniture and a nice oil heating stove. Off that was their bedroom with a chenille bedspread on their bed. They had a small portable radio in the bedroom, and they would let me lie on the bed and listen to it. (they had mattresses and not feather ticks, so you could lie on the bed and not mess it up). Off the bedroom was a door to the upstairs. I know we stayed upstairs once because there was the memory of ironed sheets and pillow cases on the bed. What luxury!

Off the dining room was a separate stairway which led to the upstairs for the hired help. Their house was always warm even though they didn't have a furnace like Aunt Euma's. Off from the kitchen was an enclosed walkway to the summer kitchen. This is where Aunt Erma did her laundry and her canning. She also did all her cooking there in the summer so as not to heat up the rest of the house. Beyond that was the outhouse. Hers wasn't just any outhouse. She had linoleum on the floor and wallpaper on the walls.... plus, a calendar and pictures on the walls. The only real problem about the outhouse was you had to pass by their chained mean shepherd dog. He was on the loose unless company came and then they would chain him. However, several years later, he became "mad" and got Aunt Erma down. She yelled until Uncle Frankie heard her...but he had bitten her several times. She had to have several shots and stitches, and I assume that was the end of the dog.

Uncle Ray and Aunt Clara lived on the other side of Bogus. They had a small two-story house, and I loved going there. I don't remember anything about the house, except for the kitchen. Aunt Clara loved cooking and it was there I had an abundance of popcorn balls. I used her recipe for years. Also, Uncle Ray always made over me a lot. Aunt Clara seemed to sit a lot as she had swollen legs. But she was soft spoken and oh so nice.

Pop had a cousin Clarence Miller that we visited. His Mother was Pop's Aunt Lydie, which was his Mother's sister. She was a few years younger, than Grandma but looked quite a lot like her.   Pop and I went to visit Clarence once, and because my parents were older, I was used to being around older adults. But his wife Cora, couldn't stand it that I had nothing to do. She said, "well, I have a jump rope here, would you like it?". I didn't know how to use it, so Pop demonstrated it for me, and that became one of my enjoyable activities.

Clarence was the banker in Hedrick, and he and his wife lived in the back of the bank and rented out the upstairs bedrooms to school teachers. He said two ladies had signed contracts to teach in Hedrick and rented the rooms upstairs. The first night there they got to wondering what would happen if a robber should try to come and gag and bind Clarence. That night Clarence had a coughing spell. Trying not to wake the boarders he stuck his head in the pillow. They thought for sure he was being robbed and gagged.

Living there by Uncle Carl and Aunt Euma a year made our visiting times fun. That gave me quite a warm feeling having aunts and uncles nearby. Most of my first cousins were all grown and many married. I was the youngest grandchild which made some of my second cousins closer to my age, except none lived nearby.

In March it became time to move again. We had lived there one year, and my father had somehow saved enough money to buy a farm.

Chapter Sixteen

The Bixler Place

The Bixler place was the only farm my father ever owned. Our address there was Salem. We were written up in "Ripley's Believe it or Not," because our property came to a three-county point. At that point were Henry, Van Buren, and Jefferson Counties. And at that point was where our mailbox stood. I was supposed to go to school in Van Buren County...but that was about two and one-half miles away and up some back-dirt roads that would have been hard to get to in inclement weather. Also, it was less populated along the way. So, Pop somehow finagled the district to allow me to attend West Grove School which was only a mile and a half away and on a gravel road. When I said our address was Salem, that was it. You might address your letter like this. Mr. V. A. Nelson, Salem, Iowa. Occasionally someone might add the letters RR. It must have been fun for the Post Office in those days.

Once again my Father had spotted the perfect tree to hold a swing, and this time he bought a new rope for my swing. Perhaps visions of the rotten one that brought Carl to a hard-seated conclusion, was the reasoning for him to do so.   Pop also said he found the perfect tree to cut for Christmas. Oh boy!

Our house was bigger than the corner house at Aunt Euma's, but it was still small. We had an eat in kitchen, with a table and four chairs, a cook stove, dish cabinet and an orange crate that stood on end to hold the wash basin.   Another orange crate served as a stand for the water bucket.   The cream separator sat in the corner.   The steps to the upstairs were off the kitchen. The living room was rather large and we had Mom's dining room table and buffet in there.   Apparently, we had it stored at Uncle Carl and Aunt Erma's somewhere, because it wasn't in our first Iowa house. The room also held our one arm rocker, a heating stove, the library table, and the piano. Off the living room was a very small door-less room that held a cot and our sewing machine where Bee spent hours patching.   I don't remember anything about our bedrooms upstairs. Sometime while we lived there, Uncle Bernie, Aunt Julie and their grandson Ronnie came to visit. We bought a blue overstuffed chair and a separate matching foot stool from them. As a hostess gift they brought us an Olive wood salt and pepper shaker set from Oregon.

In our living room window hung a flag with three blue stars on a white satin background. That indicated we had three members of our family in the service. Some households had flags with one or two stars, but ours was one of the few with three stars.

Outside our front door was a small porch and trumpet vines grew over the trellises. There were also tile flower containers which we never used. There was a huge grove of trees out front, that if kept mowed almost looked like a park. But since the only thing we owned was a field mower, it was hard to cut around the trees. Even if it did, there was still lots of stubble in the grassy places, but it looked nice from the road.

I started to West Grove school in March. My school teacher's name was Miss Stark, and she didn't give me the special treatment like I was use too. She already had her favorite student before I got there. Even though she was fairly nice to me, I could feel her coolness. My first school had twenty-seven students. My second school had twelve students, but this one only had six students. Now I am in my latter part of the third grade. Fortunately, I had my "times tables" learned by then as I don't think Miss Stark would have been too tolerant. I had to walk by her house to get to school. She often hadn't left yet when I passed by, but do you think she'd give me a ride in her car? Nooooeee. She lived with her parents while her husband to be, was in the war. Fortunately, I only had her one more year...although I will have to say she was a very pretty lady and dressed very well. She really wasn't mean but like one of the students said to me, "You don't get honeyed up like her pet does, do you?"

Remember how I said the School Superintendent's name at Indiana school was named Miss Lyons? Well, the Superintendent here at West Grove name was Miss Graw. It sounded like growl to me and I thought it a bit funny to follow someone by the name of Lions...plus she had the same mannerisms that Miss Lyons had. She sat at the desk with her coat on, so as not to touch anything unclean. Hotty Totty.

Carl had to finish out his Junior year at Lockridge. It was about fifteen miles away, but he would walk a couple miles to the neighbors, who happened to be the school superintendent, and ride with him and his daughters.

.

It was here at this house, place and time that I began to see the world in a different light. I learned I was old enough to contribute to the working world. Up until then, I really couldn't have told you much about how things were done. For the first time, I learned to gather eggs by myself. I slightly remember going with a sibling to gather eggs before, but now I was on my own. I learned you took authority under that old hen. You reached in under her rather quickly if she was still sitting on the nest and pulled out those eggs. If you moved your hand rather slow, she would indeed give you a peck. It was also a trick to carry the eggs in a bucket without tripping or cracking them when running. I also did floor scrubbing duty, even though I do remember doing that before Mom died. No, we didn't use a mop. Most of my years of scrubbing the floor was on my hands and knees with a rag and pan of water.

In addition, I learned there were ashes to be removed from the cook stove. There was a small bin at the bottom of the wood burning part that was filled with ashes. That had to be removed once a day and emptied in the coal bucket. The best way to do that unless you wanted to clean up a mess, was to put a newspaper under the ash bin, and coal bucket. There was a shaker on the side of the stove that let the ashes drop down into the ash bin. Then the ashes had to be carried out to the "ash pile". The ash pile might also have cinders in it if we used coal for the heating stove in the living room. The cinders definitely made for good traction for the car tires to keep from getting stuck in the snow in winter.

Since this was spring we didn't have to build a lot of fires for heat, just for the cook stove. But come winter I had added chores. I had to go to the hog lot and gather up a bucket of corn cobs, plus fill a bucket of twigs for kindling to start the fire mornings. I had to carry chopped wood and stack it on the porch outside the kitchen door. I was shown about how much wood that had to be brought in to last for a full day. Since I was small in size, it took me forever to fill the wood quota as I could only carry two or three sticks of wood at a time. Also, I had to make sure the kerosene bucket was filled from the barrel and placed behind the kitchen stove. That was what you dipped a corn cob in to give the fire a boost. A match box was hanging on the wall near the cook stove. Our match box was kind of bent and old, but we finally got one that had a picture on it.

The first thing after we moved besides starting to school was to locate a church. My dad found the Round Prairie Baptist church about five miles away. It was more like our churches in South Dakota. The people there were warm and friendly and once again the church was the center of our lives.

There was one family there we especially connected with; the Cline's. Now, Uncle Carl and Aunt Euma's last name was Cline, but this family was not related to them. Anyway, Joyce and Minnette were closer to Carl and Bee's age and Vaughn, Judith and Sharon were closer to my age. We were together a lot. Remember as I tell these stories especially about the church folks, the years sort of all run together.

We had lots of friends in the area. Beside the Shelton's, there were the Litton's, the McElwee's, the Huff 's, the Harvey's, the Hildebrand's, the Wilson's, and some young people that Carl and Bee hung around with whose last name I don't remember. One was Evelyn, another Elaine, another Howard, and another Lauree. Many of the young folks came to our house, and Bee and Carl went to their houses. As far as I was concerned even if there were only one or two people my age, that was just fine. People in those days often associated with those a few years older or younger as was my case. So, my main friend was Judith, although I liked her brother Vaughn and he liked me.

My dad was soon asked to teach the adult SS class. He was used to saying "amen" in our South Dakota churches and did so here, even though that didn't seem to be the custom. The reason I inserted that, is because when we moved from that church, they gave us a farewell party and dedicated a poem to my father, called "the Amen Corner". Carl became the church janitor which involved going a couple hours before the Sunday services in the winter to start the fire in the furnace. Bee joined the BYF. (Baptist Youth Fellowship). At times, Bee had to take me with her even though I was much too young to be in that group. Carl had chores and a job to do.

When we started going to Round Prairie church, the pastor's last name was Green. He had red hair, and so everyone called him "Red Green". He received a letter in the mail once where someone merely made a red crayon mark and a green one for his name. The Parsonage was in Lockridge which was at least five miles away. No one expected the pastor to both farm and preach.

One funny thing happened when Carl was janitor. Since this was a country church, it wasn't unusual to smell skunks around the area. The church did have electricity and a basement with rooms for Sunday School classes and the furnace room. We still used outhouses and were always careful to check for skunks. But one Sunday morning, Carl was thrilled to corner a skunk in the church coal bin. He was the hero for sure when he clubbed the skunk to death. He promptly put the skunk in a gunny sack and loaded it in the car. We no longer had to deal with a skunk scent during the church hours!! Indeed, we had to deal with more than a scent. It was a huge smell. And when the Pastor got there he had a situation to deal with. So, did we when we got ready to leave for church. Carl took the skunk out at home, but now our car smelled really strong. We got in the car to drive to church, and the smell was unbearable. So, Pop got his Old Spice lotion and dumped it all over the car. We rolled the car windows down and made sure to keep our hats, gloves, and coats buttoned up for the winter ride. When we got to the church, all the church windows were opened as well as the doors thrown wide open, which was the pastor's solution. Everyone had to keep their outer garments on during the whole service.

The Cline's lived down a dirt road, and when it was muddy, they would leave their car by the gravel road, roll up their pants legs and walk home. They had a wagon to ride in to get back to the road for their car. I suppose it was horse drawn although I don't remember. But come winter they had a church invited chili supper at their house. The snow was so deep no one could drive back there, but parked along the gravel road. The Cline's took the wheels off the wagon and put rudders on it and met people at the gravel road giving us a lovely sleigh ride.

We attended Farm Bureau meetings over the years, which would usually include a dinner at someone's house and were mostly people from our church. Also, there were 4H meetings, which we participated in somewhat.

One of the projects for 4H, involved doing some canning. Since we had two big cherry trees in our back yard we invited the 4H Club to come to our house to do canning. The trees were just loaded, and we had enjoyed them our first year even though we didn't do any canning then. We certainly made lots of pies though.

It takes a lot of sugar to can cherries, so we were all prepared. The jars were all sterilized, and the big boiler on the wood kitchen stove was ready to set the fruit jars in to complete the canning process. First, the cherries had to be picked from the tree. A ladder was used to reach and pick the cherries, filling several buckets. Then the cherries were washed and pitted. We didn't have a cherry pitter, so all the pits were squeezed out by hand. At last they were ready to be cooked. Lots of sugar was added, and they kept stirring the cherry/sugar/water mix until it started to boil. Someone checked the big kettle and thought there was a lot of foam on the top. Except a close look showed the foam was wiggling. The cherries were wormy!!! The worms were white and heretofore indistinguishable from the white inside of the cherry. Pounds of sugar was wasted plus all the labor and the loss of the canning project for the 4H club. Our first thought was to skim off the worms but decided against that. Hmm, what about the year before when we picked them straight from the tree for a sweet treat, plus all the pies? Most of my siblings lived to be in their seventies, eighties, and nineties. A medical thought...perhaps worms are healthy for you?

After school was out that summer, I stayed at Uncle Ray and Aunt Clara's house. They had a different house moved from some other location and their old house was torn down. Pictures showed the new house being moved, taking up the width of the road as it was being transported. I don't know where they got it, but it was a very nice large house. They had electricity, a furnace in the basement, running water and later a bathroom.

The house had a large kitchen with a sink, a huge dining room with a lovely table and buffet and a silver tea set adorning the top of it. Uncle Ray had a rocking chair by the bay window that had window seats with storage underneath. That is where I sat and talked to him. There were a big parlor and a lovely polished staircase near the front door. There were at least three or four bedrooms upstairs. I was given a bedroom all my own.

I'm not sure if they offered to have me stay there or if Pop asked, but it was sooo much fun. I had never been away from my sibling or parents for more than a night or two, so this was quite an experience. Their son Merle and wife Arlene lived there and co-farmed. Arlene taught school, but she was home in the summer. I stayed there one week that summer.

Uncle Ray reminded me enough of my dad, that I could talk to him by the hour if he'd let me. I discovered one thing though. Uncle Ray and Aunt Clara didn't go to church, ask the blessing at meal time, or read the Bible like we did at our house. So, I was determined to somehow change that. I had that little new testament that I told you MC gave me, and I would sit on the window seat by Uncle Ray and read the Bible. I told him I wanted to be a preacher like my brother MC. He would just nod his head and let me read away. I would get tired of reading after a while, but he would remind me that I needed to study if I was going to be a preacher. It could be he enjoyed hearing the Bible read.

I didn't know any preachers that chewed tobacco, and I wanted to mimic Uncle Ray who did. He had a tobacco pouch and would pull out this long stuff that looked like field grass and make a ball of it on one side of his mouth. He would go outside and spit now and then and he could shoot it quite away from the step. Since I ate licorice candy, I suppose one day by accident I spit and low and behold it looked like his tobacco spit. I never could spit as far as Uncle Ray even though I tried.

Back at our farm after my stay/vacation was over, there were a lot of new and interesting things going on. It was about a mile down to the "bottoms" where most of the planting was done. There was a nice little creek that rippled over some rocks there. Near there my Father found not one, but two Indian arrowheads and they were pointed and sharp! We kept those around for years, but somehow got lost in the shuffle. Also, my dad found wild hazelnuts and wild peanuts growing down there. He reasoned the Indians must have planted some and volunteers grew up from that. He brought them both home, but because of their size, were not really edible.

Pop planted watermelon down at the bottoms each year. When they were ready to eat, he would pick one or two and put them in the stream and the cool water in the creek that ran under the shade trees would bring them to a nice temperature. When he came home at night, he would bring one or two of them. Nothing tastes better than ripe watermelon in my opinion.

I also learned about moles. They were tearing up our yard, and you could easily turn your ankle over the raised ground when you headed to the outhouse. But my dad had a remedy. He gave me a bucket of water. I was to stand over where he thought the entrance to the mole hole was and he would watch for the movement under the ground when the moles were actively at work. When he signaled I was to dump that bucket of water down the hole and it would flush the mole out at the other end where he was standing with a pitchfork... and that's how we stopped the moles from tearing up our yards.

We took Saturday night baths. The wash tub, that also served as a rinse tub and a bathtub, was brought in on Saturday nights and set in the middle of the kitchen floor over old newspapers. That is in the winter time. Water was heated on the cook stove and the tub filled about half full with it. The men bathed last, and of course, hot water was added from the tea kettle when a different person got in the tub. We were each afforded total privacy in the kitchen. In the summer it was a different story. Pop purchased a bucket shower from the Watkins man, and it hung on the side of the wash house. It was a three-gallon bucket that was hung higher than our head. It had a spigot on it that when released, would send water down a tube into a large brush that had spray holes in it. This made a lovely shower. Nails were on the shed for us to hang our clean clothes. It was especially nice to use if I had been walking through the mud barefoot. Anyway, the spray brush did a great job. As always outside showers were not without problems. A car could drive by, or neighbors could come for a visit, even though Pop tried to make sure the shower was hidden.

Chapter Seventeen

Fourth Grade

Our family had met one of our neighbors by the name of Watson's not long after moving near Salem. They had a daughter Joy who was a grade behind me and also the teacher's pet. (I found that out last year in third grade.) Their mail box was just a short distance from our mailbox. When I say short distance, perhaps a quarter of a mile. They had a long lane of about a mile to get back to their house. Mrs. Watson's name was Margret, and she was a nurse. Her husband's name was Arlo. He did some small farming, and operated a lumber mill. They had a very nice house, and I loved to go there, as Joy was an only child and had lots of toys. However, like us, they had no electricity and no indoor bathroom.

Sometimes I could go to Hillsboro to the grocery store with the Watson family and among other things they would buy raisin cinnamon bread. I had never had it before, but Joy would break open the bag and we'd eat it on the way home. They had a panel truck, and the truck had seats along the side. As we rode along eating, Arlo would sing "Mares e dotes and cows e dotes and little lambs e divvy. . . A kettle eat ivy too wooden shoe". Otherwise known as "Mares eat oats, and Cows eat oats, and little lambs eat ivy. A kid will eat ivy too, wouldn't you."

I will have to give credit to my father as he made holidays fun and special. That summer on the fourth of July, he had gone to town and purchased a 50-pound chunk of ice. He brought it home and put it in the washtub with a whole case of orange soda pop around it to get cold. He also bought a huge bag of peanuts in the shell. People were in the habit of just dropping by, and since it was a holiday, most farmers took the day off. Whoever came was treated to Orange Vess and peanuts.

One of the things we did on the farm was take the cream to the creamery at least once a week. When we sold the cream, we would use that money to buy any groceries needed. Since we canned our vegetables and fruit, and had our own meat, we only had to buy the main staples. One summer day Bee, Carl, and I were headed to Mt. Pleasant to sell the cream. Our drive took us through the Oakland Mills, winding, hilly road. The regular cream can was fat and squatty, but Pop had just purchased a new tall cylinder can. We all three were riding in the front seat for some reason. We suddenly heard a thud but didn't know what it was. Later we looked in the back seat and saw the cylinder can had tipped over and cream was pouring out all over the floor. We stopped the car and salvaged as much of it as possible but had to face our dad concerning the loss of the cream. If that wasn't bad enough, the heat of the summer turned that spilled cream on the carpet into a putrid smell that we endured for quite some time. Eventually, we disposed of that cream can as it spilled more than once.

The students at West Grove that year consisted of Keith, Donna and Maurice Garmoe, Joy Watson, David and myself. I don't remember David's last name. In fact, I don't remember a lot about school that year, except Keith was in eighth grade, and that was his last year there. His sister Donna was in seventh grade. Maurice, Joy, and David were all in the same grade. We played games inside in the winter that we made up. We would blindfold someone, and they had to move about the desks to find us, while we were in constant motion. We also played games like "Ante Over" and "Mother May I' outside.

David was an only child and had nice clothes. In fact, he had argyle socks which was quite a fashion statement in those years. However, those socks almost got him in trouble. He was standing up against the back of the school building waiting for the question, "Mother May I?" when I noticed one of his argyle socks didn't match the other. One sock was yellow and black, the other a red and black. When suddenly it dawned on me, the yellow and black sock was a snake wrapped around his ankle. I screamed and ran inside the school while the teacher and the other students dismantled the snake.

The school did have a teeter totter, which we used in a variety of ways. We discovered if we polished the wood it could become a slide. An individual could start with the teeter on one side close to the ground, walk up the teeter and when it tipped down on the other side, slide down it. Also, we had steel rods around the school ground for a fence that was just the right height to do "skin the cat". Or we could learn to walk the bars, which I did until I fell astraddle the rod.

One room schools were pretty basic. In the front of the school was the blackboard, a roll down phonics teaching lesson, the teacher's desk, a long fold-up bench by the teacher's desk for recitations, etc. Also, there was usually a globe or large paper maps that had drop down pages and two framed pictures of past presidents on the wall. I know one was always George Washington and I suppose the other was Abraham Lincoln. The school hours were from nine to four each day except the holdouts of daylight savings time. Many farmers, including my dad, refused to change their clocks then. So, in my household when it was fall, I went to school from ten to five. In the spring I went from eight to three. So, the question was usually, "are you on fast time or slow time?"

The school day went something like this. The school bell would ring a half hour before starting time. At starting time, it would ring nine times.

After that, you had five minutes before you would be considered tardy. That would show up on your report card. The teacher would stand by her desk and ask all students to rise and repeat the pledge of allegiance. Then we would say the Lord's prayer and be seated.

The teacher would already have the flag on the flagpole upon our arrival. In the winter she had a fire blazing in the stationary pot belly stove located in the middle of the room. If our outer clothes were wet from the snow or rain, they would be taken off and hung around the stove to dry and sometimes placed on top of the stove and turned from time to time to dry the other side of the garment. Talk about wet dogs? Wet human clothes smells were just as bad, especially if several were drying their clothes at the same time. Boots were turned inside out to dry as snow would get down inside them.

An example of how classes were held: A few minutes after opening exercises, the teacher might call "Third grade reading". At which time the students would then go to the recitation bench and be asked to read aloud. When class was over she would say, "class dismissed". She would repeat the call for all the classes, and for different subjects.

Mid-morning there was a fifteen-minute recess. Some people would go to their lunch boxes and get a snack. If it was nice weather, students were encouraged to go outside. That's when you were supposed to use the toilet. However, it was more fun to ask permission for a drink of water, or to go to the toilet during regular class time, and not use up your recess time. If the teacher didn't believe you needed to go to the toilet, sometimes the students would have a puddle under their desk, and they would have to wear wet stinky clothes all day.

After recess, classes resumed. When your class wasn't called, then you were expected to be studying. Well, talk about learning to shut out sounds when the teacher had recitation...you learned to do it. We also had desk inspections. The desk had inside storage under the desk lid. You were expected to have your books neatly arranged and written lessons neatly stored. At the right-hand corner of your desk top was an ink well. A bottle of Script ink was placed there if you were old enough to have a pen. MC had given me a child-sized pen. It had a lever on the side and operated kind of like a syringe to dip in ink to load it. Quite often you might wear your pen point down, and have to go to the dime store and purchase another pen point. Some people had just straight pens, where you had to dip and write a few words and dip again. There were different shades of ink: blue, black, purple, green and red. (Wanda used purple ink, and MC used green ink, which became their life long signature colors).

At noon, the teacher would announce" dinner time". You would then march by rows to the back of the room, and the assigned person would pour water in the wash basin for you to wash your hands. (Each student brought their own towel which hung on a peg by the water bucket). There was also a shelf by the water bucket where each student had their drinking container. I had a metal fold up cup for a while. These were to be taken home on Friday's, washed and brought back on Monday. Quite often the students would forget to do that, so you asked your friend if you could borrow theirs. And quite often the towels would remain there week after week.

Most of the desks had double seats and if there was a favorite person that you wanted to sit by, you had to request ahead of time to do that. Or sometimes you just ran and sat by that person. That was quite a privilege. Sometimes you might share food if someone asked for one of your cookies etc. We would hurry with our lunch as fast as possible to go out to play. It didn't take long to finish lunch if you had eaten part of it at recess. After lunch students resumed studies and classes. At midafternoon would be another fifteen-minute recess.

Fun times included practicing for school programs usually Halloween and Christmas. Schools in the area tried not to have conflicting dates. Those programs were always well attended and supported by the community. A wire was stretched across the front of the school and wrinkled curtains unpacked from their boxes, hung and hooked on the wire, thus making a stage. The students would be behind the curtains with another area sectioned off to hide until your part. Some of the visitors tried to cram in the desk seating, while many others stood around the outside circumference of the school room. After the program, the teacher's desk and some donated saw horses with boards over them were used to display all the pies and cookies that the adults had brought to be shared. I don't remember any beverages being served, but they probably were. No one was assigned to bring anything; people just did. I suppose they used paper plates.

Confetti was still "in". Sometimes the teacher would let us add construction paper to make our bag of hand cut paper more colorful. (Wouldn't our paper shredders have been the cat's meow for something like that?). While the grown-ups were visiting and consuming the refreshments, kids would go out and soap car windows. One year Carl hid out somewhere caught some of the kids soaping our car windows and made them scrape it off with his pocket knife.

At the Christmas program, gifts were given out by the teacher. There would be a tree that someone donated to the school from their farm, which the students decorated aforetime. Usually, the President of the School board would step forward and present the teacher with a gift, supposedly contributed by the students' parents. The visitors would congratulate the students that they thought did an outstanding job. Of course, we students tried to make the rounds to people that we thought would pat us on the back.

At the close of the regular school day, you were given certain privileges (or assigned tasks). Your name would be on the blackboard as to the assigned privilege. It might be to wipe the blackboard clean or pound the dust out of the blackboard erasers. There were usually two erasers which you clapped together or pounded them on the cement until the powder from them was gone. On Friday the blackboard was washed clean, and usually a taller student had that job.

Two people were assigned to take the flag down. One pulled the rope and the other made sure the flag didn't touch the ground. If it started to rain, two assigned students would dash outside and get the flag down as it wasn't supposed to get wet.

Another job was to empty the wastebasket by the teacher's desk or empty the pencil sharpener. I can't tolerate the smell of pencil shavings! If we needed to sharpen our pencil we could do that without permission. Many times, going to the front to sharpen your pencil was a chance to drop off a note to one of your friends. If your pencil was being sharpened a lot in one day, the teacher might just call you on that.

When all the students left the building for the day, one student would remain and go to the corner where a bucket of red sweeping compound was located. He would use the dustpan to get a load and sprinkle that around the room. That was not an everyday thing, but a for sure thing on Friday's. The teacher would come early on Monday morning and sweep it up. With wooden floors the compound made sort of an oily, shiny look to the floor when swept.

In the spring of the year, it was much easier to walk to school without my heavy snowsuit. I still can remember the earthy smells of the wet spring time. It would often take quite some time before the spring rains dried up the roads. Therefore, I still had to wear boots to school. I would walk a few steps and shake the mud off my boots. Take a few more steps and repeat. Huge mud clods definitely would slow you down. The car tracks would eventually become dry enough that I would coax my folks into letting me walk without boots. It was OK as long as I could stay in the tracks, but occasionally a car would come and I would have to step out of the tracks in the mud. Then when I got to school I had to scrape the mud from my shoes on the mud scraper by the school house door, just like we had at home. It was a piece of metal wedged in the ground to scrape off the mud or snow.

Once in a while Joy Watson would walk home with me, which was very nice of her, because she still had a mile to walk back to her house. Mostly her parents picked her up on the back road though. If she did walk with me and someone would give us a ride, we would sit in the back seat together. When we got ready to get out, one of us would say, "thanks for the ride" and the other would say, "you're welcome" and then we'd get out and giggle and giggle. When I was a child it was normal for people to give kids an apple for a treat. One man that gave us a ride a couple of times would do so. The same way if I was in someone's house and they gave me an apple, I never knew what to do with the core. No one seemed to tell you where you could dispose of it, and so I learned to eat the whole apple, core and all. If there were a stem on it, I would put that in my pocket. To this day, I kind of like to eat the core.

One thing I was afraid of when walking to school was our neighbor's bull. I tried my best to be silent when I walked by that field, but if he was near the fence, or spotted me, he would stalk me the whole length of the fence. I told my dad about it, but he acted as though it was nothing. However, one day, I saw him standing at the end of our lane, watching as the bull stalked me. That was very comforting for me to know he was watching.

In April of that year, we received a phone call from MC and Hazel. They had a baby and were calling to inform us. Since we had a party line telephone, it was hard to understand what was being said but my dad thought they said they had a girl by the name of Judy Diane. That was fairly close. Her name was actually Judith Ann. Party lines were quite the thing, but at least we had a telephone. Several people shared one telephone line. Before one made a call, you would have to listen to see if someone else might be using the phone. Sometimes people would hog the line for quite some time. If that happened you might pick up the phone and put the receiver down gently the first time...but after several times of trying to make a call, you might slam down the phone. The next time you picked up the receiver, you might hear someone say, "Well, it sounds as though someone else wants to use the line, so I'd better hang up." You could rest assured if you did, that person would then pick up the phone and listen to your conversation to see what the urgency was for you to use the phone.

Everybody on the line had a different ring for their household. For example, our phone number might be four longs and three shorts. That is the ring would come over the phone, with a long ring to distinguish it from the short rings. The trouble if you were just coming in the house you might have heard only part of the ring and you never knew if someone was trying to call you or if it wasn't your ring. So, you would pick up the phone and if no one was talking, you would then say "hello". Sometimes neighbors would answer our ring. For example, if someone was trying to call us and had tried several times, a nearby neighbor might pick up the phone and say, "I just saw the Nelsons go by our house and I don't think they are at home". Also from time to time one of my soldier brothers might try and call us. If we didn't answer, and someone else did...they would give a message to the person answering, who in turn would make sure we got the message. If there were a problem in the neighborhood such as someone's barn on fire, the Operator would put out a general ring. That would be a series of many rings, and everybody on the line would pick up their phones, and the operator would give the message...such as" The Jones barn is on fire. Please grab your buckets and go help". We didn't have firetrucks for the country.

One springtime my dad told me I could skip school. Uncle Clarence Cline which was my Aunt May's husband had passed away and she was going to have a farm sale. My dad said I could go with him there. It was still dark when we left in the morning. We drove about fifty miles, and when he got there he helped her line all the machinery up. I think he may have auctioned the sale also as he had helped with auctioning from time to time. As I said before my dad was very talented in many ways.

Aunt May's grandson Marslyn was there, and he had rheumatic fever. He was probably five years younger than me. He wasn't supposed to walk so Aunt May would carry him to the bathroom...fortunately they had an indoor bathroom. I don't know where his Mother Olive was, although at one point she had TB and was in a TB sanatorium for a year or two, so she could have been there then. We went to visit her family once, when she was in the TB sanitarium.

My brothers would send letters from Germany or from wherever they were stationed. How I'd love to get the mail as very often they would send a letter just to me. If one came addressed to Pop, we would wait for him to open and read it when we had dinner. I don't know why, but the letters were mimeographed from the original letter and reduced to half the size. Apparently, there were times my brothers told something they weren't supposed to tell, as that sentence or paragraph would be neatly cut out with a razor blade. What made it bad was on the back side of the letter you would have to guess what they were saying, as of course it was cut out on both sides. Their addresses were very long and always out of a New York P.O. box. I might add here, that in addition to writing to us...Marvin had his wife Hazel, and Rex, his wife Bea, to send letters too also. It seems to me, during World War II, they didn't have much free time, so I commend them for being able to keep up with their mail.

Here are some stories my brothers told us after the service. One I remember was they went to an occupied house. Since my brothers were

Christians and if they ranked high enough to be in charge, they made sure to treat the occupants kindly. One winter they occupied a house to get warm. There was a nice fire in the kitchen stove going.   One of my brothers had some popcorn. So, they popped corn on these people's stove using their kettles. As the corn began to pop, the poor occupants thought it was gun shells going off and were very frightened. My brother offered them some popcorn, but they refused to eat it. I learned Germans did not have popcorn so no wonder they were frightened.

There was another story about asking some farmers for food. A particular farmer went out and dug up eggs that had been boiled, stored in the ground and were black. I am not sure if the soldiers ate them or not.

One situation had a terrible ending. The soldiers had gone into one house and found it unoccupied. They searched the house through and finally saw something that made them look under the mattress. (the mattresses there were huge, huge feather ticks and you slept in between them somehow). Anyway, this particular family had smothered to death, trying to hide from the soldiers.

We received a very long letter from Gordon once. Someone had carried a typewriter with them in battle, and they were staying in the farmer's barn. Gordon had privy to the typewriter, but no typing paper. He typed while sitting on a bale of hay, using toilet paper for typing paper. He made a joke saying it was probably the longest letter he would ever write.

My brother Rex was ordered to evacuate a certain village. It was very cold out and as he went from house to house to command them to leave his heart broke for the women and children. Even though he wasn't supposed to...he told them quickly to grab coats and hats as he marched them out of the village.

Another time Gordon saw some children alongside the road and they were hungry. So, he tossed them out boxes of cereal. The children ran and got water as they didn't have milk and poured it over the cereal, eating it by the roadside.

As a testimony to their Christian witness, I heard after the war was over, my brothers received letters thanking them for their kindness to them. Some asking for rationed foods, which my brothers made up boxes and sent. In return the Germans might send back hand knit sweaters as a thank you. One even searched for my brother MC when they came to the United States. via a TV program called, "Queen for a Day". Although that person didn't win, a listener knew how to find MC, and they flew him to meet the person. The story was that the Army had taken over a certain house and since MC was a Chaplain, they issued him this particular house for his wife and child. The garden was beautiful, and one day MC noticed a man walking by looking at the garden. He visited with the man and found out he was the owner of the house. MC hired him for a gardener and his wife for child care. Imagine these people that had been ousted out of their house were now able to be back in their own home, because of my brother's Godly concern.

Meanwhile back at the ranch...

Carl graduated from high school that year. He was looking for work and not only helped at home but hired out different places where extra help was needed. Since school was out, I knew I would be headed for Uncle Ray and Aunt Clara's home. But before I left, Alice Kellem, my brother Cecil's stepdaughter arrived for the summer. She had graduated from high school and evidently had been in correspondence with Bee. Since Cecil was a bus driver, she was able to ride the bus to Mt. Pleasant for free. It was a nice deal, however, her suitcases got lost along the way.

We picked her up from the bus station, and after much discussion about the luggage, she came to our house without them. She did happen to have a little travel case with an extra dress in it. But Rapid City weather was a lot cooler, and her two dresses were not the coolest apparel for hot, humid, Iowa. On the farm, we did laundry once a week, and if it rained, it might be even longer. Unless of course, you used the washboard. That was a method of hand wash that you rubbed clothes up and down over a ribbed board to help get the clothes clean. Carl introduced Alice to one of his classmates named Wilma that had also graduated and looking for work. The girls decided to go to Fairfield and get a room together. Both found work in a factory making plastic basket liners to fit inside the wooden bushel baskets. That way women could use the baskets for laundry without snagging the clothes or getting the baskets wet. We didn't get to see Alice very often as the days we went to Fairfield to shop were the days she would be working. Alice just stayed the summer since she had applied to go to college elsewhere. She and Wilma stayed in touch with each other through out their life though.

Chapter Eighteen

Summer, Fifth Grade, Malts and Fries

I wasn't privy to the adult conversations, but I stayed longer at Uncle Ray's that summer as Bee was going to attend summer school at Parsons College in Fairfield. There was a shortage of teachers, and Miss Stark had resigned from West Grove to get married. That left a vacancy and a dilemma. With Keith finishing eighth grade, we were now down to five students at our school. We had six during the previous year, which was stretching it as the schools could only stay open if they had a minimum of six students. Now it would take an act of Congress to keep a school open with five students. With the shortage of teachers, I assume because of the war, one could get a teacher's certificate if they could pass a test after six weeks of crammed college courses. So again, without any knowledge on my part, Bee decided to go to college.

Bee didn't really have the clothes to go to college, but evidently it was made known when they dropped me off at Uncle Ray's for the summer. Arlene gave her two of her wool plaid skirts. They were pretty and nice, but not what you would consider summer wear in hot, steamy, Iowa. Bee rented a room in Fairfield somewhere and also landed a job at Woolworth's to pay for her room and board. Uncle Ray's happened to come to town once, and I got to see her behind the candy counter on a Saturday. Saturday was the day for all farmers to do their shopping.

That summer was even more fun at Uncle Rays. They had spiffed up their place quite considerably since moving into their newer house. Uncle Ray was quite the carpenter and years before had built his barn with wooden pegs. Even though it wasn't painted it stayed straight and sturdy, unlike other old barns built with nails that would sag and creak. I learned the pegs were wet when they pounded them in holes. When they dried, they would swell up and keep the holes nice and tight. He was featured in a farm magazine with that barn. Now he had planted a yard that he mowed with a lawn mower! They had a knee high white picket fence around it and the grass was like a carpet. Not only that they had a beautiful garden with vegetables and rows and rows of flowers. He made an archway to enter the garden and over the archway was a Dutch windmill. I was allowed to pick flowers for the dining room table when they needed fresh ones. Gladiolus was my favorite.

In addition to all the beautiful features at their farm, their oldest son Chester had moved near them, and they had a daughter Marilyn that was a year younger than me. It was the first time I met her and boy did we have fun. We could do somersaults on the lawn and catch lightning bugs. I learned if we squeezed off the bugs light and put the light part on your finger, it would look like you were wearing a diamond ring. The somersaults did have their consequences though. We soon discovered chiggers had found their way around our underwear linings and anklet tops. The itching was terrible. We used lots of rubbing alcohol.

We didn't get off Scott free at Uncle Ray's though because Marilyn rode the horse to the hay-fork. So, when the guys would bring in a hay load to put in the barn, we would have to interrupt our play. Somehow the horse was hooked up to a pulley, and another pulley was hooked up to a hay fork that would grab a load of hay off the hay wagon and pull it up to the hay mow. The person riding the horse would start the horse walking very slowly until someone yelled "Whoa". The person in the haymow would grab the fork and release the hay at a designated place. When the hay-rack was unloaded, we could go back to playing. My job was to open the gate to the barnyard when the loaded hay rack arrived.

At the end of the week, Marilyn got paid for riding the horse, and much to my surprise Uncle Ray gave me fifty cents for opening the gate. I knew exactly what I wanted to do with my money. When we went to Fairfield on Saturday, I wanted to buy barrettes. That was a popular fashion for your hair back then. I had different sets of barrettes. One was a set of red airplanes. Others were shaped like a knife, fork and spoon. The ones I got on Saturday were shaped like a large ribbon. I couldn't believe it cost me the whole fifty cents for a set of two! I had only been paying ten cents for barrettes before this time. Not only that, I found out I had to have tax money. Arlene was good enough to pay the tax. Oh, and you know what else we did on Saturday shopping? We parked our car someplace around the city square, and everyone went their way to do their own thing. If you got back before the others, you sat in the car and watched the people go by. No one locked their cars, so it was no problem to get in the car. Plus, in the summer you left all the car windows down. Occasionally you might see someone you knew and would honk the horn. They would stand by the car and visit awhile. Or, you could laugh at the way some quirky people dressed, talked or walked. Before you left town, you walked over to the popcorn stand and bought popcorn for a dime. Wow, that was living.

Uncle Ray's always had different foods for me to enjoy. One thing was ice tea. They had long handled ice tea spoons that you stirred the lumps of sugar with. When we stirred the tea with the ice cubes, it made a clinking sound that I still like to hear. Also, we sat at the dining room table, not the kitchen table. All this seemed so classy. Aunt Clara made wonderful corn fritters and served them with syrup. Yummy yummy. I was asked to set the table from time to time and I had to make my bed...but other than when Marilyn came over, I was pretty much free to do whatever I liked. (Years later, Marilyn's life ended in a head-on car collision not long after she graduated from high school).

That summer Aunt Clara and Arlene decided I needed to have some new clothes. They had some material, whether from feed sacks or store bought, which they made me school dresses. I don't think I was as grateful as I should have been because they would interrupt my play for me to come and try a dress on now and then. I didn't like one of the dresses. They created their own styles and made one with a ruffle around the collar, and without buttons. They had to pull real hard to get this over my head. I felt I looked like a clown with that ruffle around my neck. But by the time I left, they had made me five dresses. There was one for each day of the week. What wonderful relatives I had.

Another interesting thing that happened at Uncle Ray's was when a man pulled off the road and knocked on the door. He was dressed in a suit and carried a briefcase. He also had a huge camera with him, and a large pole for which to set the camera. He talked with Uncle Ray for quite some time, but it wasn't until Pop came back for me that I learned the purpose for that man's visit. I ran and stood by Pop while he and Uncle Ray sat under the shade tree. Uncle Ray began to share how a man from one of the well-known magazines...I'm not sure if it was "Life" or "Look" magazine, had stopped by and wanted to feature his farm in the magazine. He wanted me to be running through the field, and we would be paid one hundred dollars! I could hardly believe what I was hearing. ONE HUNDRED DOLLARS. That's one hundred dollars. When Uncle Ray said it was going to be sponsored by Camel Cigarettes, my dad said "no". I just couldn't believe he turned down such a money-making idea. I did brag about that to my friends when school started, which I think they never did believe me.

Things were obviously changing back home. Carl was going to be a Senior in high school, and my dad was lobbying to keep our school open even with five students. I hadn't realized he was President of the School Board. Not only was he successful in overriding the minimum of six students, but Bee was voted in for the teacher.

Our neighbor Joy and I got together a few times during the remainder of the summer, and she and one of her friends came to our house with a bike. The girl's name was Evelyn, and she had actually lived at the Bixler place before my Dad bought it. Anyway, she taught me how to ride her bike. The only other time anyone that I knew had anything similar was a scooter. I had been to Linby to visit Uncle Bernie, and there were some kids going up and down the sidewalk with a scooter. I talked one of them into letting me try it, but I couldn't get the hang of it.

In no man's land across from our mailbox, I discovered a huge and I mean huge blackberry patch. I soon found out I needed to wear long sleeves if I was going to be picking blackberries. This particular year the berries were huge, and I would hide myself in the center of the patch eating blackberries until I could hold no more. A time or two I picked enough for a batch of jelly and also blackberry pie. I guess it was a secret place as I never saw anyone else there.

Gordon came home for a furlough and brought his girlfriend Lucy for us to meet. She was from Louisville, KY and had a very soft accent. I was immediately charmed by her as was the rest of the family. (And yes, when Gordon was discharged from the service he married her) I'm sure it was quite different for her as she had a job in town and lived where she had modern conveniences. But to us, washing from a wash pan and all of us drinking out of the same dipper from the water bucket was the way things were. We did give her the cot in the sewing room though which gave her some privacy. At that particular time when they were there, we had twin lambs we were feeding. I fed them cow's milk from a glass pop bottle with a very strong nipple that was made to fit over pop bottles. Lucy watched me feed the lambs through the fence hole. I had to hang on to those bottles for dear life as they would vigorously suck and might pull the nipple off and spray milk everywhere. When she returned home, she found a couple of porcelain twin lambs and mailed them to me for my what not shelf. I really, really, liked her then. Pop named the twin lambs Larse & Nettie.

School started and was definitely different with Bee, excuse me, Miss Nelson. I sometimes would call her Miss Nelson at home which brought a smile, but if I said Bee at school, I would get the "look". But Miss Nelson made school interesting.

Arlo Watson and Joy would often stop by our house and give us a ride to school. If we had to walk, that would use up our time to get the housework done. In fact, Arlo began to do it so much we depended on him. He and Joy would come to our house and wait for us while we finished washing the dishes and doing other household things. We seemed never to have our work done before they got there.

At school, art was especially fun. I can still remember some of the things we did in art. One, was when Miss Nelson brought a bar of Ivory Soap for each of us and we drew a duck or elephant or some simple animal on the outside of the bar. Then we took pocket knives and shaved off the soap to create that animal. Another thing we did was to make shadow pictures. We had someone trace the outline of our head and shoulders from the shadow, on white paper. Then we transferred that cutout to black construction paper which we centered on white paper. We put a piece of cardboard behind that paper and made a picture frame around it. Then we gave that to our parents. The other thing I remember is she cut a piece of glass, probably eight by ten. We would find something we liked to paint, such as a horse. Then we would lay the glass over that picture and draw around that picture with a special pen and black ink. Then the picture behind the glass was removed and we would take black electricians tape and put that around the glass so no one could get cut and it sort of made a frame. We also would gather leaves in the fall, put them under a sheet of paper and rub our pencils over them to make the veins of the leaves stand out. Also, we made ink blob pictures. We would fold our paper in half and pour some ink in the center of the paper. Close up the paper and smear the ink around, open it up and try to guess what the design was.

Another thing all teachers did at the beginning of the school year, was to pump the well clean. When a well was unused for some time, it would gather leaves, mice, etc. So, the pump was removed from the platform, and each year the debris cleaned out by hand and pumped clean. But Miss Nelson made it fun for us. She gave us all war bond stamp books. She would give us each a stamp (they were ten cents) every day we pumped out the unclean water. For the first few day of school, we hauled water from home, but after the well had started pumping clean water, we used that. No city or country inspectors testing the water. If it was clear and it tasted good, it was OK to drink. This was part of our P.E. Never had P.E. before. Now she also added jumping jacks at the beginning of the school day. In the fall for our P.E. she brought a gunny sack and we walked up and down the road and collected milkweed pods. She took them to the receiving place in Salem. Again, she gave us war bond stamps for our book for collecting them. The milkweed pods were used for insulation for jackets for the soldiers. We also collected tin cans and other things.

Speaking of water, when we got ready to wash our hand she did it differently too. She had one of the students pour water over our hands and into the wash pan. The previous way was for us to put our hands in the washbasin using the same basin that others used.

Miss Nelson also made a chart for Health. Yes, it was the gold star method. If we brushed our teeth, did physical exercises, was at school on time etc... we got a gold star. Brushing our teeth was new to most of us. Wanda did get me a child's toothbrush once. When she was home, she used a liquid toothpaste called Teel, which smelled a bit like red hots and came in a glass bottle. But we didn't have toothpaste, so Pop told us to use baking soda or salt. I preferred the salt on my toothbrush.

The road by the school turned into a triangle with three roads going different ways. In the center of that triangle was a little pond with tadpoles, which were collected and brought into the school for a science project. In the fall we would also have the brown plant/flower that we called cattails. They were dried and made into a bouquet with other fall flowers.

Since I don't remember which grade I was in when we did these things, I will tell you that Bee taught me in both fifth and sixth grade. I assume some of these things were in either or both years.

One winter we had lots of snow. Snow suits were the big thing back then. Kind of like ski suits. I wore snow suits to school through most of my seventh grade. (Later when I went to city school snow suits were considered childish). But my last snow suit was dark green and very very nice. I probably wore hand me downs before.

We would often bring our sleds and slide down Watson's Hill. When we moved to the Bixler place, I didn't have a sled. So, Pop bought one at an auction for thirty-five cents. The glider was wobbly, but he fixed that with a screw, and the rudders were very rusty. During one of the first snows he put a rope on the sled and threaded it through the back-car bumper. He took me out on a slightly snow graveled road and said..." Just lay on the sled and I will pull you along with the car and the rocks will knock the rust off. But if we hit a big bump let go of the rope." Sure, enough that worked. So, I took mine to school and rode down Watson's hill. It was a washed-out road that only they traveled with their car on rare occasions. It made a good place for sledding because no other cars used it. Once in a while, Margaret would ride the horse up to school and she and Joy would ride double all the way home down that road.

During free time, we would play fox and geese in the snow. We made a round track in the snow with our feet, like a pie with pie wedges. The center was the fox den. The fox would step out of his den and go up and down one of the pie shaped pieces while the geese tried to get to his den. That usually satisfied us for fun for several days. One year we made an igloo to prove that a person could be fairly warm in one. Back in the school room our wet clothes would be hung over the sides of the furnace to dry.

One of the Christmas's on the Bixler place I received a xylophone and a game of Tiddly Winks. The xylophone had eight glass tubes, a different one for each note. There was a small wooden mallet for which to tap. Today's toy makers would have been sued making a toy with glass. One ends of a tube did get broken off but was still usable. Another Christmas at the Bixler Place, I received a beautiful yellow and rose gold bracelet from Carl and Wanda. Wanda also sent me a green and red plaid jumper with a white satin blouse. Bee gave me a soft white head scarf, and from Pop I received a winter coat. One of Carl's lesser gifts he received, included two small ceramic dogs with magnets on the bottom of them. One was black, one was white. We had more fun playing with those...putting one on top of a glass and the other on the bottom., to make a dog chase.

MC came home from the service for a furlough and managed a visit to us. We have a picture of him standing outside wearing his Chaplain coat and hat and I was wearing my Christmas head scarf and coat. It was always funny when MC came home. He was forever running late to get where he wanted to go. The train would come in to Mt. Pleasant where we would pick him up. On his return trip, we would say, "MC, it's time to go or you'll never catch the train". About then we would hear the train whistle somewhere near us, and he would say, "Run get in the car and let me drive". He would grab his suitcase, get under the steering wheel and push the pedal to the metal and off we'd go trying to out race the train. We always made it, but it was nip and tuck.

Carl had a girlfriend. He was dating one of the Cline girls, and when it came to New Years, he was talking about bringing her to our house to watch the old year out and the new year in. Well, I asked to stay up also as I wanted to see this change. I was really tired, but managed to keep my eyes open. When they stepped outside at midnight (probably to get a kiss) I ran out also and looked up at the sky expecting to see some wondrous thing happen. When nothing happened, I didn't say a word as I didn't want anyone to think I was uneducated.

Oh yes, speaking of Carl dating. he too was stuck with me from time to time. On one date he wanted to go see the Harlem Globe Trotters. It sounded too wonderful to me to see a guy shoot the ball backward and do all kinds of tricks and I asked to go. So, Carl took me on his date. But his dates younger sister Judith, was telling me that her sister and my brother Carl kissed. I said, "On the lips?" She said, "Yes". She had seen them. Well, like I said, we never kissed in our family and I wasn't about to miss out on something like that. So, on our way home after the ball game I lay down in the back seat pretending I was asleep. At some point in time and somewhere they pulled off the road and stopped. It was dark, but I did see through my squinted eyes Carl looking back to see if I was asleep. And then it happened! His arm went around her shoulder and they kissed. Judith was right. They kissed ON THE LIPS. I had seen that happen when Gordon was inducted into the army, but only once and I could never imagine that happening to some of MY family. Another date that I made a threesome was to a Youth for Christ meeting at the High School auditorium in Fairfield. I had never seen so many people. I'm sorry, but that was not the highlight of the evening for me. Afterward we went to Maid Rite and had a hamburger, French fries and malt that Carl bought me. I had tasted hamburgers before, but never French fries and a malt. I thought that had to be the greatest food combination I ever had the pleasure of indulging.

One interesting thing that happened that spring was Joy showed me how to find and pick morel mushrooms. She told me they were good to eat. When I took them home, Pop showed me how to soak them in salt water to draw the ants out. After that they were washed, drained and washed again, them floured and fried. They were sooo good. Just a few years ago I found some for sale. I paid a fortune for them because of my wonderful childhood memory of eating them. I was not disappointed. They were perfect. Some things such as fried squirrel, fried pheasant, and fried rabbit did not carry the same thrill of taste as I remembered them. They were just not the same. Roasted skunk and snake links didn't taste as good either. I am just kidding. I wanted to see if I could repulse you.

I don't know if there were some Sunday evenings that Round Prairie didn't have church or if Pop just wanted to try different things, but I remember him taking me to a Quaker service not far from us. In fact, it was very close to the school I should have been attending. The church had no electricity and used kerosene lamps affixed on the wall. They also read every word of their sermon in a monotone voice. I think it was just the novelty of that service that prompted my dad to go there.

Chapter Nineteen

The Huffs Place

Carl got a job working for the Huffs doing chores and working in the fields. It was going to be a long-range plan, I discovered.

Back at the Bixler place, Pop was busy getting the grove ready to look nice for our family reunion. Saw horses with planks were covered with white tablecloths. People started arriving with their picnic baskets. I think I came back with Uncle Ray and Aunt Clara. Pop had mowed around the trees the best he could with the field mower, but of course, it left stubble and was not like Uncle Ray's front lawn. Still, it was a nice place for a picnic. We probably had our program as we usually did at our reunions, but we also played croquet. I remember Pop got a croquet set at a farm sale for fifty cents. We had played it the last two summers as we did have a nice flat place in our front yard.

I spent some of the summer riding the horse to the hay fork. I did a few days of that the summer before too. Pop did pay me at the rate of ten cents a load. His friend Paul also hired me, and he gave me fifteen cents a load. I didn't care for Paul very much. His wife had a stroke and couldn't talk. His daughter had graduated from school, but was physically unable to work...so Paul hired school girls to do his housework. He was friendlier than I was comfortable with, but since he was Pop's best friend, I said nothing. Bee was busy in the sewing room when she had a chance. She patched Pop's shirts and did other mending. It was during those times she taught me the books of the Bible in their order, using a tune to an old hymn that we sang at church.

The flies in the house were just terrible that year. We had fly stickers all over the kitchen. I was bored, and so Bee gave me a job. She said for me to take the fly swatter and kill flies. She would give me a penny for every fifty flies I killed. I think I killed some on the screen door that was on the outside of the house because I wanted to make a nickel. Two hundred and fifty flies? I sure did.

One time I went with Joy to Mt. Pleasant so her mother Margaret could visit a sister. All the farmers and people in our area were Caucasian...so it was quite interesting to me to find Joy's Aunt lived next door to a black family. I only remembered seeing a black person one other time in my life. Anyway, there was a little girl our age by her aunt's house. As I told you before, the back of Joy's family vehicle was fixed up almost like a play house. So, we invited the little girl in to play with us. Her name was Patricia and I thought she was the sweetest, most soft-spoken girl I had known. When her mama looked outside and couldn't find her little girl she must have panicked, for she screamed at her to get in the house. She probably was concerned we might kidnap her.

Soon it became clear other changes were in the offing. The Huffs had hired Carl for a year starting in March and going to the next March. They had two daughters. Mollie Rae, and Lenora. They were younger than I even though Mollie Rae was a lot taller. Common sense tells me Carl had been in training for the care of the farm and animals so that the Huffs could take a year sabbatical and tour the southern states.

Pop still was President of the school board, and he had a really big fight on his hands to keep West Grove School open with only four students to attend, since Donna had now graduated from eighth grade. Once again, he was successful. School started with Miss Nelson again being our teacher. She bought a nineteen twenty-nine Chevy car for seventy-five dollars. Old, but it worked and it sure beat walking. I'm sure Arlo was glad he didn't have to wait for us anymore.

I don't remember how long or when the transition occurred, but it became obvious that Carl would need help in running Huff's farm. It was decided that Bee and I should move over to the Huffs to help out. Now it was even scarier as I now lived even farther away from school. Since Bee had a car, we assured the school board I would continue to attend West Grove School. This move was going to leave Pop alone to manage the farm.

Wanda was still living and working in South Dakota, and was engaged to a man named Fritz. She had written a letter to my dad that summer I imagine telling him of her impending marriage. The reason it's not clear to me was beneath the address to my dad were the words underlined "Personal". Since I was the one that gave the mail to my dad each day, I remember saying to him," Does that mean it's just for you?" He said, "yes".

When Bee and I moved in with Carl at the Huffs, it was like a dream vacation. They had a house with a garage underneath it. We could get out of the car in the basement and head right up the steps to the kitchen without ever getting wet. It was a full-sized basement, and all the walls were cement, not like some of the basements I had seen that had dirt walls, AND they had electricity. There was also an indoor bathroom with toilet paper., not catalogs. (We used the Sears or Monkey Wards catalogs for the outhouses). There was a furnace in the basement instead of a pot-bellied stove in the middle of the room. There were water faucets in the kitchen, an electric stove, and enough bedrooms that we all could have our own. Not only that, they had two ponies I could ride. There was a Shetland pony named Ginger and a palomino named Tony and there was a saddle for him.

I don't remember moving our clothes there, but obviously we did. The Huff's place was six and one half miles from the school, and a quarter of a mile from the Round Prairie Church. I didn't think about how Pop was going to manage the farm alone; I was just excited about moving. The bedroom I used had a saying right above the bed which read, "He that holdeth his tongue, proveth himself the better man". My room was behind French Doors and was much colder as they didn't have a register in that room for some reason. Nonetheless, it was MY room.

The living room/dining room combination had a built-in china cabinet, a fireplace, nice furniture and a player piano. In case you have never seen a player piano, it looks like an ordinary upright piano with a sliding door in the top section. There are little paper rolls perhaps ten inches long, to insert through the sliding door. Kind of like a music box works. Each roll plays a different melody as you pedal it. The piano rolls included songs such as "Tennessee Waltz," and" The Yellow Rose of Texas." I didn't have to ask anyone if I could play them...I just did.

I did have chores there too. The Huffs raised around five hundred chickens. I gathered the eggs and would prepare them for the egg crates which were in the basement. The eggs had to be washed and candled. Candling was holding the eggs up to a light bulb to see if there were any dark spots. If there were dark spots, that meant it had to be discarded. I believe each crate held twenty-four dozen eggs and we had at least a couple of crates. Twice a week the egg truck would come around and pick them up. So, I had to have the eggs washed and in the crates, ready for market.

We all seemed to enjoy the lack of parental supervision, that is we were much more relaxed. Much of that had to do with all the conveniences too. They had a small portable radio that sat atop the refrigerator, and on Saturday's I listened to a kids' program called, "Archie". I can still hear" Archie...ARCHIEEE", and he would reply with his young male changing voice, "coming Mother."

Elaine, one of the girls from church, was a young school teacher. She bought a small car called a "Crosley". It was probably about the size of the "Smart cars" today. One church service, the young men from the church, began leaving the building just before the benediction. Parents were raising eyebrows. Unknown to them, someone had decided to carry Elaine's car up the steps and put it on the landing. When we came out of the church, much to everyone's surprise there set her car. The young men all played dumb, and now the question was "how to get it back down the steps". I don't remember how that played out, but I'm sure they had to carry it back down again. Elaine's car was often the source of entertainment. Again, poor Bee had to take me with her. Sunday nights after church, three or four of us would get in Elaine's car and take off to unknown territory. I was, of course, the youngest. The fun was to go down country roads that none of us had ever been before and twist and turn and see if we could find out way back home. As you know at night things look different, and since church time started at eight pm. by the time of dismissal. It was really dark. One night we got lost, and it was very late. We decided to turn around in someone's driveway and see if we could back track, when we were met in the driveway with a not too happy farmer. We had a lot of explaining to do with nervous giggles.

The letter from Wanda had unraveled my dad somewhat, and he wanted her to come home. He hadn't approved of her engagement to the young man because he wasn't Protestant. I also can't help but wonder if he needed her back at home, now that we were gone. I think it took her awhile to give her notice and wait until Dr. Collins had found a suitable replacement. She was obedient and broke off her engagement.

In the meantime back at school, Bee's friend Elaine, taught at the Vega school, not far from us. Bee had conferred with the Watson's about using their cabin for a combined school "fun day". The Watson's had first lived in a cabin when they moved to their property while they built their current home. So, when they moved out, they just left it fully furnished. This was going to make a perfect place for us to have a wiener and marshmallow roast down in the woods. Their cabin was located about a mile from their new home, and the road to it had long been forgotten. On this particular day, Vega and West Grove were meeting for this wonderful time. Just as we arrived at the cabin there came a real down pour of rain. Instead of a wiener roast, we found a kettle and heated the hot dogs over the stove. It had been so long since Joy had been there, she really didn't know where anything was. Our biggest problem was finding matches to light the stove. Eventually, some were located.

We were all huddled in this one room cabin with the rain pouring outside. We ate fairly quickly and then decided we had better leave because what had once been a road was only a faint trace of clay. I believe we had three cars there, and they were all mired in that clay. There were the two boys from our school and thankfully Vega school had more male students. So, they and the teachers went out and pushed and pushed the cars out of the mud to the top of the hill and back on the main road. The boys were wet and covered with mud it seemed. We girls were left to clean up the mess inside the cabin when suddenly Vaughn stuck his head in the door and let us know how lucky girls were.

Bee was prone to getting sick with probably appendicitis attacks. So, a couple of times she would have to dismiss school early, and I would drive her car home. Remember I was only in sixth grade. Fortunately, one of the things I had already learned was how to shift gears. On Sunday's before we moved to the Huffs, Pop would often linger inside the church visiting. It was on such occasions that Bee used that time to help me learn to use the shift stick. When I was still young enough to sit on Pops lap, he would let me steer the car, otherwise I had no previous experience in driving. Once when I was driving her car home I was following a tractor pulling a wagon going up a hill. The tongue disconnected from the wagon and started rolling backward toward her car at a pretty good speed. As we were praying, the wagon suddenly jackknifed and went into the ditch. Another time when I was driving home I did just fine until I got to Huff's driveway. It was narrow and if I missed it, we could go into a very deep ditch. Well, I had to scoot down to reach the clutch and brake. This made me unable to see the driveway, and I missed it! A post stopped me from totally tipping over, but I was so embarrassed because Vaughn was there mowing the lawn and saw it all. It cured Bee of her sickness pretty fast when she thought we were going to tip over.

For some reason Carl must have borrowed Bees car, or it was getting repaired, and we had to walk home from school. Yes, we had to walk the whole six and a half miles, and we did that more than once. Talk about HER getting sick! Well if I walked very long I would get terrible side aches. So bad I couldn't walk. So, Bee would pack me on her back. Yes, me a sixth grader, and even though I was skinny it was still quite a load. We certainly didn't want anyone to see us like that, so if a car started coming our way she would put me down, and we would bend down and look at the side of the road as though we were gathering flowers. Speaking of flowers, I did love to pick violets, pansies, and sweet Williams in the springtime, which could usually be found along the sides of the road.

One day after school we were walking to the Huffs when it started pouring down rain. We just happened to be by the Bixler place so we went in and decided to spend the night with Pop. We found one old dress that I had outgrown in length that I could wear to school the next day. Probably Pop was glad to have someone there for the night to cook supper and help with the chores. Since we didn't have electricity there, we used lamps. I may not have described this chore before, but daily they had to be filled with kerosene. Because my hand was small, I could reach in the lamp chimneys and clean them. This was usually done first with a newspaper to get most of the suet out and then washed with soap and water. Before lighting, the wicks were trimmed straight across to give a better flame.

Sixth grade wasn't much different that fifth. We still did the usual stuff except for one not so fun day. We girls did notice a swarm of bumble bees around the girl's outhouse and Joy got stung on her ankle. I had no idea of the pain she was going through when her ankle swelled up and probably didn't sympathize with her much...that is, until I got stung on the ankle. I was sure mine was much worse than hers and limped around for quite a while. Miss Nelson told us then to use the boys' outhouse. We hated that because it had no door on it. However, it did face the opposite way toward a field.

Gordon and Rex had come home for a furlough and came to visit school dressed in their uniforms. I was so proud of them. I would see Bee get this squelched smile on her face every now and then. What they were doing as they sat in the back row, was raising their fingers like asking permission to go to the bathroom or get a drink. On the serious side, Rex and Gordon did teach us the proper way to fold a flag. We had done as others had done in the past and folded it in the middle but from that time forth it was folded properly.

Everything was fine at school until we found out that David and his family were moving. Now that left only three students at school. We were tiptoeing around, hoping the school superintendent didn't come for a visit and shut us down. But something almost did shut us down during the winter. Bee had learned how to stoke the furnace at night so that there might be a few coals left over to start the fire the next morning. Apparently, she stoked it a little too much one night. One of the neighbors passed by and saw this bright red furnace glowing through the school house windows. He stopped and somehow tamed it down. Nothing was locked in those days...not schools, not houses, not cars. The fellow let the school board know about it the next day and Bee was admonished.

The Huffs had a rubber tired wagon. The only wagons our family ever used had wooden wheels which made a lot of clatter. The morning after Halloween, Carl woke up to find the wagon missing. He somehow knew it was a Halloween prank...and went looking for it. After a day or two, he finally found it. There was an old vacant store in the country with a portico, and somehow the pranksters had put that wagon on its roof.

I don't know how or when this happened, but suddenly we found out Pop was very sick. Bee told me one time the name of his sickness but I didn't write it down, and now have forgotten it. He was too sick to do anything and had to use the outhouse continually. Soooo we brought him to the Huffs. Fortunately, there were twin beds in Carl's room, which was located very close to the bathroom. It was getting colder out and having a furnace made it all the more comfortable for my dad. We filled in doing the chores for a time back at the Bixler place. Some didn't expect him to recover from that illness, and the farm was sold along with the livestock. I have no idea where the furniture was stored, but Carl must have had the bulk of the responsibility. Just that spring Pop had sheared the sheep, and I remember the awful smell when the wool came off. If he nicked the sheep with his sheers he would rub them with oil. Also, when the bugs would burrow into their fur, I remember how he would get "sheep dip" and apply it to those areas. Two of those sheep had been my pets. Now Pop was bedridden. He could do nothing.

Wanda finally made it home, and took care of Pop until he was able to be by himself. She then became nanny for Uncle Ray's son Morris and family. Morris was discharged from the Navy and lived in the area for a few years.

One of my chores at the Huff place was filling the water tank in the house. It was much like a horse tank located in the walk-up attic. We would turn on a switch, and it would pump water into this tank. Somehow that was piped into the bathroom and kitchen. The Huffs had warned us never to let the tank overflow, or it would ruin the ceiling and other things. So, it was my job to check and make sure the tank never overflowed nor allowed to run dry. I hated that job. It scared me to pieces. They kept an old piece of carpet on top of the tank to keep the bugs out of the water and I would have to peer under it and constantly watch to see where the water line was. I guess I did a good job because nothing ever happened.

Chapter Twenty

The Fight About Ice Cream

Who would have ever thought that ice cream would be a tormenting factor at the close of a church service? Well, it happened to me, and since I consider this part the most pivotal part of my life, I decided it deserved a separate chapter. My father was now feeling well enough to attend church services and do a few light things around the house. I so thank God that He had prepared a comfortable place for him to recuperate. Only God could have timed everything so perfectly.

We had young new pastors at our church, Calvin and Lois Heather. Wanting to get better acquainted with them, my father said that if church didn't let out too late that night, we could invite them to our house for homemade ice cream. I enjoyed company as much as the rest of the family and for the pastor to accept our invitation would be a high honor.

I didn't reckon with what was going to happen at the close of the service. An invitation was being given for people that didn't know Christ to come to the altar, seek forgiveness of sins and accept Him as Lord and Savior. It wasn't until this moment that I realized I had never done that. For the most part, I was a good girl. We didn't go to movies, dances, swear, smoke, drink or chew and I lived in a Christian home. My brother was even a minister. My father read the Bible to us every morning and had prayer time with us every morning before breakfast. Suddenly I realized I was responsible for my own salvation experience. Just doing all the above didn't make me a Christian.

The problem was there was a tug of war going on. You see when you are about to make a stand for Christ, that's when the enemy will fight you, and the fight was over ice cream. This is what was going on in my mind. "Well, if I go forward and it takes a long time to pray, then it will be too late to ask the pastors over for ice cream". So, I determined to do it another service. About that time the pastor said, "You know you are here tonight, but what if you are in a car accident on the way home and killed. Would you be ready to meet God?" Myself said, "Well that's silly we live the first house down the road from the church, how could we get in an accident?" Continuing thoughts, "you have to back out of the parking area onto the road. What if your tail lights aren't working and someone hits you?" These thoughts ran on and on.

About that time two older girls seated in the back row started down the aisle. We always sat near the front and gentler thoughts started coming. "You can go at the same time they do, and it will be easier if someone is going with you". Angry thoughts, "But what will people think, since you have always told people you were a Christian?

The others were about two steps from the altar when I suddenly jumped up and stood with them. At that time the pastor asked us to be seated in the front pew because he wanted to talk with us. Since the pastor gave this bit of instruction for "All eyes closed and no one looking around", my dad hadn't realized until then I was sitting in the front pew. He turned around and rushed up to where I was sitting with tears streaming down his face and said, "Do you want to ask Jesus into your heart tonight?" When I nodded yes, he said, "Papa has been praying for you". I thought. You have? I didn't know he prayed other prayers from the ones I heard.

After our time of prayer seeking forgiveness and promising to follow the Lord to the best of our ability, we DID still have time for ice cream. Don't ever let the enemy talk you out of accepting Christ as your Savior, as I almost did. The benefits far outweigh the pleasures of sin.

There used to be a Pepsi commercial that said, "the pause that refreshes" and I invite you to take that pause right now. It's not so much as what I have to say...it's what the Bible has to say.

If you have never accepted Christ as your Savior, admit you are a sinner. Ask Christ to forgive you and determine to live for Him forever. The Bible says in Romans 3:23...For all have sinned and come short of the glory of God. (That's me, you and everyone else.)

Romans 6:23 says. For the wages of sin is death, but the gift of God is eternal life through Jesus Christ our Lord. (I want to accept this gift, and be saved from hell)

Romans 10:9 and 10 says, that if thou (me) shalt confess with my mouth, the Lord Jesus and shall believe in my heart that God has raised him from the dead, I shall be saved. For with the heart man believes unto righteousness and with the mouth confession is made unto salvation.

Ephesians 2:8 and 9 reads, for by grace are you saved through faith, and that not of yourselves. It is the gift of God, not of works, lest any man should boast. (It is the gift he has given us...we can't get into heaven by our good works...because if we did some would boast about all the wonderful things he or she has done.)

Perhaps you could say a prayer like this. Dear Jesus, according to your word I am a sinner. I also understand that I deserve to die for my sins. But you did it for me. You died on the cross and rose again and are now in heaven. With my confession, I acknowledge that you did this for me, and that I have been a sinner. I want to now ask forgiveness for my sins and accept you as my Lord and Savior. I want to learn more about you by studying the Bible and talking to you daily through prayer. Direct me to a Bible teaching church. In your name, I pray. Amen.

Of course, we will always have problems. We live in a sinful world. But I don't run to the Devil when I have problems. I run to God. He is the great comforter. I don't need alcohol or drugs to drown out my sorrows. I need to feel God's presence. God has sustained me for over eighty years as I write this.

As one preacher said, "Try God. If you don't like Him, the Devil will always give you back your sins."

I would be thrilled to hear from you if after reading this, you accepted Christ in your life.

NOW MORE OF HOW LIFE WAS IN THE NEXT CHAPTERS.

Chapter Twenty-One

A Special Christmas

Christmas that year was very special it seemed. Wanda came home for a Christmas vacation. We were able to chop down a tree from the farm, and we purchased some electric lights for the tree. We put the tree near the picture window so the lights could be seen from the road.

Miss Nelson had a very good Christmas program. People couldn't believe the program she had with only three of us. We presented one play that was all singing. Of course, I was one of the star singers. Smile. Either that year or the year before, she started me on the "Nancy Drew Books". I just loved them, and even in my eighties, reread the ones she gave me. I would like to interject here that when Miss Nelson arrived at West Grove, there was an old phonograph there, but the needles were shot. So, at the first opportunity, she bought new needles so we could play some old records to listen too. A couple of the songs I remember were, "Dinky, Dinky Par Le Vou", and "When the Rain Drops Pattered on My Old Tin Hat".

Christmas day arrived, and I don't think I had ever seen such a stack of gifts. Bee, Carl, and Wanda were all working, and I got gifts from all of them, plus my dad. The rest of us drew names as our family was enlarging. Some of the things I received was a purse from Wanda, some mittens and bed socks that Bee had knit, a stocking cap from Carl, different from the ones now. It hung way down my back much like you see a Santa hat, only much longer. Pop and Rex went together and got me my first complete Bible. They even had my name engraved on it. It was a beautiful slim brown Bible and had a great concordance in the back that Bee showed me how to use. Wanda had purchased some waxy type things that to throw in the already light fireplace which made different colors spray up in the fire. Very festive.

The Huffs would send home oranges from time to time for us to store in their basement for them. They said we could eat some of them, especially if we saw that some were going to spoil. They had some unusual looking oranges in the crate called Kumquats. They told us the correct way was to eat the skin and all. They were so good that if I EVEN THOUGHT one might go bad in a few days, I would eat it.

I rode Tony quite a bit and would often get the cows for Carl to bring to the barn. It was a bit tricky though as there was a corn field between the pasture where the cows grazed. Thus, the cows would want to turn into that field before I could get them past it. One time they got in the field, and Tony and I had quite a ride getting them out of there. I was so scared because I had heard my dad say that cows didn't know when to quit eating and would founder themselves to death. I was also worried the owner of that field would be upset because some of the corn was trampled down. Somehow, I managed to get them out of the field and to the barn.

One day Carl asked me if I would like to ride Tony double with him and go fast. I didn't want to, as I was frightened to go fast, but I gave in and off we went. Tony was running very hard and fast until we got to the stream. Instead of jumping over it, he abruptly stopped and threw us both off. It knocked the wind out of me, but otherwise, I was unhurt. Carl knew immediately what happened and began to pump my stomach.   That was the end of riding fast!

The Huffs had quite a brooder system. I don't know where Carl got the chickens, but I remember the brooder system that spring. The chickens were elevated on a wire so the droppings could go beneath. All you would have to do then was slide out this rack and clean off the droppings. Their housing was at eye level so we didn't' have to bend down and was only tall enough for the chickens.

By the side of the house was a mulberry tree that was loaded with fruit. I don't know why, but I thought I needed a dish to eat the mulberries from when I climbed up the tree and sat on a branch. The horse Ginger was usually standing under that tree, so afterward I would get on her and ride bareback around the yard. They also had a tree that produced green gauge plums. True to the name they were green and even though we didn't care for the taste, we canned them. I don't think we ate them canned either.

Our pastors the Heather's were going to South Dakota, and it seemed like a good time for Wanda and me to catch a ride with them and visit friends. They were to pass by close enough to our friends the Hollingsworth's so that we could stay with them. To top it off, Mrs. Hollingsworth was very ill, and Wanda could help out with housekeeping. After all, she had lived with them and worked for them when in high school.

The Heather's had friends in Sioux City... a single man they probably met in Bible College, and it was arranged that we spend the night there. The problem was his parents were not believers; just he and his sister who was still in high school. We arrived very late at night to this very, very fancy house. Everyone was already in bed. Not wanting to wake his parents, the young man met us at the door and didn't turn on any lights. I don't think he knew the Heather's had Wanda and I with them either. He used a flashlight and took us up a long winding staircase. He took me to his sister's room and whispered in her ear to scoot over, that a young girl would be sleeping there. He took Wanda to a private room, and the Heather's to another. That's how large this mansion was. We were waked in the morning before day light, and we left the place, not speaking to or meeting any of the family. I have no idea what the girl looked like whose bed I shared, but that was an experience. We stayed a week at Hollingsworth's and returned back home.

Cecil, Irene, Billy and Linda came to visit us at the Huffs, and Irene made Chow Mein. We had never had anything like that before. She left things for us to make more after they left, but none of us knew how to fix it. One day Carl took Billy, (Irene's son younger than me) and me to Fairfield. As we got out on the main road, we saw a hitch hiker. Carl decided it would be fun to give him a ride. We let him ride in the front with Carl, while Billy and I rode in the back seat. The rider was a fairly young fellow, and he wanted to know if we knew a certain song, which we didn't. So, he began to sing "Well, I was born on a farm out in Ioway, A flaming youth who was bound that he'd fly away."

Chapter Twenty-Two

The Stoops Place

It was March and time to move on. Only twice in my life when I was ages four and seven did I remember anything about the move. Both of those times you have read the details as I recalled them. Seemingly I did little to help as that part is completely free from my mind. All I know is we were now at the Stoops place, and now we had about fifteen miles to drive to finish out the school year.

We were renting again and this time from Ralph Stoops. He happened to be my cousin, Clarice Bradfield's, brother-in-law. The house was a very nice large two-story house. There was no indoor bathroom, but there was electricity on the first floor. The upstairs had no electricity. I guess they figured at bedtime you were to go to sleep and wouldn't need lights.

There was a huge eat-in-kitchen, a separate pantry, a huge dining/sitting room, a sewing room, and down the hall was a parlor. Off the hall was the staircase that led upstairs to three very large bedrooms. I had my room, Bee and Wanda shared a room if they were both home at the same time, and Pop and Carl had the back bedroom. Their bedroom had a vent in the floor which let the heat come up from the kitchen. Otherwise like all our other houses, the upstairs was completely unheated.

There was a screened in porch off the kitchen with broken pieces hanging down. Mr. Stoops told my dad that he would pay for the screen if he would screen it. He did, and it looked so nice. Off the dining room to the back of the house was another screened in porch. The screen only had a few tears in it, so my dad patched those. To the front of the dining room was just a floored covered porch and still another porch over what was probably supposed to be the front entrance.

We had our orange crates in the kitchen for the wash pan and water bucket. A kerosene cook stove that came from somewhere plus our table and chairs completed the furnishings. The cream separator was located on the porch until winter; when it was brought into the kitchen. We had the towel on rollers on the back of the kitchen door. When the towel got worn, it was cut up in small rags for wash rags. Notice I said wash rags...not wash cloths. I don't think wash cloths appeared until I graduated from high school and got a job.

The pantry had a counter top, but it was a mess. So, Bee and Pop went to town and bought some wine-colored linoleum, tore off the old stuff and replaced it with the new linoleum. The first thing Bee and I did was play jacks on the new smooth counter top. We played there any chance we got.

I don't remember us having any chickens there, but we did have a few cows. They did a small amount of farming, but not much as Pop and Carl went into the lime spreading business. They had purchased an old lime truck and would leave early in the morning to haul lime for the day. Pop was still regaining his strength.

After I had accepted Christ as my Savior, I read my new Bible and began a real prayer life for an eleven-year-old. I decided from that Christmas on I would pray every day for a bicycle. I knew that would take a miracle because the basic rules with my siblings were this; what one got we all got. I knew, for example, a wrist watch was the gift that all my siblings received upon graduation from high school, and I would get one as well. None of my siblings had a bicycle, and I shouldn't expect one either. Yet, I knew within my heart I would get one. My birthday was in April, and I would be twelve.

Since Carl and Pop got up around four A.M., I didn't have to get up until probably six A.M. The day before my birthday; I scouted around the barn, machine shed, and wash house. There was no bicycle to be found, but I wasn't discouraged. On the morning of my birthday, I heard my dad and Carl come in the house, and it was still dark outside. Pop said to Be, "You'd better get Edythe up". Wow, I knew it, I knew it! Why else would they be getting me up while it was still dark? So, I faked being asleep and came down the stairs rubbing my eyes as though trying to wake up. They were in the dining/ sitting room, lacing up their boots to go on their route, and there stood a BICYCLE. A RED BICYCLE. It had a sheepskin cover on the seat. It didn't matter that it was a boy's bicycle. It didn't matter that I could see it had been freshly painted with some red on the tire rims. It was a real BICYCLE. I KNEW GOD ANSWERS PRAYERS. I believe God let me see the power of prayer through that one request. Concerning the fact that my siblings didn't get a bicycle...I found out later from one of my brothers that Pop went to each of my siblings and asked them if it would be alright if he gave me a bicycle. Most of them were married, and had children who owned bicycles, so of course they wanted me to have one. Today, people would laugh to learn that was the first bike for a twelve-year-old., when now even two-year-old get bikes.

I was thrilled to learn that Taylor school where I would be attending was only a quarter mile away. I didn't know any of the kids in the neighborhood yet, but with Uncle Vern's family of children and grandchildren, we had lots of fun thing happening. However, there were two boys that had just gotten motor bikes that rode up and down by our house. I found out later they were cousins, and they were very nice looking. They would pause their bikes and whistle whenever I was out on the porch; which was quite flattering.

It was a sad time to leave Round Prairie Baptist as we had so many friends there. However, we continued to visit with one another from time to time. The new church set up was quite different. There was obviously a shortage of pastors for Stockport. So, one Pastor was hired to serve two different denominations. One Sunday we would meet at the Christian church and the next we would meet at the Friends Church. The Pastors name was Valentine Krumm. He had several children who were evidently out of control. One Sunday Pastor Krumm was preaching, and one of his teen age boys jumped up to leave the church. The pastor stopped preaching and ran out the door after him.

I don't remember socializing with any of the church folks, except with our relatives. The church relationship or teaching wasn't the same as what we had in South Dakota or at Round Prairie...yet God provided a warmth with all our relatives. Uncle Vern's had about six of his children living in the area. They were all married except Lorna Jean, and many had children, some just a few years younger than I and some with just babies. We would meet at Uncle Vern's many a Sunday afternoon and make homemade ice cream. Lorna Jean was now walking with crutches and out of bed. She and I went to Birmingham and got permanents. We waited and waited for Uncle Vern to pick us up as it was now five o'clock and the shop was closing. So, Lorna Jean suggested we start walking. It was fifteen miles back to Stockport. I said, "how are you going to be able to walk that far on crutches?" She said, "sometimes these crutches are a blessing". I soon got the point as about that time a truck driver stopped and asked us if we wanted a ride. He was headed to Stockport!

Wanda appeared at our house one day as she had been taking care of our cousin Morris's children. She had been to the doctor and was diagnosed with something called "milk leg". She had to have an ace bandage wrapped tightly around it and stay off it as much as possible. Nothing to do but quit her job. As she was recovering she and Bee served together as surrogate mothers.

Wanda had an idea. She said if I would get up at four A.M. with the rest of them and help with breakfast and the daily chores, we could go back to bed after the men left. It was summer time ...so we girls fixed breakfast, washed the dishes and cleaned the house. As farmers, the houses had to be cleaned every day. The men would track in from the barn, so the kitchen and dining room floors had to be scrubbed (always on your hands and knees). The halls had to be dust mopped. The porches swept, the furniture dusted as we had to leave all the doors and windows open to cool the house.

Living by a gravel road sent volumes of dust in the house when a car passed by. We kept the parlor shut up, so we didn't have to vacuum or dust in there until we had special company. Of course, the beds had to be made...the feather tick fluffed up, and on Mondays, the wash had to be done. The clothes hung on the line and Tuesday was ironing day. But...with all three of us working, we could be back in bed by six and sleep until eight A.M.

Yes it was summer. My cousin Clarice's, wife Wilda, and daughter Caroline lived one mile away. Caroline was about six years younger than I, but ages didn't matter that much to farm people. We hung out with people of all ages. The churches in town all went together that year to hold VBS. I think there were four churches...and we met at the high school. VBS was always two weeks. Wilda drove my cousin Caroline, her niece Jerri and me each day to VBS. I was going to be in seventh grade, Jerri was going to be in fifth grade, and I think Caroline was going to be in first grade. The first day we were told to write our full names on a paper and hand it in. Jerri whispered to me that she didn't know how to spell her name. I said WHAT...GOING INTO FIFTH GRADE AND YOU DON'T KNOW HOW TO SPELL YOUR NAME? She said "well my real name is Geraldine, but I've always gone by Jerri and I've never learned to spell it". Well that made a difference, so I shut up.

Two things I remember about VBS. One we learned a psalm, and two, we sang "Break Thou the Bread of Life". I learned the Psalm so I could get a prize if I could say it by heart at the program. The program was going to be held on the Sunday following the two weeks of VBS. But the Saturday before the program I got the Measles....oh no. Two things were terribly wrong. I wouldn't get my prize and Gordon, and Lucy arrived and I wouldn't be able to do things with them. Doing things meant visiting the relative's homes in that area and having special meals together. Bummer, Bummer. The folks let me sleep on the cot in the dining/sitting area to be by the family and not be alone upstairs. Lucy thought I would like to see how I looked, so she brought me a mirror. I was really covered with the measles. The rule was to keep all the shades drawn and as dark as possible to prevent any weakness to the eyes.

When I got over the measles, I got to go to Clarice and Wilda's a lot, and play with Caroline. She did something I had never done, which was to dress up her kittens in doll clothes. We were doing that one day when all of a sudden, the cat bolted. We never did find the kitten and get those clothes back.

Wanda decided I was old enough to stay by myself when she and Bee would go to town. I didn't like that too much until I found out that every time they went, they would bring me back something. One was bubbles that you could blow from the jar just by waving a wand. Before that, the way we would blow bubbles was to get a straw from the barn...mix up some soap in a wash pan and blow away. That is until one day I discovered you could take an onion top for a straw and make bigger bubbles. Beside bubbles, they brought me something to mix up and make my own balloons. As far as making the balloons...whatever it was made of had an ether-like smell that nearly put you out. They brought other things like silly putty and a stick like thing that had notches on it with a propeller on the end of the stick. If you rubbed another stick over the notches, it would make the propeller go around and around. Plus, they came home with new dresses for school. So, it wasn't bad staying alone.

One day I got a little lonely, and Pop seemed to be home that day working in a field down the road apiece. He had driven the car down there...so I decided to ride my bike where he was. When I arrived, he told me he needed me to go to Clarice's and get something. "You'll have to take the car", he said. Now I had driven the car before, but not alone. I said, "well what about my bike?" Pop said, "I'll ride it home". Never in my life had I seen my dad ride a bike. So, I started off to Clarice's. Now the stop sign on the main road was up a hill. That meant you had to have your foot on the clutch and the brake and gas pedal. But if I would scoot down to put my foot on the clutch and brake, I would most likely kill the engine. So, I prayed, "God don't let a car be coming down the road because I'm not going to stop at the stop sign". I could tell there wasn't a car coming because there was no dust flying...so I zoomed up the hill through the stop sign. When I got home, an hour later...there sat my bike. I would love to have seen my Dad ride it. But I never saw him get on it...ever.

A time or two, Wilda would hire me to do her dusting. Wow...I never thought about getting paid for that kind of thing. We all just helped each other with no thought of pay. They had a beautiful high polished stairway to their upstairs, and I loved to make those steps shine. Plus, a time or two, she left me to watch Caroline while she went to town with her sister Esther. Once she left, and it was way past dinner time. I couldn't find anything to eat, so I went to the garden and pulled radishes. I found some bread and butter and sliced radishes for a sandwich. I had never heard of that before, but that tasted so good. I still like a radish sandwich.

Wilda's sister Esther was Caroline's favorite Aunt. Caroline had never quit sucking her thumb, and it was time for her to start school. We had party line phones, and one of their neighbors by the name of Floy loved to listen in to phone calls. We could see her sitting by her picture window with the phone receiver in her hand every time we passed by. I don't know when she did her work One day Esther called Caroline and said. "If you will quit sucking your thumb I'll get you one of those new dolls that feels like real baby skin and takes a bottle and wets its diaper". Caroline said, "Oh Aunt Esther why did you have to say that on the phone? People might be listening." Esther said, "Oh I don't think so". Caroline said, "well how about Floy?" Esther replied, "Oh I doubt she's listening". About that time Floy said, "Oh yes I am". The dust flew between Esther's and Wilda's house that day while they chuckled over that story.

Another incident that happened was when Wilda, Caroline and I were going to Stockport. We were supposed to stop and pick up Esther. Esther had just finished cleaning up her kitchen from breakfast, and poured the bacon grease from the skillet into a cup. People always reused the bacon grease to cook with other foods. Anyway, we honked the horn for Esther to come out and she yelled, "Let me finish my cup of coffee, and I'll be right out." She came out all right spitting and spewing. Thinking she had her cup of coffee, she had downed the bacon grease.

Cecil and Irene wanted to take a trip to New York that summer and asked Wanda to watch Linda and Billy. Trips were long and slow back then, so we had the kids for two weeks. Billy got to help out at Clarice's farm as well as ours since the men exchanged work. Lime truck business had slowed down for the year, so it was more farm work. Uncle Vern was a trucker also not only with lime business but with hauling grain and cattle. Once in a while he would stop and ask Billy, Caroline, or me if we would like to go riding with him. We went to the elevators while they would weigh and unload. Uncle Vern always had something to snack on. Something real unique. He had ginger snaps and cheese sandwiches and they was so good. I still like that combination.

Cecil and Irene came back from New York to get the kids back to South Dakota in time for school. They brought me a bronze colored image of the Skyscrapers. Irene was a little hurt as Linda didn't want to go home with them. She wanted to stay with Wanda. In the meantime, Bee had gone to Michigan to find work in a factory and stay with brother Rex and wife Bea who had just built their first house.

Sometime during that summer, Pop took me to Des Moines to the Capital to see the governor. My father spoke to someone and without us having any security check, Governor Bleu came out to meet us. He was my grandmother's first cousin and after making the relationship connection, we chatted a short while. Before we left, he asked me if I would like to sit in the Governor's chair, which I did. He was Governor from 1945 to 1949.

That fall, I couldn't wait to go to Taylor school. I was pleasantly surprised to find quite a few students. This is one school I don't remember how many students there were, but I guess about twenty-five. My teacher's name was Miss Dawson, and she was awesome. (I just did a little rhyme time in case you didn't notice.) There were four different families there with the last name of Dorothy. Three of those families had nice looking boys in the seventh and eighth grade, and they were all vying for my attention. How lucky was that! Finally, one of them won ours. His name was Donnie, and he had a very cute sister that was about Carl's age. I was now the newest kid in the neighborhood. Two of the Dorothy boys had to walk by my place to and from school, while Donnie had to go the other direction. So, the two that went by my place were sure I would like them the best...that is until Donnie would walk me home and then turn around and walk the other direction to his home.

Every day was fun. There were boyfriends, girlfriends, and a wonderful teacher. Our teacher had a fiancé' in Germany, and he would send Marzipan candy shaped like real fruit, and Miss Dawson would share it with us. I don't remember where she lived, but it seemed like it was about fifty miles away. So, one weekend, she invited Patricia, Esther and me to her house. She lived with her widowed mother in one of those big old farm homes. We had a wonderful time laughing, giggling, and visiting with her mother. Her fiancé' said if we sent a picture of ourselves to him, he would make us rings with our picture in them. Miss Dawson carefully measured our fingers with string for the size and sent the pictures to him. The rings were some brown plastic with our picture in it. Esther was also a Dorothy, and she was a grade behind me but came from a wonderful Christian family. I still keep in touch with her, through visits and correspondence. She told me recently that was the one that taught her how to ride a bike.

The Gideon's came to our school and said if anyone could say John 3:16, we would get a new testament. I thought everyone would raise their hand, but when I looked around, I was the only one that did. I was a little ashamed, and now I am ashamed that I was ashamed...because I was the only one to recite it. He then told the rest of the students...if they learned it, he would come back in a month, and pass out more New Testaments upon their recitation. Oh, how far our schools have come. NOT! I hear its permissible in Russian schools to read the Bible. But not our country. We were only FOUNDED on Christian principles.

I felt like I needed to get glasses that year in school, but the only glasses for young people were horrible looking. Wanda had seen some glasses with gold frames around them that looked quite classy. So, she went with me to the optometrist, and those were the kind I got. The doctor said I had astigmatism. I wasn't sure how the boys would react, but when I walked into the school with my new glasses on, Donnie thought I looked great.

We found out when Miss Dawson's' birthday was, so we girls decided to have a party. Wanda and I made our family candy recipe, popcorn balls, and fudge. There was a church building just a few yards from the school, so Esther helped me carry the stuff down to the church and place it inside so the dogs, or vermin wouldn't get it. We girls were so excited and naturally I got to be the one to tell Miss Dawson at recess we were going to have a party for her. She was so surprised she immediately dismissed class for the rest of the day. Quickly Esther and I had to run over to the church and bring the treats over. In the meantime, Wanda had made some more candy and taken it to the church. How did we get in the church? Well, what do you think? We simply opened the door and walked in. Churches weren't locked. Not even crooks would have the guts to take something from a church. They respected God even though they didn't respect man.

It's funny...I don't remember anything about a Halloween or Christmas program. I just remember doing 'readin, 'riting, and 'rithmetic and the fact that even though there were three or four of us sitting on the recitation bench, Donnie always saved me a spot by him.

Patricia asked me if we were going to Stockport to watch the high school Senior play, one evening. I said "yes". After all EVERYBODY attended school productions. She asked if she could have a ride. I said sure. She lived almost two miles from the school and a mile and half of that was on a dirt road. So, the night of the Senior Play it poured down rain. I mean poured. Our family decided not to go until we heard a knock on the door. Patricia had walked all the way in the rain to our house. It was so dark, I don't know how she managed to find her footing on the road. Her boots had so much mud on them it had to have been difficult to walk. We quickly changed our minds and went to the play. After the play was over, we offered to take Patricia home, but she said she was afraid we might get stuck. Besides her parents told her she had to walk if she wanted to go. She came from a split family, and I don't think she had an easy life. In fact, it seemed to me she did most of the family housework.

My brother Carl started dating Donnie's sister Vivian. She was about the cutest girl I knew. I don't know how they met...but usually, farmers knew everyone in the neighborhood.

Again, Christmas was so much fun that year. Pop cut a big tree, and we put it in the parlor. We still had some of the electric lights left from the Huffs, and we had piles of presents as well as our candy sacks. Grandma Nelson was visiting Aunt Lora and Uncle Vern, so we had her come out. We had an oil stove in the parlor which we lit, and it was nice and warm. We never lit the stove in there unless we had company coming. For some reason Lucy and Gordon decided to send me a Christmas present that year even though they hadn't drawn my name. They gave me bracelet with a clover charm, and a beautiful figure sweater.   My present from Wanda was an electric lamp with a blue deer figurine base and a pink lampshade. We figured out that we could use a long extension cord from the hall way and thread it through the banister to reach my bedroom. Yippee, I had electric lights. Naturally, Wanda let the light shine in her bedroom, so she didn't have to light a lamp.

Pop and I were invited to Uncle Vern's for Christmas dinner as for some reason we were going to be alone. In their huge kitchen was a table that seated lots of people. They had many grandchildren that I sort of knew...not having lived around them until that year. I just remember the grand-kids and I had to share a chair...that is two to a chair. After dinner, we headed to the parlor to open Christmas presents. There was our tan Indian rug that we had in South Dakota. It looked so beautiful. I reasoned that Pop must have given it to Uncle Vern for payment in moving us. Anyway, I didn't expect any presents as I had my opened mine at home. Imagine my surprise when I was included with the same gifts as their grandchildren. They had wrapped a half dollar in aluminum foil and hung them on the tree. Uncle Vern said. "go to the tree Edythe and get your present". I couldn't get over it.   Aunt Lori who was Pop's sister was always working...gardening, cooking, doing dishes and caring for Grandma when it was her turn to keep her, so I spent more time around Uncle Vern. I never remember her sitting down to visit.

I never saw Uncle Vern without a smile. Problems if he had them, didn't remove that smile. In the summer time, when we would see him, he'd say, "Better stop by and we will make a freezer of ice cream." And true to his word, we would have homemade ice cream. In the winter he would say to me, "go to the kitchen and get the dishpan, take it to the cellar and fill it up with apples." He was a favorite Uncle...even though he was only an uncle by marriage.

Christmas was now over, and a couple of things stand out in my mind. A family lived down the road from us that had eight boys. The Mother was pregnant and with every pregnancy had to have complete bed rest. They moved her bed into the kitchen/dining area where she could direct the family's affairs. Pop took me with him to visit and pray for the lady. The house looked immaculate and apparently ran like a smoothly oiled machine.

The other incident I remember is one night after we had all gone to bed, I heard a car stop in front of our house. We had a hand twist doorbell on the front door, and I think it was the first time it we ever heard it used. (Friends always used the kitchen door.) I warned Wanda who quickly put on a bathrobe, alerting Pop as she headed the stairs. They apologized for waking us, but they said they were lost, and had been driving around in circles and we looked like a friendly house. Wanda gave them directions, and I remember Pop saying they were probably drunk.

Carl was still dating Vivian and Easter was in early March that year. Carl came home after a date and gave me a beautifully decorated chocolate Easter egg. He said Donnie had sent it to me. I didn't believe him at first. I was shy and embarrassed, but of course pleased. But once again I found out...we are on the road again. This time we were moving to a farm near Ollie, Iowa.

Chapter Twenty-Three

The Ollie Farm Owned by Aunt Euma and Uncle Carl

Most of my Seventh-grade year had been so wonderful, that I assumed it would continue. Again, I don't recall anything about moving and getting settled in the house. But one good thing...there was a letter waiting for me from Donnie when we arrived. Sigh. I guess Carl gave him my address because I was so surprised. Carl stayed behind in Stockport, having taken over the filling station from his Bradfield cousins.

I found out I would be riding a school bus. Because we lived on a dirt road, Willis our neighbor who just graduated from high school was hired to transport me the mile to the bus stop. He was a very shy man, and I was a chatter box I suppose. Anyway, this would be my first city school.

My class room consisted of only the seventh and eighth graders, and my teacher was Mr. Chandler. He was quite large, but he could get around pretty fast. The system was so different from a country school. We probably had twenty-five to thirty students in that classroom. It was toward the end of March, and everyone else knew all the ropes by that time...except me of course. The girls were not friendly. Even though I grew up on a farm, I had never seen the birth of any animal. For some reason, my dad didn't think that proper for ladies, and when they asked me sexual questions, I hadn't a clue. Not only that, I was undeveloped and was still wearing children's clothing. The smallest size then for young ladies was a "nine" and I wore a size twelve in kids clothing. Also, I came from a "religious" family and didn't do a lot of things for entertainment that they did. We didn't go to dances, movies or have smokers in our house and went to church every Sunday, prayed before our meals and read the Bible.

I must have asked questions as to how to do this or that, because one day the teacher said, "Now let's go over the test papers we had yesterday". I hadn't saved mine...so when everyone pulled theirs out of their desk, I had none. He said, "Edythe, where is your paper?". I said, "I didn't know I had to save it". He said, 'DO WE HAVE TO TELL YOU EVERYTHING?" I didn't cry, but almost. So, of course, I looked like the class dummy. Not only that, we had hot lunches served there and I had brought my lunch.

I tried to interact with the students...but not even the boys would look at me. I had three or four vying for my attention at Taylor, and now this was my first time that I had no friends, girls or boys. None. I even thought about trying to hang out with the sixth graders, because country school kids hung out with everybody. But here, Jr. High kids didn't do that! I must have shared things with Wanda because she got me some more "adult" looking clothing. I even tried to let the girls know that I had a boyfriend! None of them seemed to have one. I brought a letter to school once that Donnie had written me, but they weren't impressed.

One of the nice perks that came from town school was a movie room. We perhaps saw a movie once a week. They were usually sponsored by Good Year Tire, or Proctor and Gamble. The one movie I'll never forget was entitled, "The Longest Way Around Is the Shortest Way Home". It was about someone who left home because they were just sure things were better elsewhere, only to discover that there was no place like home. It reminded me of the Bible Story of the Prodigal Son.

Summer came none too quickly. No matter where we lived we went to all the area fairs; Fairfield Centennial, Ollie days, Stockport days, Sigourney Fair, Fremont Fair, Donnelson fair...you name it. I also think my dad enjoyed meeting up with his friends. Pop said we could go back to the Stockport Days. I was so tickled as I could be with Donnie. I happened to meet my friend Judith there. I always ran across friends at the fairs and I looked for Donnie. There he was, but he was with another girl. He had paid her way to ride the Ferris wheel and was waiting for her to get off. He spoke to me, but barely, and that ended that! He eventually married that girl and my brother Carl ended up marrying Donnie's sister Vivian.

An older cousin of mine had broken her foot and was on crutches and wanted me to come and help out for two weeks. My father was a little hesitant as she had been married a couple of times and he wasn't sure her reputation was good for me to be around. However, she had been married to this man for quite some time, and she had a young son perhaps eight years old, that need attention also. So, he agreed to let me go. It was quite a distance away so I stayed nights also.

Those days were like none other. When her husband would be gone, another man would often show up bringing dry cleaning, etc., and he would stay for quite some time. I did dishes, made beds, mopped the floors, and helped with some cooking, and ironing. One night she and her husband and son decided to go to a drive-in movie. It was my very first. Of course, I had to go along...but I never told my dad. She knew my dad didn't allow things like that...so I think she thought that was great sport to take me to my first movie. I so wanted to be obedient that when we got to the theater, I lay down in the back seat and pretended to be sleepy, so I didn't have to watch it.

One early evening my cousin had hopped out on her crutches to the barn to visit with her husband. She came back in and was crying. She told me to look at a certain place on her body where her husband had whacked her a good one. He had hit her so hard it left a hand print even several minutes later. He had seen the man with the dry cleaning leave the house. She told her son and me that we had to get away from the house immediately. The only phone in the area was in a certain direction.... So, she said, "Let's go the opposite way and hide in the ditch in case he starts out to look for us". So, we lay in the ditch until dark.

We then turned and went back by the house again where her husband had all the lights on, and we could see him walking around. Our passing by started the dogs barking, but for some reason, he didn't come out and check. We walked slowly as she was on crutches. We hoped a car would come along and when the first one came in our direction she flagged it down. She asked if he would drive us to the country store which was five miles away. He wasn't too keen on the idea, since he was her husband's neighbor, and he made very little conversation on the way. When we arrived at the store, my cousin called her dad. We had to wait at the store for quite some time until he arrived.

We stayed the night at my aunt and uncle's house and the next morning got up early and went back to her husband's house. Yes, it was her husband's house. He owned a farm when she married him. My uncle had a coupe car, and it had a HUGE trunk. It was a new car, so the trunk was spotless. She threw a sheet down on the trunk floor, and we started carrying out clothes and personal items. Then her husband came in and confronted us. My uncle said, "We had better sit down and talk". In the meantime, I kept carrying out clothes and other items. I remember my Uncle saying, "Well if you can't get along, I guess you will have to part". I stayed at my aunt and uncle's house for the night again, because I knew when I went home I would have to explain and it wouldn't go over very well. Besides, I was to be paid in the morning. Thankfully when I got home my sister-in-law Irene, and children Billy and Linda arrived. It seemed Billy was getting in to a lot of mischief in Rapid City and it was decided for the three of them to spend the summer on the farm. Wanda then took a job caring for Mrs. Brown, an elderly lady in Hedrick.

Billy and I had a lot of fun. We worked in the garden, pulling weeds and gardening. Irene did the cooking, laundry, and house cleaning. Linda and I had to do the dusting. Irene also sewed me some clothing for school. Pop would send me up to Pekin in the car to the corner store for things. Billy would go with me and because once again the stop sign was on a hill...we worked together to get the car across. If I took my foot off the gas pedal, the car would die. If I took my foot off the clutch, and try to zoom across the highway, it would kill the engine. So somehow, Billy would work the brake or the gas pedal, and we would make it.

On the fourth of July, Pop said he would take us to Sigourney to the carnival. He said we were invited over to the Anderson's (people that owned the hardware store in Ollie) for the evening to look at some home movies. They had been to the Black Hills, and taken lots of pictures, but didn't know the significance of some of them and needed an explanation. So, Pop volunteered Irene to be the moderator of the movies since they lived in the Black Hills.

Upon arriving in Sigourney around noon, it started to snow. We had worn light sweaters but had no idea it was going to start snowing. It was too cold to get out and do anything, but Pop did get us a pint of ice cream apiece. After driving around, a bit, we went home and he lit a fire in the cook-stove. I'm sure we had taken the pot belly stove down for the summer to give us more room. When the chimney was dismantled we filled up the chimney hole with the flue cover. The flue cover even though was almost to the ceiling had a picture on it. Usually, we had saved a pretty picture from a calendar to glue on each year. I went ahead and cleaned the lamps for the evening. We usually had three lamps. One with a mantle on it. It made the brighter light, but the mantle itself would dry out and get brittle. So, if it got bumped while carrying it, it might disintegrate, and have to be replaced. We also had a Coleman lantern that you could pump up with air to make a brighter light as it started to dim. That lantern was made to use outdoors.

Linda went with me to gather the eggs and feed the chickens that night, while Billy helped Pop with the milking. After the milking and separating was done (it was still the fourth of July, so it was Pop's day off) Irene had supper ready. Soon after we headed for the Anderson's and found out their power was off. Fortunately, they had a generator which I didn't know such things existed. They lived right night to the hardware store/food locker and it was a necessity to have a generator. They put a fire in the fireplace as it was still snowing and quite cold. They started the movies while Irene moderated them. Afterward they served us ice cream in very pretty dishes.

Pop decided we should go to St. Louis and visit our former Pastors the George's. Since Irene knew them also, it was a fun trip. We spent the night with the George's and Sis George served us breakfast in their breezeway. I thought that was so cool. Pun intended. She made oatmeal for one thing and I asked the cream to be passed. It was in a tiny pitcher and I thought that was odd (not knowing city folks used it for coffee only) I emptied the cream pitcher on my oatmeal. She came back from the kitchen and said, "oh my, I thought I had filled the cream pitcher". I was embarrassed to find out they didn't use cream on their oatmeal, but milk. In the afternoon they took us to see the St. Louis Zoo. That was quite the interest for Billy, Linda Kay and me. Then because we had never ridden on a trolley, their son who was ten years older than me, said we would take the trolley home. That was a real experience. The older adults took the car home.

Summer moved on, and it was soon time for me to start to eighth grade. I found out that some of the neighboring country schools had closed and we would have extra students to join us. Now they would be the new kids on the block and I decided to get acquainted with two girls, Trilla and Betty. They were from different country schools and didn't know each other either. Even yet, though we live in three different states, we still get together from time to time...write, call, or visit. I thank God for those great friendships.

The Black Hills school started later, so Irene stayed on for another week or so. I took Linda to school with me one day. No one else in the class was an aunt at that age, so I felt really proud. Of course, everyone made over her, but I'm sure she was bored.

Instead of recess in seventh and eighth grade, we had gym. We had a basketball team, and I had never even held a basketball. I was so scared about being made a fool, that I explained to the teacher that I had a heart problem. My heart diagnosis was a heart murmur, and I also suspect angina. It probably wouldn't have prevented me from playing basketball, but I wasn't taking any chances. So, Mr. Chandler said I could be the chaperon. He would send me into the girl's lockers to make sure everyone was decent so that he could come in and speak to the girls. We played a few different schools and could skip classes during that time.

Not too much to report about eighth grade, except one of the boys was not responding to Mr. Chandler. He walked to the back of the room, picked the kid up with one hand and grabbed a paddle and paddled him good. The kid never made a sound. I felt sorry for him as he had a hearing problem and thought perhaps that was the reason he didn't respond correctly.

We had eighth-grade graduation. I wore a beautiful white taffeta dress, and I believe I had green shoes to go with them. Other than that, I don't remember anything else about it. Many students ended their schooling with eighth-grade as did some of our classmates.

Chapter Twenty-Four

The Pekin Church and Community

We were only two miles from the church that Pop chose for us to attend. It was a Methodist church at Pekin, which he had attended as a boy. Once again, it was nothing like the Tabernacle, the Yankton Assembly or the Round Prairie Baptist. People were always friendly at church, but other than that, they didn't seem to fellowship with one another except those that were related.

The young people were a conglomeration from different schools, and none attended Ollie where I went. So, we had Ollie, Packwood, Hedrick and Farson schools represented. We often had pie suppers, wedding showers, baby showers, and Christmas programs held at the church which allowed some social time.

My dad soon became elected as the S.S. teacher for the Adult Class. They met in the front corner of the auditorium and our young people's class met at the very back with a teacher whose name was also Edith. Wanda became the primary pianist. We also had a youth choir. We didn't practice we just had chairs by the piano that constituted a choir area. We usually sat there through the entire preaching service. It seemed the pastor usually asked my father to close in prayer. Now Pop usually stayed seated in the front row after teaching his class and often fell asleep during the sermon. The usual closing of the service went like this: "May we all stand and Mr. Nelson would you close in prayer". However, he was not always the one that was asked to dismiss in prayer. He would wake up when he heard the people standing. Not knowing if he should pray or not, he would look at me in the choir section and if I nodded my head, that meant he was to pray. If I didn't, then he knew someone else was supposed to have the closing prayer.

After I got a saxophone, I would often play a saxophone special. Dale, another young person would often play a trumpet special, or sing a solo. Later on, when they were really desperate, I would play the piano. Evelyn and Ella Mae were two grades ahead of me, and they played the piano sometimes. Evelyn's last name was Capps, and she was a distant relative of mine that we had never met until we moved there. I think we figured we were fourth cousins. She and her brother attended church, but neither of their parents did.

One Easter I wore a beautiful turquoise and white plaid coat, white hat, gloves, and purse. We couldn't find brown shoes to match my brown dress, so Wanda found me a pair of black wedges, (back then we called them wedgies) and had them dyed brown at the shoe store. Everyone dressed up especially for Easter. Now came another problem for me. There were no such things as stretch hose, and my legs were so skinny that when I tried on hosiery, they bagged around my legs. Wanda heard of a store in Ottumwa called "Yonkers" that carried children's hosiery, and purchased some for me. I wore children's hosiery all through high school. Hosiery had a dark seam that you had to line up perfectly straight on the back of your legs. The hose was turned inside out so the seam would stand out more. It was a fashion statement. To get them connected to your garter belt so that they lined up straight was no small feat. Ladies and girls with crooked seams were talked about.

About three events happened with that Methodist congregation that stand out in my mind. I think I was perhaps a freshman and someone heard there was a young evangelist speaking at the Ottumwa Colosseum that was pretty good. So, a carload of us went to hear him. His name was Billy Graham and he was not well known in our area. That would have been about 1949 or 1950. When we arrived at this huge auditorium there only were two or three rows of people gathered across the front. I remember thinking..." why did they have such a big place with only fifty or one hundred people". Anyway, he kept my interest. Little did we know how famous he would become.

Another situation happened at a later time when Bee was living at home. Ella Mae had heard about some goings on in Linby. Linby was about two miles from Pekin. My Aunt Erma lived on one side of the street in Linby, and My Uncle Bernie lived across the street from her. There was one gas station in town, which also handled some groceries. Other than that, there were no other businesses. At one time it had been a thriving town with a hotel, stores, churches, and schools. The old hotel there had stood vacant for years, but Ella Mae was telling us that some of her friends had decided to check it out. Of course, they went at night with a flashlight to make it spooky. They were walking through some of the rooms noting that the beds, dressers, etc. still stood. She said when they got to one room, they saw that the bed was unmade. One of the girls said, "Well you can tell if it been recently used if the bed is still warm". They felt the bed, and it was warm. About then they heard a scuffling down the stairs. So out the door, they flew.

Now we were all up for a challenge, so we talked Bee into driving us younger ones up by the hotel. The main part of the hotel was dark, but there were lights down in the basement. We saw through the basement window a man standing there mixing something like a scientist would do. We paused the car to all peer in the window, and suddenly Bee killed the engine. She couldn't get it restarted for a few minutes and we nearly all panicked. When it did start, we spun out of there rather quickly. I couldn't wait to ask our Aunt Erma the scoop the next time we paid a visit. The report was that a doctor from Chicago had apparently left rather quickly and somehow found out about that old hotel in Linby. No one knows whether he purchased it or just took up residence there. Eventually, he opened up for business, and yes, he did mix some of his own medicines. He lived there, practiced there, but never hung a sign. My cousin decided she would risk his services and she felt quite comfortable with him, as did some of the other occupants in Linby.

One time we had a pie supper at church. Each family was to bring a pie and it was just Pop and me living at home. I had never baked a pie before, but I endeavored to make a mincemeat pie for that occasion. Pop quickly purchased a piece of my pie, tasted it and nodded his head to me that it was good and it sold out quickly. Our fellowship hall and children's Sunday School class was downstairs in the church basement. The entrance was outside which had the old-fashioned cellar doors that you opened up and laid back to walk down the steps. Like at our home, we had to go outside and pump water and carry a dishpan in to wash dishes. There was no outhouse there, but the neighbors were kind enough to let anyone use theirs.

I remember my dad's rule that no farming was done on Sundays. It was a day of rest. Chores of course and some cooking were done. It seemed like there would be several years when it would rain and rain and the farmers couldn't get their crops in. Sure, as anything the first nice day to plant would occur on Sunday. Several men would be absent from church on that Sunday, except my dad. The wonderful thing was this...he may not have got his crops in that day, but he always had good crops, and he still had a day off!!!!

Lastly, I remember the church bells ringing on Sunday morning that we could hear two miles away. They would ring nine times – a bell for each hour. My Dad would hurry in from the chores, run the milk through the separator while we girls, or myself, finished up with that job. He would then come up from the basement and get dressed for ten am. church. On Sunday's we ate breakfast before the chores, so we could get the dishes done, except for washing the separator. We didn't have night church there except on rare occasion Pastor Parrot (the Pastor at Pekin) would have a special service. He lived in Ottumwa which was about a 20-mile drive. His wife didn't always come, which I thought unusual...but I didn't question things like that. During one summer he decided to have a service for us young people. He read a chapter each week from 'IN HIS STEPS" by Charles Shelton. To me it was boring. One time he invited another church youth group to come. We were all supposed to stand and say when we were saved. The visiting church would say when they were saved AND sanctified. I had never heard of being sanctified before, so that was interesting.

You might think the different styles of church were upsetting, but everything seemed to be taken in stride. After all, nothing changed at home. Every morning before we ate breakfast, Pop would read the Bible and have a prayer time. (By the way, nothing ever sat on top of the Bible. It was highly honored) Sometimes, I would leave without breakfast, hearing the bus honk, while we finished the prayer. I don't think it bothered me that I didn't have breakfast. That's just what we did. If we got sick, Pop prayed for us to get well. He would lay hands on us according to the scripture in the Bible and pray for us. My school mate Betty and I recently got together, and she said, "I thought of your Dad as being the kindest man. I remember him reading the Bible and praying before we went to school". That pleased me.

We had very good neighbors, The Grant Hollingsworth's. They lived a quarter mile from us and once again...we had to walk a little more than a quarter mile to get our mail. We two families were the only ones on that mile road and the mailbox was at the cross road. One year I purchased some lavender material and wanted to make a skirt. I don't know how I thought I could make a skirt, but I started it and then went to Mrs. Hollingsworth and asked her a question. She very kindly showed me how to do it. I wanted to wear it to "Ollie Days". The carnival was there, the school band played, and I met up with my cousin Marilyn. About half mile up the road from the Grant Hollingsworth's. going the other direction, lived Grant's brother and sister-in-law. The main reason I am mentioning this is that when Grant's brother died, his sister-in-law Rhoda, began driving a car, which she had never done before. She was 78 years old and started driving like an old pro. They didn't have children, so I assumed she realized it was either do or die...so she went for the "do".

Chapter Twenty-Five

The Last Summer before High School

Pop and I were the only ones left at home. I know Bee was in Michigan and Wanda was working in Hedrick. We still kept in contact with our Round Prairie Church friends and visited some from time to time, although Judith's family had now moved to Corydon, Iowa. I think that was probably a hundred miles away.

Judith came for a few days visit and we had the bright idea to ride bikes to Hedrick and see Wanda. The problem was, there was only one bike. I knew Evelyn from Pekin church had a bike, and I thought perhaps she would loan hers to me for the day. So, Judith sat on the cross bars of my bike, and I pumped away for almost two miles to pick up Evelyn's bike. We then bicycled fifteen miles in to Hedrick and certainly surprised Wanda when we knocked on the door at Mrs. Browns. She fixed dishes of ice cream and brought outside for us to eat on the patio. We visited awhile and started back home. We didn't realize it, but the wind was at our backs pedaling to Hedrick, and we thought it a breeze. Pun intended. Coming home? Yikes we had to face the wind and again using a play on words; we were winded.

Sometime that summer, Wanda also found out that Round Prairie had a Baptismal service at the river and I hadn't been baptized. She made arrangements for me to be included. Stockport and Pekin churches just sprinkled and we believed in immersion. So, we drove back to Round Prairie that Sunday. We met out at the river after church and the service was typical of baptismal services in that era. Women would make a circle holding blankets with outstretched arms for a changing room. People were baptized in regular street clothes and then would change into dry clothes. This particular Sunday, as we left the banks to get in the water, it started pouring down rain. They went ahead with the baptismal service, and I declared that I was doubly baptized, under the water and water coming down. The problem was that by the time I got to the makeshift dressing room, the blanket closet was wet, my baptismal dress was wet, and trying to get it off with no roof over me was a pain. Everyone kept saying," hurry up", as they were getting soaked also. But my clothes were stuck to me and to top it all my "dry clothes" were now mostly wet. I remember to this day the dress I wore to be baptized in, and I literally ripped the seams apart getting it off me.

Being alone that summer, suddenly made me aware of all the household duties. Before it seemed to mostly go over my head. I learned how to start the fire in the kitchen range. Yes, I knew that you had to shake down the ashes to the ash bin. Twigs, paper and corn cobs, were all the starting equipment. The match box was behind the stove, and one gallon can of kerosene sat outside the porch door. So, I soaked a corn cob in the kerosene, (a corn cob fit just perfectly down the spout), placed it in the stove and struck the match. Then layered degrees of thicker wood on the top. We had a spiral handle to lift the stove plates off to add more wood as needed. On the side of the stove was a boiler we kept filled with water. (add another responsibility) that I'm pretty sure held a bucket of water. When cooking, the fire had to be hot enough to make the skillet sizzle with a drop of water. If fixing something in the oven, the trick was keeping it at an even temperature to make the baked goods turn out properly.

Baking reminds me of a funny story. Aunt May, Pop's sister, had come to stay a few days. After her estate sale, she took turns living with different family members. She decided to bake a cake to help me out. We didn't really have recipes back then. We just shared ingredients. I think Carl and Vivian were coming for supper. I pointed to where we kept the spices, and she began adding ingredients. The last ingredient to add was the vanilla. As she took the lid off, the bottle slipped from her hand and it fell into the batter upside down. So, as she pulled the bottle out, most of it emptied into the batter. We were excited to have a nice cake for dessert. It raised so nice and looked beautiful. After supper and while doing the dishes, one by one people began to use the outhouse rather quickly. Questioning the problem, someone spotted the emptied bottle of what Aunt May thought was the vanilla instead was Fletcher's Castoria. It was the same color and size of the vanilla and shouldn't have been kept by the spices. But it was, so we all suffered the affects. I guess the laughter was worth it. The Sears catalog lost several pages in the outhouse that night.

Summer was a great time for reunions and fairs. We attended them all. In addition to the "Tandy Webb Reunion", we also created the "Nelson" reunion. Someone would go around five a.m. to the Chautauqua Park in Fairfield to hold down several picnic tables. Because reunions were such a popular thing if you didn't do so, you might not get enough tables. Food and programs were the usual agenda with everyone arriving after church. As far as fairs go, Pop would often enter our horses, Jake and Ike, in the horse pulling contests. His nephew, my cousin Chester, would be the one to drive the horses during the contests. We would watch my second cousins, Danny and Bea Mitchell ride their ponies in the different venues. I was always so proud of them and would tell everybody we were related, even though we seldom visited. They lived in another farming community.,

My favorite fair item was the pulled taffy. It was thin, perhaps two inches wide and twelve inches long and handed to you on a piece of wax paper. If it was still a little warm, it was even better. I don't recall ever buying anything to drink. Usually, someone had a gallon jug of water in their car, or they would set it under a shade tree. No one took your stuff.   I think those jugs may have been old pickle or vinegar jars wrapped with damp strips of overalls to make kind of an insulation. Everybody used the same spout. After all, we were friends!

Outhouses at the fairgrounds were no different than at home. They were a little more crowded of course. When finished you could wash your hands at the pump outside. Someone would pump while you put your hands under the pump and wash. No soap, or towel, but your dress was OK for drying. Yes, women and girls wore dresses to the fair.   The Ferris wheel and merry go round were the only rides I could enjoy without getting sick. Also, it was always interesting to hear the medicine man do his pitch. He would usually have a trick that he was going to share. But you had to wait until his pitch was done before he let you see the trick. He then would coax someone into buying his potion, and if successful two or three from the crowd might buy. No one wanted to admit they were the only one suckered into buying his home-made stuff.

My dad also found out about some new type of ice cream that came out. He said it wasn't supposed to melt as quickly as the regular ice cream. There was a new place in Fairfield that carried this type, so we drove there to taste it. In fact, we took some neighbors with us. I don't remember the name, whether it was Dairy Queen or Tastee Freeze, but we thought it was quite the thing.

One day Pop needed some rope from Sigourney and asked me to get it. I turned fourteen and had not driven twenty miles alone before, but I did that day.   All the paved roads then had curbs, and were only two lanes. It was very hard to keep from hitting the curb if you were meeting an oncoming car. I happened to pass a stopped police car at the Martinsburg Y. But he didn't pull me over.

In July I decided I needed to get a student driver's permit. I would be starting high school in the fall. I'm sure the permits were only meant to drive to school if needed. However, it became accepted as a regular license. The day I went to get my permit was extremely hot. Air conditioners were unheard of for cars, much less homes and shops. I had the windows down in the car, and the side windows opened as I drove to the Sigourney courthouse. I didn't give it a thought that someone should have driven me there as of course, I hadn't passed the test yet. I went in and took the written test. A patrolman accompanied me on the driving test. I was scared I wouldn't be able to parallel park, and therefore fail the test. Again...remember it was hot...very very hot that day. The courthouse was in the center of the town square. When the officer got in the car, he had me drive around the square until I had completed the four blocks. Then he had me pause the car in front of the courthouse and let him out. He told me to come inside and pick up my permit after I found a parking place. So just like that, I had my student license with no parallel parking.

It was almost too hot to sleep nights that summer. There were no breezes blowing day or night. Every window and door was open. We would bring our pillows and lay in front of the open door to try and get more breeze. Sometimes Pop suggested we lay out side away from the heat of the house. We would grab an Indian blanket and lay on the hard ground. I in my pajamas and Pop with a pair of overalls on, one strap undone. We would count the stars as they came out, swat mosquitoes and finally fall asleep. About two a.m. Pop would wake me and say that we should get in our beds and give our back a rest.

The next two chapters involve becoming a "farmers daughter". That is, the basic knowledge of what it took to do country work in and out of the house. The learning process probably started from birth and continued until I finished high school. So, follow me as I walk you through how things were done then.

Chapter Twenty-Six

How I Learned Do Things the Farmer's way

WASH DAY. Buckets and buckets of water had to be pumped and carried in the house. A big boiler was put on top of the fire blazing wood stove, filled with water and brought to a boil. No matter how hot the weather, we had to make a fire in the stove. When the water came to a boil, lye was added to "break" the water to make it like soft water. Before using we had to skim away the lye. It would float up to the top, and then we took a cup and skimmed it off. Otherwise too much lye could burn your hands.

The hot water was then carried down the steps in the cellar and dumped in the washer. In good weather, we opened the flap door on the porch floor and carried the water down that way. That was the shortest trip to the washer. Can you imagine carrying buckets of water down some wooden steps without tripping or spilling it? Somehow, we did. (In icy or snowy weather, we had to carry the hot water through the dining room and down the inside stairway across to the other side of the cellar). Then we had to carry the wash tub in from the wash house, down the stairs and fill with cool rinse water.

We had a gas washing machine, and it was started much like motorcycles were started. The muffler was strung across the floor and stuck out the window. It was not bad in summer but freezing in winter to have the window open and of course no heat in the basement. If you drove by the road when the washer was going, the "putt putt" could be heard for quite a distance. It was a hard job to get the washer engine going, and Pop and Bee were the only ones that could get it started. So, if you heard the" put-put" slowing down, you quickly ran down the steps and added more gas, so it wouldn't die.

The dirty clothes were sorted. Whites got washed first. Then the light-colored clothes. After that the overalls and lastly rugs and mop rags - all in the same water, just in separate loads. After the clothes had been agitated for a while, they were then hand fed through a ringer. You had to be careful not to get your hair or clothing caught in the wringer. Sometimes while trying to get the clothes to "catch" to go through the wringer, you might shove your hand a little too close and get it caught. Yes, I did. And fortunately, there was a side release bar to get my hand out. But I saw Wanda and Bee both get their arms sucked into the wringer up to their elbows before the release bar got pushed.

When it went from the wash water into the rinse water, you stomped it up and down with a plunger to get the clothes rinsed. Then you ran the clothes back through the wringer from the opposite side of the washer, to get the water out. If clothes needed to be starched, there were two buckets of hot starch. The starch we used was "Argo starch". It had to be cooked and stirred until smooth. After the first batch of clothes was in the washer, we would make the starch. One bucket was medium starch for dipping the body of a garment. Collars and cuffs of shirts or blouses, were dipped in the heavy starch. You had to have the starch hot so that it would spread evenly on the clothes. If it was too cool, it would clump. So yes, you would dip and then ring the clothes quickly so as not to burn your hands. As each load was finished, they would be carried up the stairs in the clothes basket and hung on the clothes line.

Before we hung the clothes, we took a clean wet rag and wiped around the metal clothes line to remove any dirt. A clothes pin bag was fashioned around a clothes hanger which you could slide up and down the clothes line. After hanging clothes up one day, Wanda taught me the right way to hang up clothes so as to make the clothes on the line look nice. Who would ever have thought you had to have a nice-looking clothes line? Well, I learned. The socks were mated and hung together, the overalls together, the sheets together, and so on. Whites hung together, and coloreds hung together. After that, I observed when passing people's homes, how their laundry looked on the line. Not everyone's looked as nice as ours.

Clothes on the line were checked from time to time to see if they were dry and when they were, they were brought in the house to be folded or prepared to iron. Sometimes it would start raining, and we would make a quick dash to grab the clothes from the line and bring them in the house. If they weren't completely dried, we hung up ropes throughout the house and finished drying them that way. Even in the winter, we would hang the clothes outside, and they would get partially dry, and sometimes were frozen stiff. It was always funny to see frozen long underwear flopping in the wind. They would thaw as they were finished drying in the house. It was always embarrassing to have unexpected guests pop in to visit you, with all your underwear strung in the sitting room where you had to dodge different articles of clothing to find a chair. Nothing smelled better though, then sun-dried sheets on your bed. We only had one set per bed usually. So, if the sheets weren't dry, we slept on flannel sheets until the cotton ones dried. Flannel sheets were used in winter and cotton in summer.

There is an art to sprinkling clothes. Yes, you get the clothes dry, and then you prepare them for ironing by sprinkling them. It hardly makes sense, unless you realize that it has to be an even sprinkling. We filled a glass pop bottle with water and added a sprinkling top with a cork that fit inside it. It looked like a tall salt shaker. Each piece was laid out and sprinkled evenly. The shirt collars and cuffs had to be extra damp for ironing. The items were then rolled up and placed in the laundry basket. This was done to better get the wrinkles out of the clothes when ironing. An hour or two later you could begin to iron.

We had a gas iron, as well as the flat iron's that we heated on the back of the stove. We usually had two or three irons being heated. One handle was used to transfer and disconnect from the one being used and the one being heated. Those irons were really heavy...they were all iron! The gas iron, on the other hand, was pretty good, except when light you had to adjust the flame often. Otherwise, it would flare out and burn your fingers. The wooden handle on the iron was scorched so we had to wrap rags around it. (this all changed after we got electricity) Our ironing board was made by one of my brothers in workshop. It was very, very heavy...but it lasted the duration of my father's life. Old sheets were wrapped around the board to make a padding.

From my instruction of ironing my Uncle Carl's undershorts and men's handkerchiefs, I graduated to ironing men's overalls. We didn't have to iron the solid blue ones, but we did striped ones. Pop wore striped overalls if he went into town or if someone was coming over as they were considered dressier. It doesn't sound like much of an ironing problem unless you happened to be like me and got dizzy ironing stripes. From overalls to embroidered tea towels, (now appropriately called dish towels) to the art of ironing men's starched shirts, table cloths or gathered skirts, rounded out ironing day. If for some reason something came up and you couldn't get all the ironing done that same day, you would have to shake the clothes out to prevent mildew. Then re-sprinkle them the next day.

Yes, our backs hurt a lot from working in the garden, or doing the average amount of lifting. Sometimes it was to pull the living room rug off the floor. Hang it over the clothes line and use a rug beater to get rid of the dust. Or sometimes it was taking down the lace curtains, washing them by hand to get out the coal and wood smoke, and then setting up the curtain stretcher. That was a job as we had to measure all sides of the stretcher to get the right length and width of the curtains, then fasten the curtains over those tiny nails. Starching added to the weight to lift. We might be able to stretch three or four curtains at one time depending on their thickness. It might take a day or two to dry, but it beat trying to iron them as we could never get them the right shape. I remember Wanda telling me, "lay on your back on the hot porch floor until you feel it ease the pain". That worked really good at times.

DOING DAIRY WORK. I had occasionally milked cows, but now I learned to get the cows in their stalls and put the kickers on, as the cows seemed to enjoy giving someone a swift kick. Stepping into the milk bucket was also enjoyed by an ornery cow. The first time Pop hadn't come home, and it was time to do the milking, I decided to do it. So, I put the hay in the manger and called the cows in. The cows were trained to go to their own stall, and after their heads were locked in the stanchions and the kickers on, I started milking. My dad's idea of a herd of milk cows was always seven. When the milking was finished, I had to strip the cow's teats, remove the kickers, unloose the stanchions and turn them back out of the barn. The stanchions were a thing that had to be closed when the cow went to the manger, as it kept her head inside so she didn't try to bolt while you were milking. So, I finished all that and Pop still wasn't home. The three-gallon milk buckets were full and waiting to be carried down the basement steps to run through the milk separator. I couldn't really lift two milk buckets full...one in each hand like my dad, so I did one at a time. I carried it a few steps, and set it down, and repeated the action all the way to the house. Then went back after the others. Pop suddenly came in the driveway and headed to the barn, when I hollered at him. "I've got the milking done", I said. All he said was "OK". Now I know he was proud, but he never said that. His way of letting me know he was proud would be when he told it to some of the neighbors in front of me. Like," Well, it was late when I got home from town, but thankfully Edythe had all the milking done".

Once I was in the barn alone milking. My dad had hauled hay all day filling the hay mow and was in the hog lot. I noticed Bossie acting a little unusual. I looked up and saw a three-foot long bull snake hanging over the cow's head from the hay mow. I had a full bucket of milk under that cow, but I jumped up and ran out in the hog lot. I yelled, "there is a snake in there hanging from the hay mow" ...he yelled back, "well where is your bucket of milk?" I said, "it's underneath the cow". He said, "you'd better hope the cow hasn't kicked it over". It hadn't. I loved that cow!

One of our cows tried to jump a fence and in the process cut off one of her faucets on the barb wire fence. Pop used medication on it to prevent infection and after it had healed, it was quite interesting. Normally you milk with two faucets at the same time. However, in this case, if you started milking with one faucet, the area without a faucet would automatically start pouring. (Thought you'd like some interesting facts).

There were certain ways for caring for dairy and produce. The cream was refrigerated in gallon cans until we went to town. We also had a container of cream that was for cooking, and for churning to make butter. We drank skim milk, but we used pure cream for our cereal. This is opposite of what people do today. A gallon of skimmed milk would be saved for drinking or cooking, and the rest was taken to the hogs. When our five-gallon cream cans were full and we collected several dozen eggs we would head to town. Mr. Buttery would test the cream for its fat content and check the eggs to make sure none were cracked or broken. His creamery was attached to his grocery store. If we bought groceries from him, he would give us two cents more per fat content, and two cents more for a dozen eggs. That was always fine. However, his groceries were higher. So quite often we would sell our cream and eggs and then go across the street to Mr. Miller's grocery as Pop liked that store better.

To make butter, the cream had to be a few days old. I could tell when it was ready to churn as it would get a little dry scum across the top. We had a gallon butter churn. We put enough cream in it to fill about three fourths of the jar. Then we screwed on the metal top lid which had two wooden paddles attached underneath it. In the lid was a small screen to drain off the buttermilk. There was a crank on the side of the top and a place for you to grip with your hands. I never was sure why it took longer to make butter than at other times, but it did. I learned a little rhyme as I churned to help while away the time. I would say, "eerie irie ickery um, how do wish the butter would come". I would say that over and over. When chunks of butter started to form, I would get a little excited. Then bigger chunks would come until finally, the paddles wouldn't turn any longer.

We had a butter bowl and a large concave wooden paddle, to work the butter and squeeze out all the buttermilk. The butter was pushed to the side of the bowl, then the liquid drained. When I thought it was about to be finished, I would take the salt shaker and lightly salt the mound of butter and work that through. I would then shape the butter like a mound in our round butter bowl. Some people had a little press that they could make a design. Our design was in the bottom of the bowl, which looked sort of like a sheaf of wheat. So sometimes I would turn the butter over to show that imprint. Pop liked to drink the buttermilk that was drained from the butter, but it was nothing like the buttermilk sold in stores. This buttermilk, was very thin and watery and a little cloudy looking. Just guesstimating, each batch might make a pound to a pound and half of butter, and was stored in the cupboard, not the refrigerator.

Aunt Euma had a different way of making butter. It was customary if you were invited to someone's house for a meal, to take some kind of food. Aunt Euma usually rode with us when we were going to one of hers and Pop's siblings. She would put cream in a fruit jar and shake it back and forth all the way to that person's house. When we got there, it would be ready to be drained and worked. The same results would occur if you ran a cow when it was milking time you might get small chunks of butter from her faucets.

GROCERY SHOPPING. The meat in the meat counter was never

precut and was butchered from large pieces as you told the butcher your choice of meat. The cheese was ordered and cut from about a twenty-five-pound piece. There were no grocery carts so we would carry our purchases to the counter by hand. Every item in the store was priced and marked by hand. Ladies personal items were wrapped in brown paper. By the time the clerk hand wrote each item on the grocery pad, Pop would have it added in his head. The clerk would add it, and very often Pop would say, "I think you added that wrong". He got a big charge out of knowing he had correctly added in his head. If the grocer was trying to win you as a customer, you might find a candy bar on the top of your grocery sack. The grocery man would carry your groceries to your car, which was parked right outside the door. Of course, one bag of groceries was usually all we bought. After all most people canned a lot of their meat and vegetables, and had cows for all dairy products. So, our groceries usually consisted of flour, sugar, spices, cereal, cheese, dried fruits, and Karo.

ANIMAL FEED AND STORAGE OF IT. We had a corn bin and a corn crib that was filled when the corn picking season was over. It was quite a trick to get a bucket of corn from the bottom of the crib without all the corn crashing down on you. It was kind of like a sneak attack. In the fall before the corn was picked, we would clean out the corn bin. It was smelly, and there were usually just a few ears of corn left in the bottom with the chance the remaining corn would have mildewed. If the silo or corn bin had oats in it, we could count on there being mice. So, as we would clean the bins with a shovel and broom, there would always be a nest of newborn mice. I have to admit they were really cute. All pink and about an inch long. I hated to make them see their demise, but that was part of the job. The manure pile also was sure to contain mice nests. The barn had to be cleaned of the manure and shoveled out to make a stack. When it had partially dried, it was then spread over the fields for fertilizer. There was a piece of equipment called the fertilizer spreader and woe be to the person that had to ride in the wagon part and feed the fertilizer through the spreader.

When I fed the hogs, I would call," Porgy Porgy Porgy". They would come running as I filled the trough with something from the slop bucket, or extra milk, and pitched out the corn. Sometimes we would add oats to the milk to make it thicker. The cows were called by "sic boss, sic boss".

I might add that if we were going to feed the chickens corn, we had to put the corn through the corn sheller. There was a crank on the side, and you got it cranking really good and then with the other hand you would reach down and feed the corn cob into a slot where the grinder was. You made sure the bucket was under the spout to catch the corn, and then you would get out of the way, because when the corn was all ground off the cob, it would shoot the cob back out the slot where you entered it and you could get hit in the eye.

CARING FOR CHICKENS. Gathering eggs was a daily chore seven days a week. I think I mentioned this before, but there was an art to collecting the eggs. If the old hen was sitting on the nest, you used your authority and quickly reached in under the hen to get the eggs. But if you sort of put your hand out front, and moved it back and forth, you were certain to get pecked. Also, sometimes if the nest was empty you had to check to see if snakes were getting the eggs. Then there was the ugly job of cleaning the hen's manure off the eggs. We had to wash the eggs and clean them before we put them in the crates. We would put the clean ones in the crate and separate those to be cleaned in a bucket. They were the icky ones that we hand washed. And while speaking of eggs, sometimes in the winter the eggs would freeze. Pop seemed to know when that was happening and often during the day, he would bring in some frozen eggs. We would let them thaw at room temperature and eat those, rather than sell them.

Also at times, we would have an egg that had no outside shell. They were still good. Just imagine a hardboiled egg with the inner skin that you peel off. Of course, those couldn't be sold, and those type of eggs let us know something. That meant the chickens were not getting enough oyster shell. So along with the feed, we would have to add more oyster shell for them to peck at. A fun thing for me was when the pullets would begin to lay. The eggs were often half the size, and as a child, they were saved just for me as the yolk was only a speck. That was just great as I preferred the whites or albumen.

Once in a while a hen would decide to lay her eggs out of the hen house. We would find a nest by the side of the corn crib or in the weeds. You could pretty much tell if the eggs were old and rotten if they were shiny and especially if there were a lot of eggs there. So, you might test one...throw it on the side of a shed and if it stunk...they were rotten. I heard that sometimes my brothers would have rotten egg throwing contests to see who could dodge the quickest.

The chicken feed came in maybe twenty-five-pound cloth bags. They started making the bags out of printed material and women used them to make dresses, curtains and other things. That sometimes posed a problem, because when you started sewing, you might find out there was not quite enough material, and would dash into town, hoping they still had the same print. Sometimes yes and sometimes no.

When the chickens were big enough to be "fryers", they would get weighed. We had a chicken hook which was a long wire with a hook on it, for you to grab a chicken by the leg and drag to you. You would then tie some binder twine around the chicken legs and hang them upside down on the scales. They needed to weigh between two to two and half pounds. Nothing bigger than three pounds. If that chicken was the right size the next job was to kill it. Pop used an ax. He laid the chicken on a stump of wood while hanging on to its feet, and it would lay still as he would chop its head off. Then he would hold it to keep it from flopping around while the blood drained out.

Bee's method was to wring the chicken's neck off. However, I would lay a broomstick on the back of the chicken neck and pull hard. When the head came off, I would run like crazy because it would flop all around and spray me with blood if I didn't get out of the way. I always tried to do it in a grassy area, otherwise a chicken could get pretty dirty.

Next, we had to have a bucket of hot water nearby. We would grasp the chicken by the feet and dip the chicken up and down a few times and then pull the feathers off. We usually had a container for the feathers. Now the water couldn't be too hot, or it would cook the chicken. But the water couldn't be too cool, or the feathers wouldn't come off. To quote a phrase from the Little Red Riding Hood story, "it had to be just right".

After the feathers were all plucked and put in a disposal container, the chicken head was thrown over to the hogs, and the hot water bucket emptied. Then we took the chicken in the house to clean it. Now came the difficult part of cleaning off all the pin feathers. Next, we reached down the chicken's neck and pulled out the craw. We had to be very careful of getting the whole sack out, otherwise, if it broke, we would have all the tiny stones to contend with. Then we cut off the chicken's tail and pulled out the intestines. For sure you wanted them to come out in one piece. Not only did it stink, but you had to scrub and scrub the chicken to make sure none of the feces was left on it. I am pretty sure we learned to master that withdrawal very quickly.

The next step was the process of cutting up the chicken. The feet were totally dismembered and discarded. Then the legs were removed and separated from the thigh. Next, the wings were cut off and carefully folded. Then came the breast, and the ribs. The back was broken in two, and the neck was cut off. The gizzard was next. There was a particular greenish colored sack you had to peel off it. The heart and liver were separated., and the sweet bread removed from the back. Cold water was in the dishpan, to wash and wash each piece of chicken to make sure it was clean and blood free.

We canned our chicken for many years. We had to make sure to center one drumstick in the fruit jar, and then pack the other pieces around it. They were of course sealed and canned in the wash boiler on the old range. The reason we had to center the drum stick is that once the chicken was cooked in the jars, we still wanted to get them out in whole pieces. The only way was to carefully pull the drumstick out first, and then the rest could be rescued. Once the food lockers came to town, we were able to prepare the chicken, have them wrapped in butcher paper and frozen. We paid so much a month for the locker and were given a key to use. It was left with the proprietor with our name on it. Sometimes we used the locker to freeze corn on the cob, and fruits. Later on, we used it for pork products. We still canned most of our vegetables, jams, jellies.

If people wanted to buy chickens, or we wanted to give some to town folk, we would catch a couple of chickens, put them in a gunny sack in the back seat of the car. It was nothing to ride a distance with chickens clucking. In the winter we would often kill an old hen to bake. They say it takes an old hen to make good gravy.

BUTCHERING. We didn't butcher many cows that I can recall but we did butcher hogs. My dad did not think that was something for women to watch, so neighbor men were usually on hand to help with that job. That was done in the early winter when it was freezing. Large pieces of pork were cut and hung in the wash house. A chain was hung from the ceiling, and a flat tin lid from a barrel was fastened to it next to the hog meat. That way if a rat tried to get a bite, he would slip off the lid and not be able to get anything. Before the hog was hung, certain parts were set aside to make lard. The fat was trimmed off the skin and put on the stove and cooked. When it looked like there was a lot of fat boiling out, the pieces were squeezed through a ricer and the left-over pieces were then put back on the stove, heated, and rendered once more. The rendered pieces were called cracklings and could be eaten, which we seldom did, but gave them to the chickens and dogs. Similar pieces are sold in the store today as pork rinds. Sausage was cooked and placed in fruit jars along with the grease or fat that came from them. This too could be used as lard for frying. I have never cared for sausage.

When it came time to eat some of the hog, Pop would bring it in the house and saw off pieces with a meat saw. Our favorite was the tenderloin. We would also have pork roast and pork chops. He liked hog brains. They were usually fixed the day after the hog was butchered. I would break a couple of eggs in with the brains and stir them up along with some crumbled up crackers and they looked similar to scrambled eggs. Fortunately, it wasn't a requirement for me to eat.

One part of the insides I did like was hog heart. The heart was sliced, filleted, pounded, floured and fried. If we purchased beef steak, it was fixed like people call country steak now. Most of our meats were fried with good old lard. I think that lard has come back to haunt me in my later years. Much like when the grease took a while to turn into a solid mass, all that fried food has turned into a big roll of solid fat around my middle.

CARE OF ANIMALS AT THE OLD BARN. We had sheep at the Ollie Farm. The farm grounds were split with several acres connected to the house area and then a quarter mile down the road, there were another 40 acres. This acreage had a barn and a windmill. So, for identification purposes, I'll call this the "old barn". This was also the area where our mail box was located. Quite often it befell me to check the sheep which were kept in that pasture. I remember going there once when it was dusk. I could barely see ahead of me. (we didn't use flashlights). I was bringing the sheep up to the barn for the night. One sheep had some little lambs following it. I couldn't see the lambs well enough but was getting tired of waiting for the lambs to move along. So, I thought, I'll just reach down and carry them. When I did, I discovered they were wet. I suppose they were new born and since I didn't know if they were bloody or water wet. I quickly put them down. I would lift one up on my shoe and hop along. Then stop and use the other foot. It took forever to get to the barn. When I finally got them to the barn and walked home, my Dad wondered what took me so long. When I told him. He said, "well the next time just pick them up under your arm and carry them"

When we first moved to the Ollie Farm, I discovered that we had inherited Banty chickens down at the old barn. They were so colorful. At first, we would collect the eggs from there, but then my dad decided just to let them hatch. I thought they were so cute. We also had lots of pigeons at the old barn. I can't remember who the boy was, but there were three or four of us down at the old barn, when someone said, "I hear if you put salt on a pigeon's tail you can catch them". So somehow, we got a salt shaker, and one of the boys crawled up in the haymow and was trying to put salt on the pigeon's tail. He leaned over just a little too far and fell from the hay mow to the ground. Fortunately, there was hay down there for the horses, and he had a soft landing.

I would often have to turn on the windmill at the Old Barn. For those not understanding windmills, there was a long wooden handle when released let the windmill spin and pump the water. If there wasn't much wind it might take hours. If there was a lot of wind, it might only be two or three hours to fill the horse tank. We would try not to let the water run over. Not only was it messy for a while, and wasteful, but it caused the ground to get really hard packed when the horses came up for a drink. I discovered that I could see the old barn out of my bedroom window upstairs, even though it was about a quarter mile away. From there I would check the speed of the windmill, without having to run down there. Also, I could see the Old Barn but not all the way to the ground by the water tank.

One day Pop asked me to check on the horses. So instead of going to the barn, I went upstairs and looked out the window. I didn't see any activity, so I assumed they were all right and told him so. He depended on me to oversee that. After a few days, he decided to go check on the horses himself and there lay Ike, dead by the horse tank. He was the huge white horse he used in horse pulling contests. When an animal died, a person could call the rendering works, and they would come and haul the animal away. They could use the hides, and the insides for other animal food. So, when the rendering works came out, they said the horse had been dead too long and couldn't be used. My poor dad had to dig a hole on that hard-packed ground deep enough to bury the horse as he couldn't be drug to softer ground. I felt terrible because it was my fault. I knew for him to dig in that hard ground was very hard labor, not to mention the smell. He never said a word to me, I think knowing my guilt was eating me up. Later he told me the horse must have been struck by lightning when he was getting a drink from the horse tank.

Windmills were an interesting thing. There were little wire notches to climb on all the way to the top of the windmill, should a blade need to be replaced or if it needed to be oiled. Thankfully, I never did that, although it was kind of fun to climb about half way. Being small, I would have to climb a little bit to pull the wooden latch down; and if the wind was strong, I might have to hang on to the wooden latch using all my weight to bring it down. The idea was to get the windmill to pump enough water to fill the horse tank. In addition to watering animals, the horse tank was also a source of a poor man's swimming pool. Of course, we wanted to get in while the water was fresh and had no slobber in it. One year someone gave me a swimming suit. It was wool if you can imagine, full of moth holes and made me itch terribly, but I wore it anyway.

Chapter Twenty-Seven

Gardening

I didn't care much for the planting of a garden, but it was fun to eat the final product. The ground would first be plowed, cultivated, and then run over with the drag to break up the clods. Often a regular garden hoe would have to break the clods down even farther and then it was raked to make the ground more pliable. Pop would put stakes from one end of the row to the other and then use binder twine to connect tightly between the two stakes. He then would hoe underneath that binder twine to make nice, straight rows. He used a 3-pointed hoe to make the planting row trenches.

Carrots were planted with onions in the same row as it took the carrots a long time to come up. We preferred the white icicle radishes to the red as they were much sweeter. However, we did plant both. Peas, green beans, tomatoes, leaf lettuce, cucumbers, beets, cabbage, potatoes, turnips, sweet corn, popcorn, watermelon, and muskmelon were the norm.

Why people would plant their gardens close to the road, I don't know. It would often be an easy step for some young person to jump out of the car, drop a watermelon or two when they were ripe, eat the hearts of the melons and escape.

Planting potatoes was a more tedious job. We would take our old potatoes from the cellar that had sprouts, cut off a piece with a sprout and an eye, and drop three or four pieces in a "hill". Carrots, and turnips were stored in sand in the cellar once they were harvested for winter. Turnips lasted longer than carrots. In fact, they would last all winter. I ate turnips like an apple. My dad wanted his sliced, cooked and served with butter. (we called our basement the cellar. I just tried to be dignified when I called it a basement)

Canning day was quite a process. We brought up the empty jars from the cellar, washed them and the lids and dropped them in boiling water to kill all the germs. We had the old fashioned gray lids that required jar rubbers, and those lids could be used for several years. However, the newer ones with the separate screw on lid and the flat insert was much easier and safer. The old gray lids could leak causing the canned product to spoil. Usually, my Dad would take a table knife and push down around the bottom of those lids, perhaps securing the seal a little more. We had a long-handled fork for scooping out the lids. We tried not to touch the interior of the jar, once it had been in the boiling water so it would be completely sterilized. When opening a canned item in the winter, you knew for sure it was spoiled if you heard a hissing sound. You quickly ran outside with it, because it would spray all over. Also, if the lid was loose, that indicated it wasn't sealed.

Green beans had to be picked, snapped and washed. The quart jars were then filled with the beans and covered with water up to the neck of the jar. A tablespoon of salt added on top. These jars were then put in the wash boiler on top of the cook stove, and wait for the water to come to a boil inside the jar. Once it did, it was 45 minutes for the beans. I can't remember how long it was for the other vegetables. The wash boiler could hold twenty-four jars at one time, and it set over two of the stove lids. We had to maintain enough wood to keep the water boiling in the jars. Some people had canners, and others used a pressure cooker. After my cousin's pressure cooker exploded once and scattered food all over the ceiling, I shied away from those.

Peas were picked, shelled and put in pint jars. We filled them up to the neck with water and added salt. We always served those creamed. Uck. Canned corn was also done in pints. We shucked the corn outdoors, putting the corn on the cob in big dishpans. When we had a dishpan full, we would bring it in the house, cutting the kernels off with a sharp knife letting them fall in the dishpan. We used the same process as we did peas for canning. Unfortunately, the corn would turn a sort of grey-yellow once it was canned. The remains of the cob and shucks were pitched over the fence for the hogs.

Tomatoes were blanched in hot water to slip off the skins. They were quartered and put in jars. Usually, there was enough juice from peeling the tomatoes to pour over them, so we didn't have to add water. The tomatoes that were not whole were put in another kettle. Some tomatoes had worm holes or partly rotten and only half of it good. The smell test usually let you know if you had cut off enough of the rotten part. The less than whole pieces were cooked in a kettle on top of the stove until they were almost pureed. We would then strain those and make juice. I don't think the juice had to be cooked as long, but I can't remember.

Wanda made sauerkraut and pickles. I think the pickles were called fourteen days and seven-day dill pickles. They went into a 3-gallon crock jar. Vinegar, water, and salt were the main ingredients, along with dill weed. We sometimes grew dill too. We kept the crock outside and a plate over the ingredients with a rock on top of the plate to keep the ingredients immersed. I think Wanda added something daily, although I can't be sure. She also made bread and butter pickles in pint jars. Dill pickles were done in quarts. They were scrubbed with a brush and washed before processing. She also made some pickled beets.

Jam was made from cherries, berries, strawberries and grapes. We didn't have a strawberry patch but we did have a grape arbor. The grapes were picked when they were a dark purple. Once in a while, I would crawl under the shade of the grape arbor and eat grapes and spit skins. Pop would ask for a grape pie now and then. I didn't care for that either. All our pie dough was made with flour, salt, and lard. When I was first married (living in town) I went to the store to buy lard for baking. My in-laws were used to Crisco and thought it unusual to use lard. My husband's grandmother didn't think it odd though. I made pies for Thanksgiving and took to her house. When she tasted my pie she said, "Oh this is the best crust! I bet you used lard. See how flaky it is". That made my day.

The jam had to be cooked until it thickened, put in pint jars and hot wax, (paraffin) was poured over the top of the jam to seal it. A lid was added. However, they didn't have to be processed in the washer boiler. Jelly was more tedious in that after cooking the fruit, you would have to strain it through a cloth. We used sure jell at times. Other times, it was just cooked until you held the spoon up from the kettle and it would slowly drop from the spoon. Then it was done. It consisted of fruit and lots of sugar.

Peaches, apricots, and beets were canned much the same way that tomatoes were canned. They were blanched first so that you could slip the skins, quarter the peaches, and half the apricots. Then processed. Skins were thrown to chickens or hogs. Beets lost a lot of their redness when cooked. (except for the pickled ones).

Popcorn was unique. After picking and shucking, we laid the ears of corn on our roof to let them thoroughly dry. If you didn't get all the moisture out, you would have tough popcorn. They were kept on the roof so the mice and rats wouldn't get to them. We liked the white popcorn better than the yellow popcorn, but it was harder to shell. Shelling the popcorn was hard on your hands. The kernels could literally make raw spots. We would take two ears of corn and rub them together to get a spot loosened. We usually put the shelled corn in metal containers and stored them in the cellar. We also popped our corn in lard. Get out the iron skillet, put in a couple of heaping spoons of lard, cover the bottom of the skillet with corn, put on a lid and shake the skillet until all was popped. Add salt only for seasoning.

The last of the gardening usually was digging the turnips, beets, and potatoes in the fall. When the vines started to die on top that was a good indication the potatoes had reached their full potential. Sometimes we would dig the potatoes before they got very big, like shooter marble size, and cook them with the green peas. They were tasty except for the fact they were always creamed together, and creamed peas and I were not friends.

Creamed potatoes were OK. Pop would take the hoe and dig down until he felt it hit a potato. Then he would try to scrape around the dirt very carefully. I would try to dig them up with my hands so as not to damage the potato. When I thought I had them all, he would take the hoe and dig around a little more to be sure. When that was done, and the potatoes were carried to the house, I would get out the wash-pan, fill it with water, grab the hand brush covering it with soap and try to get all the dirt out from under my fingernails.

But aside from the canning and winter prep, eating fresh was the best. Usually, we couldn't wait for the sweet corn to get ripe, so sometimes Pop would bring in field corn when it was first tender. It was good but very chewy. However, a mess of sweet corn for a meal was usually twelve ears a piece. We had a vegetable brush that we used to get the corn silks out from between the rows of corn. Now I will tell you this. The kernels were much smaller and ears shorter than you see them now so it was not a problem to down that many ears of corn at one meal.

Cucumbers, were peeled, sliced, salted and put in water. We must get every bit of the skin off. We did not add vinegar and onions in that mix as some people do today. We each had our salt dishes for radishes and carrots. Green beans were cooked with bacon. Tomatoes were also peeled and sliced. If you left any skin on the tomato, you might hear something like, "Did you notice that so and so brought some sliced tomatoes and didn't get off all the skins?" Watermelon was eaten with the juice dripping from your chin. Cantaloupe and watermelon both required the salt shaker. Potatoes could be eaten raw with salt as well. Cabbage was sliced and made into coleslaw. We used sugar, vinegar and pure cream for the dressing for the slaw. Leaf lettuce was wilted. Freshly washed, you made a mixture of hot vinegar and bacon grease to pour over the lettuce.

Black walnuts and hickory nuts probably would not be considered gardening, but we would gather the walnuts and hickory nuts, put them in the driveway and drive the car over them to remove the outside green shell. Sometimes we would put them in the corn sheller. Then you had to let the outside of the walnut dry out. If you know anything about black walnuts and hickory nuts, you know they usually have to be cracked with a hammer. I told you at Christmas time we received in our sack a variety of nuts. Bee and I would crack hazelnuts, pecans, and English walnuts with our teeth. Once in a while Bee could crack a hickory nut that way too. We didn't have nutcrackers, unless you would call a hammer and the bottom side of the flat iron one.

Chapter Twenty-Eight

High School

The next two chapters deal with my high school years. Since they pretty much all run together, I didn't really distinguish one year from another, except for "Freshman Initiation". I was given a handwritten instruction after school began that fall, as to what to wear on initiation day. A gunny sack dress, an onion necklace and blacking on my face in spots. I got the blacking from our suet in the chimney, onions probably from the cellar and a neckline was cut from the bottom of a gunnysack. Arm holes were cut on the sides. Before the day ended, we all met in the gym and went through a paddle line. All the upper grades made a tunnel with their legs straddled and each of them held a ping pong paddle. You had to crawl through this tunnel as fast as you could because each person gave you a swat. Might not sound hard, but crawling on the gym floor left your knees with floor burns. Then we each had to do a trick of some kind. My trick was to stand on my head. I was given a pair of someone's gym shorts, which happened to be pink. I couldn't stand on my head, so I was propped up against the wall, and of course, my gunny sack dress fell to the floor exposing those pink gym shorts. I was so embarrassed I cried as I was afraid the boys would think those were my underpants.

Besides the initiation, the only other outstanding thing that year was I got a boyfriend. La la la la la. His name was Frankie, and he was a sophomore. He was quite chubby, but he had the cutest dimples. During special programs in the gym, he would hold my hand. Of course, I still had my BFF who were Trilla and Betty. The special programs consisted of different groups that were booked to come for entertainment. One was the Minstrel group that put on a play. Different magicians showed us their tricks. A one man show asked someone for a penny. He then took a bottle of coke and poured it over the penny eating off the residue down to the copper. He said that's what our stomachs would look like if we drank Coke.

We always had basketball games that the whole area would come to see. People were charged fifteen cents at the door which also bought a piece of pie. The two churches in town took turns providing the pies. My dad always came to all the games. I think he came as much for the pie as for the game. There were other snacks for sale as well. The new fad was to buy a bottle of pop, and a pack of salted peanuts. You poured the peanuts down the bottle of pop and ate and drank them that way. Frankie bought me a bottle of soda pop and peanuts, but our love affair was short lived. I have no clue what happened, but one day when I smiled at him, he didn't smile back. He steered clear of me the rest of his school years. I thought it was odd, but it didn't upset me too much, except I never got another boyfriend in high school. I had a couple of "blind dates" which didn't materialize into anything. Perhaps the one thing I regretted was that Trilla and Betty both had boyfriends and I didn't. Trilla and Betty were popular with the guys. One funny thing happened later when I was a senior. Seniors were often given free tickets for dances, etc. After almost four years of no contact, Frankie called me and wanted to know if I wanted to go to a dance. Because as he said, "You did get some free tickets, didn't you?" When all the people hung up on the party line they knew at least one boy called me for a date! I didn't go, but it was nice to know he still thought of me.

Christmas that year was what Pop called "the plastic Christmas". Plastic made items were becoming more popular and available. He got each of us three girls, plastic rain coats, and plastic closets. Most houses didn't have closets, so hooks were hung on the back of the door. Pop THOUGHT he had three plastic closets, but only had two. He called Wanda aside and let her know the mistake he had made. That morning we all three opened our packages of rain coats, and only Bee and Wanda received the closets. Wanda later informed me of the problem. Pop wrapped his presents after we were in bed on Christmas Eve and discovered he was short a closet. She said he felt just terrible about the mistake. I hadn't thought a thing about it as Bee and Wanda often got things I didn't because they were older. Brownie cameras were the "in thing" for young people. That Christmas, I received two. One came from Rex as he drew my name and the other was from probably Bee or Wanda, as we three gave gifts to each other in addition to the names we drew. I returned one and got to keep the money.

We usually purchased film at the drug store to insert in the camera. There was a little round spot on the back of the camera that showed a number which represented how many pictures was left on the film. We could buy a twelve-picture film, or a twenty-four-picture film. I personally might keep two or three rolls of film before mailing them off to the "Brown's film processing company, as one stamp would cover as many as I could fit in the envelope. They had a special heavy-duty bag for mailing, and you circled on the back how many pictures you wanted to be made from each roll. Most of us usually purchased doubles as we often would give pictures away to family and friends. Most people paid by cash, placing the coins in a special pocket and the dollars in another. There was about a two week turn around, but oh what fun when they came. They always returned the negatives and if you wanted more pictures made of a certain pose, you would return the negative with your next roll of film, indicating what you wanted.

Wanda got married when I was a sophomore. How she and Harold met was interesting. Up until the summer before I was a sophomore, we only had dirt roads. That summer graders and gravel trucks passed our house daily preparing the road for gravel. Wanda and I always sat on the front porch to shell peas, snap beans, etc. We noticed that some of the truckers were young and would often honk at us. So, we made sure we shelled peas and snapped green beans daily, even if it was just enough for dinner and supper. One guy, in particular, stood out. He had red hair and was very cute and was close to Wanda's age. We would recognize him because he always wore a white t-shirt. Believe me, we ate dust as those trucks passed by, but it was worth it. So, when the truck would pass by, and the guy with the white t-shirt honked, we would wave back. I'm not sure how he knew we identified him but someone figured it out. One day nearly all the truckers had on white T-shirts and honked. I'm sure Harold got razzed that day.

I don't know much about Harold and Wanda's dating, except he gave her a portable radio for Christmas. We could listen to "Hit Parade" on Saturday evenings if the battery held out. Pop would use it to hear the stock market report at noon as to whether he should sell some of the livestock or not. We would listen to the basketball tournament when the Ollie High School girls went to state, and first thing in the morning when the news came on with this song...." oh what a beautiful morning, Oh, what a beautiful day" and the announcer would say..." And I'm sure it's even more beautiful wherever you are". "W-H-O" were the radio call letters for the Des Moines radio station.

Wanda and Harold had a private wedding, however, the community wanted to have a shower for her which was held at Pekin Methodist Church. Wanda had me hand her the gifts while someone else did the recording. I felt important. She sat on the platform, and the pews were almost filled with guests. She was well thought of.

As soon as they married, they bought a trailer house, and moved it to our yard. (By now we had electricity...that story is for later). They also bought a TV and since my dad liked to see a good fight we would go over and watch wrestling. Usually only about two channels were available. And again, while I'm on the TV subject, the doctor in Ollie had a TV in his office on main street. In the evening after he closed, he would turn the TV set toward the sidewalk and people would gather around and watch TV, even if it was mostly snow. The programs signed off before midnight.

Harold and I hit it off right away as my first brother-in-law. We teased and tormented each other. I found out he liked hazelnuts and he found out I liked olives. So, for years, I would give him hazelnuts at Christmas trying to disguise the wrap, and he would do the same with me with olives. One year he put a jar of olives in an oatmeal box and I had to guess what it was. Another year, he gave me a whole GALLON of olives. Soon in to their marriage a draft notice came for Harold. He had to quit his job, so they sold the trailer and Wanda stepped back into helping with the household chores at the house. But Harold was only gone about two weeks if I remember right, when we received a telephone call. He said, "come and pick me up". He was at the bus station. When he had his physical, they found out that Harold only had one kidney, so he was excused from the service. After his return home, he got a job in Sigourney where they rented an apartment. Now it was back to just Pop and I.

I suppose Bee felt sorry for me and somehow found out about a school teaching job and came home to fill it. She left her job in Grand Rapids, Michigan as a factory worker, applied for a country school near Fairfield and was hired. As it turned out two of her cousins' children were her students.

One day when I came home from school, it began to be very windy. Mary Poppins was not a movie yet, but somehow, I got the idea to get an umbrella and see if I could fly. My dad had inherited his mother's umbrella, which was formerly used by "Bell Boys" at a hotel. It was so big; I could hardly get it to pop open. I stood on the side of the porch, and indeed it did lift me off the porch and up for several feet. I panicked and even more so, when the wind turned the umbrella inside out. I was sure it was broken. When my feet hit the ground, I ran back in the house and tried to fix it. I don't remember if I fixed it or not, but looking outside I saw that the outhouse was demolished. That's how strong the wind was!

I didn't realize what a blessing the loss of the outhouse was. The original outhouse floor was so warped that you could never get the door closed. It was a two holer, so you used the one behind the partially opened door. And in the winter snow filled up the opening and upon seating we would get a very cold reception. We kept an old piece of broom inside the outhouse for sweeping out varmints and the snow. Anyway, that day my dad gravely said, "Girls you will have to use the barn tonight." He had to have been one amazing person because when I got home from school the next day, there stood a brand-new outhouse and he didn't buy one already made. The extra pieces of lumber and sawdust proved it. We now had a door that closed. Yippee!

Even though my sister Bee was ten years older than I, apparently, we looked quite a lot alike, and since we were the same size, we could wear each other's shirts and jackets. One incident I never lived down. Our bus driver's name was Don Winn. One day, Bee had stopped at the Ollie grocery store on her way home from school. About the same time Mr. Winn had finished his route and was in the store. He looked at her thinking it was me and said, "Didn't I just take you home?" Anyway, she thought it was funny since she was ten years older. My bus pickups went something like this. Since I didn't know when the bus was coming, I would wait in the house until I heard the bus honk. Because of inclement weather or other incidents, the bus never arrived at the same time. If I wasn't going to school that day, someone would stand out on the porch and wave the bus on.

Bee decided to take her school checks and buy a bottle gas cook stove, and matching maroon couch and chair from the Sears catalog. When the stove arrived, it had a big chunk of enamel out of the corner of it, and the couch had a chip out of one of the wooden legs. Pop puttied where the enamel was missing on the stove and it looked pretty good for a while. Eventually the putty turned yellow in color. Sears offered to send her new ones or accept a discount. She opted for the discount. We did have to have bottle gas delivered, but it seemed to last a long time. To find out when we needed to purchase more gas, we would rap on the tank and if it had a hollow sound, it was time to re-order. The stove was such a blessing. We used it for quick things in the morning when we both were going off to school. The kitchen was often quite cold, and Jack Frost made patterns on the windows by the kitchen table. So, during breakfast, we would often try and guess what the designs were. Trees, mountains and the sky were examples.

Speaking of the kitchen table it reminded me of when more of us lived at home.
My dad had a game he played to get us to come to the table quickly. We never ate until all were seated and thanked the Lord for our food. So... if you were the first one at the table, you could yell out real loud, "FIRST," or if second, "SECOND". I remember seeing some looks of amazement on our guests faces when dinner was called. We kept that up even when it was just the two of us and how we laughed.

The couch and chair that Bee bought were a wonderful addition to our parlor. Our guests now had a place to sit other than the dining room chairs, the one arm rocker, and the chair we got from Uncle Bernie. Most of our work was done standing up, so if you sat down, it was usually to eat or visit.   Probably the only time the couch was used in the winter was on Sundays or if we had overnight guests as the parlor wasn't heated on a daily basis. We had an oil stove in the parlor.   It was much cleaner than the wood, coal, and ashes. We did have a coal bin in the basement, and we only got one load of coal a year. It was nice to use especially if we had lots of snow.   Otherwise we used wood that was carried to the porch daily from the wood pile. Sometimes if there was ice on the wood pile, I couldn't break the pieces of wood apart, as they would be frozen together, so we used the coal. Coal was hard to get a fire started. Soft coal started more quickly, but hard coal burned longer. (there were two kinds to choose from).

Pop, Bee and I often engaged in a winter sport. I'm sure the animal activist would have turned us in, if there was such an organization. Mice were often a problem, especially in the winter. When no lamp was in the kitchen, and we were sitting in the dining room around the pot belly stove, we would hear noises coming from the kitchen. We had no radio, no TV, and the only sound was the crackling of the fire. So, we would spring to our feet to see if the mouse trap had any vermin. If not, the game was on. We would often catch the culprit running when we brought in the lamp. At that point, Bee would grab the yard stick and Pop the broom. I was the router. They would each lay on the floor, and I would start the chase. Pop would use the broom to slide the mouse over to Bee, and she would take a swing with the yard stick. The mouse would be batted back and forth while we squealed, "he ran behind there, or he's over here". After he had worn himself out, he was then captured and tossed over the fence. OK, so we didn't shoot a deer or a coyote, but it didn't take bullets or other ammunition, and there were no yearly license fees.

I will never forget the day we got electricity. Electric poles had been installed up and down the road for several weeks. Now all that was needed was an electrician to bring the wiring in from the road to our house and wire the house. My dad found out that my mom's nephew was an electrician. Since Aunt Euma and Uncle Carl owned the house, they were paying for the installation. They didn't think it was necessary for the barn or any outbuildings to have electricity, so we just had the basics. I was embarrassed when Aunt Euma gave us some old light fixtures she had in her basement that today would probably be worth a fortune. However, they were waaaaay out of style. We didn't have a two-way switch on the stairway; therefore, we would turn on the light from the bottom of the stairs, go upstairs and switch on a lamp. Go back downstairs and turn off the light switch. The day that my cousin Floyd was finishing up wiring was the day Bee was expecting her friend Bill from Shepherd Air Force Base to come for a furlough. We were supposed to pick him up from the bus station in Ottumwa at a certain time. However, my cousin fell through the rafters in the dining room, and we had plaster and dust everywhere. After we had swept up what we could get off the floor, and cleaned off the table, things were still covered with white dust. So, I got the bright idea to put furniture polish on the floor, use the dust mop and make it look shiny. Wrong! It made it worse. Then we tried to mop the floor, and it just wouldn't work. Usually, a person mopped the linoleum covered floor, then waxed it. But it was getting late, and Bill used a pay phone to let us know he was at the bus station waiting. So, we left the floor a swirly mess of white dust and headed off to Ottumwa. We supposed Bill had taken the bus, but instead had hitchhiked from Texas to Ottumwa and was dropped off at the bus station. He knew he could wait there and be comfortable. We picked him up and got back home about nine pm. Then we made supper. It was late, but we had lights! My cousin came back the next day and plastered and repaired and Pop found a piece of ceiling wallpaper and papered over it. It must have looked great with probably mismatched wallpaper and turn of the century light fixtures. That was soon overlooked as we had electric lights!

To say that I had a stubborn streak may have been an understatement. It was more like pouting. One year when it was just Pop and I at home for Christmas season, he didn't bring in a tree. (He probably didn't feel like climbing a tree and sawing the top off to drag in from the field). So, I said, "aren't we going to have a tree for Christmas?" He said, "well, do we need one?" I said, "well where are we going to put our presents?" Christmas Eve afternoon, he came in the house with a tree. He had been to town and purchased one for fifty cents. I decorated the tree that evening. We didn't have tree stands but used an old paint can filled with rocks or sand. The next morning, we opened our gifts, those that were mailed to us, and ones we bought for each other. Wanda invited us over for dinner later. We made a couple of other relatives stops as was the custom and then headed home to do chores. The day after Christmas when Pop was out in the barn, I took the tree down. I was so angry that we only had the tree one evening before Christmas that little more than twenty- four hours later, I took it down. When Pop came in from his chores, he saw the tree was on the porch to be chopped and ready to burn. He never said a word, and neither did I.

Chapter Twenty-Nine

Still More of the High School Years

Starting school in the fall was always exciting. The first day, students could pick desk seating. We always hoped that we could get one close to our friends. We had a large bus route though, so by the time I got there, most of the seats by my friends were taken. Entering the study hall, the first two rows of seating were for the freshman. The next two were for the sophomores, the next two for the juniors and the last ones facing the windows were for the seniors. Sometimes if the classes were small, there might be a row of empty seats to separate each grade.

The pencil sharpener was always at the front of the study hall connected to the railing. Teachers suggested we use Number Two lead pencils. It was a softer lead. On the other side of the railing was the library, which I never used. Bee had bought a consolidated encyclopedia from a traveling salesman, so I used it. This was a huge book, and everything from A-Z was in one book. It didn't have all the information that the Colliers Encyclopedia did, but enough that I could get by. I didn't study that much as people can probably tell. I hated studying. There was a certain amount I had to do though. So, I carried books home, sat at the dining room table after chores and supper dishes were done and studied. I didn't get bad grades. More of an average student, I suppose. One of the things I liked to do was write articles for the Ollie Sparkler. (our school newspaper) Those that contributed were considered reporters.

I don't remember what year it was, but Betty and Trilla got picked to be cheerleaders, but I think it was our sophomore year. The coach, who doubled as the principal, was the one who appointed them. I think Mr. Ewart, our Superintendent, felt sorry for me because he knew they were my friends and he offered me a job filling the pop machine. In Iowa, it was called pop. In Michigan it was soda. How weird. In Iowa soda was something you got at the ice cream store, for Pete sake. Anyway, I had a particular time that I was excused to go fill the pop machine down in the gym. This is when Betty and Trilla and others would practice their cheers. There was a storage room off to the side where the pop was stored in cases. The Pop machine had a slot for each flavor. So, I had to carry the twenty-four bottle cases of pop to the machine to fill it. I always had to fill it when the boys were having basketball practice. I was very embarrassed because I could barely lift those full cases and I hated for the boys to see me as a weakling. Anyway, Mr. Ewart told me I could have a bottle of pop for filling the machine. I would have to collect the money from the machine, keep a tally of what flavors and how many bottles of pop we would need to replace the ones sold. The money was then taken to the office in a bag. I always got my bottle of pop, but I would stand in the storage room to drink it. Yes, I was shy.

The students got to vote on the cheerleaders our junior year and I got voted in as a substitute. We had gold satin blouses that snapped at the bottom, so they wouldn't pull out of our slacks when we were cheering. Our slacks were black, and we wore black and white saddle oxfords one year. My senior year I became a full-time cheerleader. The outfits were furnished by the school, but we had to furnish our shoes. So, we purchased black suede oxfords. Shoes with removable kilties were "in", and Trilla discovered a place where you could purchase gold kilties and we were so cool.

Letter sweaters had big pockets, and you sewed your school emblem on the pocket, which in our case, were black sweaters and a big gold" O" for Ollie. We had different things we received awards for...a bugle for the cheerleaders, stripes for X number of years in music and band. Even a typing pin. The more stuff you had on your letter sweater, showed the more things you were involved in. Yes, I had a letter sweater. It was wool and very scratchy; however, that didn't stop me from wearing it.

Jeans were the fashion for girls to wear, that is neatly rolled up to pedal pusher length. I only had one pair of jeans. For one thing, I was so small around the waist; I was hard to fit. My classmate Nadine, gave me a pair of green jeans. (That was before the TV program Mr. Green Jeans!) She was much taller than I, and got the wrong size, which fit me perfectly. Now I had two. Most adults still thought dresses should be the preferred attire. Neon sweaters were "in", as were silk scarves to wear over our sweaters with scatter pins to hold them in place. I had a green neon sweater and pink neon anklets.

Girls would wash their hair at night, and pin curl it with bobby pins, or use metal hair rollers. If we woke up in the morning and our hair was still wet as it often was in the winter or humid weather, we would fashion a turban our curlers and go to school like that. We had no such things as hair dryers.

A permanent was an all-day event. The process in getting your hair curled was unbelievable. You had to have electric clamp like things plugged into hair rollers, and the normal setting time was four hours. They were so heavy on my head that the beauty operator would have to come and hold my head up. I saw a movie at school when electric milkers had just come in, and supposedly someone got the electric hair rollers mixed up with the milkers. So, the poor cow's faucets were curled, and the person's hair had four bunches of hair pulled up straight on their head. "Tony" and "Lilt" came out with home permanents, and that was a great innovation. They were called cold waves. Thankfully, those long days at the beauty shop with those huge contraptions were over.

Long skirts were in for a while. They came down to the ankle, and a bit of the skirt at the hem was pulled up like a triangle with lace sewed behind it to look like the olden days when your petticoat showed. Betty and Trilla had deep wine-colored corduroy dresses. I don't think they purchased them with the others knowledge. I wanted to be like them, so I bought the same colored material and a pattern. After having some trouble with it, Trillla's Mom finished it for me. I was so grateful for her kindness to me. She was a special lady.

Home EC was fun. We did sewing and cooking. I made a summer dress with a bolero. On one occasion our class cooked a complete meal and invited some of the teachers. Whoever was in charge of making the tapioca pudding burned it a little. That was to be our dessert. So, Mrs. Nihart, our teacher, had someone run down to Mr. Buttery's store and purchase a can of pineapple to disguise the burned taste. We added that to the pudding, but didn't disguise the burned flavor completely.

We had lots of slumber parties. I remember Betty and Trilla coming over several times to the house to spend the night. On occasion, if Wanda knew I was having them over, she would have a meal cooked and placed in the kitchen for me. Wow, what good sisters I had. Nadine, Carol, and Linnie also spent the night at different times. In turn, I also remember staying at Trilla, Betty's, and Carol's house. One night when we were staying at Trilla's, it got cold. We were sleeping on the fold out couch in the living room. They had an oil burner stove, so since we had one at home, I was sure I could light it. However, after it began to shake like it was going to blow up, Trilla had to awaken her Mother. I'll admit I was scared. So, the stove was left off for the night. Many people today have king size beds, but back then we only had double beds, and all three of us girls would sleep in one bed.

One slumber party was held where Nadine was babysitting. She had the approval of the children's parent's and invited all the girls from our class to come over after school as it was within walking distance. The parents of the children worked nights. Nadine's job was to arrive after school, and the parents would go to bed and sleep until about ten P.M. She cooked supper for them and us, and I was amazed that Nadine knew how to make meatloaf. We shushed around until the parents got up and went off to work. I can't imagine how they slept with nine or ten girls giggling and carrying on.

Another slumber party which involved all the girls from our class was at Carol Smith's house. I think the bus was pretty full that night as we traveled to her place. Most of us didn't ride on her bus route, so that made extra people on that bus. I don't know how we did it, but it was to be a picnic, and we all brought food. Evidently, we brought the food to school, and it set out all day. We were afraid of the potato salad that one person brought, and when that person wasn't looking, we would give a pitch with our fork of potato salad out in the grass. Carol's parents were ministers and kept certain rules. We went upstairs to the bedroom for the evening, and after dark, we decided to walk to a nearby cemetery in our night clothes. There was a porch roof that we stepped onto from the bedroom window and then slid down the posts. To get to the cemetery we had to walk over a bridge. Just as we got to the bridge, we saw a car coming, and we all got behind different beams hanging over the side. It happened to be Betty and Trilla's boyfriends thinking they would ride out to see what was going on. Apparently, they didn't see us behind the beams, or maybe we looked too ghoulish, because they didn't stop. We ran back to Carol's house, but we now had a dilemma. Her folks didn't know we had left the premises, and there was no way we could climb the porch posts and get in the bedroom, so we sheepishly and quietly had to go through the kitchen and back up the stairs to the bedroom. I don't know if Carol got in trouble the next day or not.

Riding the bus was always an experience. In the spring when it was muddy or in the winter when the snow plows only plowed the main roads, the buses couldn't always make it to everyone's house. However, the kids would egg the bus driver on by saying..." Oh, I know you can get down Doolin's Road because I saw a car pass by there". So, he would try and drive down the road and get stuck. That was the whole idea of course, so that we would be terribly late for school. Sometimes the older boys would get out and push, and the mud would spray all over their clothes. And if they didn't have on four buckle boots, their shoes would have to be cleaned before entering the school room. On at least two occasions students coaxed the driver into going down a snowy road and the bus got stuck. So, the boys agreed to get out and push. But instead of pushing it back on the road they would push it in the ditch. A couple of hours late for school was a day that left us happy.

One of the boys on the bus liked me a little bit and Christmastime that year, was when "Rudolph the Red-Nosed Reindeer" became popular. He gave me a powder dish with a reindeer statue lid. Another incident was not nice. One of the boys on the bus tried to raise up my dress, and in my trying to keep it down I sprained my hand badly. Of all the times for my dad had to be in the house when I got home, that was not the right time. When he saw my swollen hand, he headed straight for the school. The

Superintendent lived across from the school house so no doubt that's where he went. The kid was kicked off of the school bus for a few days, and I had to see the coach the next day. The reason was that he also acted as the nurse. He had me double up my fist, and he gave it a sock. Evidently, I had some fingers dislocated. He put some "Heat medicine" on it, wrapped it up and life went on. The offending kid never acted discourteously to me after that. He was just as friendly as ever. I was afraid he would be a bully, but he wasn't.

School bus chatter could be used to make sales. If you heard of someone wanting to buy something you might know where someone had that for sale. In our case, we were trying to get rid of puppies. It wasn't uncommon for people to dump dogs, especially pregnant ones by a farm house. One winter evening Pop came in the house and said someone had left us a dog. She had crawled under the porch and he wanted us to throw her some scraps as he thought she was about ready to have puppies. Sure enough, we soon found a litter. When the puppies got big enough we tried to give them away. A boy on the bus wanted a puppy to train to hunt. So, we gave him one. There was a woods not far from our house and in warm weather we kept our windows open. A year or so later, I kept hearing someone call, "Here, Edythe"...here Edythe". So, I mentioned it to the kid that had taken our puppy. Yah, he said, "I named her Edythe since we got her from you." What an honor. Glad we didn't give him a pig.

We never got rid of stray cats. They depopulated on their own. You could wake up in the night hearing the worst screams ever. You've heard of cat fights, or someone being so mad they could have scratched someone's eyes out. Well, that's what happens when there are real cat-fights. I also had a pet raccoon, but he learned how to open the latch on his cage with his paws, and then he would walk the clothes line upside down. If he got loose, he also killed the chickens. He was soon unfriended.

When cheer-leading for basketball games in other towns, we would meet at the school and ride the bus. However, we had to have our transportation to and from the school. A couple of times, I remember staying with Trilla at her grandma's house about four blocks from the school. She would fix us oatmeal in the morning and her dining and kitchen would be so nice and warm. I always wished I had relatives in the school district.

Quite often Pop would let me drive the car to school. Since the seats were low down in the car, when I pushed on the clutch and accelerator, I couldn't see out the windshield very well. The car was kept in the garage, but the garage door wasn't slide-able. In other words, we had an open garage. However, the door laid up against the side of the garage with a bit of it hanging over into the door opening. I don't know how I did it, but one day as I was backing out of the garage which was on an incline, I somehow caught the corner of the garage door in my front bumper, and it lifted it straight up and stayed on the bumper. I didn't realize that's what happened and I thought I wasn't backing up. I thought maybe I didn't have the car in reverse, until I hit the hog pen wire fence. Again, I don't know how I had the strength to lift that big heavy garage door off the bumper, but I did and propped it up against the fence. When I came home from school the night, my dad had it nailed to the side of the garage as though nothing happened. That meant he had to carry it up the incline which was probably four car lengths. He said nothing, nor did I. That was often the way Pop handled things.

I didn't consider what my dad had to do when I stayed overnight at someone's house. The chickens had to be fed, the eggs gathered and cleaned and crated. The milk separator parts put together, then dismantled, and washed after usage. The wood carried in, and the fire built. Then he had to fix his own supper. Heat the water, and wash and dry the dishes. Build a fire the next morning, fix his own breakfast and do the dishes.

Speaking of fixing the fire in the winter, I had a certain routine. When I got off the bus, I would start the fire in the kitchen and pot belly stoves. A snack was eaten while making sure the fire was "catching". I might fix a graham cracker and frosting sandwich or grab a handful of peanuts. My dad had bought a can of Spanish peanuts and as I shoved a handful in my mouth, I felt this tickling sensation. And then I saw it! The peanut can was full of red ants. After my snack, making sure the wood was "catching" and before I did chores, I would go into the parlor which was not heated. With my coat on, I would play the piano for quite a while. It seemed to keep the lonesome blues away. Sometimes my hands and the piano keys would be so cold I could hardly play. I learned that most things we do in our life help launch us into other things. If I had been told to practice the piano, I probably would not have enjoyed it. So, I really didn't realize I was practicing. I had two lessons from Mrs. Church at Round Prairie, who taught me to read the notes when I perhaps was eight years old. When I was in seventh grade, Wanda took me to Mrs. DeGood who gave me two lessons on chords. Then when I was a Junior, Mrs. Boyenk gave me two lessons on timing. So, over the years I had a total of six lessons. All that to say this… With the years of playing in the cold parlor, I learned to play well enough to assist different churches when they needed a pianist. Also, one of my friends showed me how to use the pedals on an organ, and years and years later, I played for a funeral home. No, I don't say I was self-taught. I say God blessed.

Thanks to my sister-in-law Vivian, after she graduated from high school, gave me her saxophone. She showed me the keys on the instrument. I practiced it at home that summer, and when school started, I joined the band. We even had a marching band, which Betty and I both were in. Our senior year, we got band uniforms and boy did we look sharp. (in our opinion). I was also invited to play at different churches, which was so enjoyable. When I graduated from high school, I gave the saxophone to my niece Judy, and I don't know where it went from there.

Oh, I will have to add something about songs while we are on the music subject. I guess my dad was my music agent. Without me knowing it, he would say to me; you need to get a song ready because you are supposed to sing at such and such a place. One of the places he took me was to his old church in Mt. Zion, Iowa on New Year's. I don't know what I sang, but some of the other kids sang, "Slap her down again, Pa, slap her down again," and "Don't Fence Me In." The Pastor apologized for some of the songs, saying the kids didn't get to do their school Christmas program because of the snow. Hence, they sang them there. I didn't think those songs were Christmas songs, but to each his own.

Often Pop would hear a song on the radio, and drive into Fairfield and buy the sheet music. He loved music. Naturally Gospel Music was his favorite, however, if there were "clean popular song" he enjoyed them too.   He bought songs such as, "I'm a lonely little Petunia in an Onion Patch" "Mocking Bird Hill", and "Cruising Down the River on a Sunday Afternoon."

During the winter many evenings were spent with him playing his harmonica, and I would sing. Or we would sing from an old song book in which my mother had hand written popular songs of her youth such as "The Letter Edged in Black" and "The Little Red Hen" and sing those. We also played Chinese Checkers. We had a Carom Board for playing American Checkers or Carom. I wasn't good at Carom, but Bee and Carl would play that when they lived at home. They shot the checkers with their fingers into the corner pockets, and their shooter finger would get so sore they would have to tape it. Pop also enjoyed putting puzzles together. We sometimes had one in progress on our dining room table.

Although this incident might not fit in time wise, there is always a bit of sorrow in life. Grandma Nelson passed away when I was fifteen. She was ninety-nine years old and had mentioned once her goal was to live to be one hundred. She would tell us over and over that the only bad thing she ever did in life, was to pull a little girl across the ice when she didn't want to go. She said "I've ask God to forgive me, but I can't forget it."

The viewing was at my Aunt Euma's house. My brother Carl and it was either my cousin Virgil or Clarice that sat up all night with the body. They had been told they couldn't fall asleep because mice were prone to come to dead bodies. They were really concerned about this and did their best to keep from falling asleep. Perhaps that's why they call it a "wake". I am not saying that with humor, just saying I'm glad that practice has ended.

One of the times when it was just Pop and me at home, several of the cousins had moved in the area. I'm saying within a 20-mile radius. That particular year, my cousins, (Pop's nephews) decided to have a once a month get together. Many of my cousins were old enough to be my Dad...but it was still wonderful fun for me. The first place we were invited to was Morris and Helen Nelson's house for supper. They served oyster stew and relishes. I loved the oyster stew...but the relishes included a lifelong dream. OLIVES. Since that introduction as a child when I didn't get to taste them, I finally got to eat an olive, and I loved it. The next place we gathered was at the home of Virgil and Emma Jane Bradfield. I don't remember the food, but I remember her coffee table. Most people didn't have coffee tables, so this was of great interest to me. It looked like a miniature dining room table in that it had drop leaves. And the last place I remember gathering was at William and Agnes Steele's. She served gingerbread cake with whipped cream and a maraschino cherry on top of that! Talk about the best of the best. That has also become one of my favorite desserts. Well after that year, Morris and family moved to Greenbelt, Maryland to be near his brother Wallace.

Wallace was with the FBI. I found his vocation quite interesting. He would come for a visit, but could only stay a short period as he had to constantly report back to Washington. He couldn't call from a party line, so he would have to drive 20 miles into Fairfield to use a pay phone. I talked to him about working for the FBI, and he had some papers sent to me for an application. So that school year I took "Law" for one of my classes" and "Government" for the other. The only words I can remember from my Law class is "the writ of habeas corpus." I really did enjoy those classes but opted out of going any farther to apply for the FBI.

I did quite a bit of babysitting in my high school years. I don't think the pay would have been as good as the FBI, but it required less studying. After all, I had nieces and nephews and second cousins that I took care of. Thus, I had hands on experience. Mr. Ewart would ask me to baby sit for his son Mickey, their only child. I got twenty-five cents an hour. Pop didn't like me driving back home late at night, so he said they would have to pick me up. At first, it was OK, but it was a five-mile trip out...so that made them have to drive twenty miles total to cart me back and forth. And a pretty girl Beverly who rode the same bus as I, asked me to come and spend the night while here parents had a night out. She was I believe in seventh grade and very mature, but still too young to be responsible for her siblings by herself. I believe I got two dollars for the whole night. And some neighbors down the road from us also had me baby sit...so I usually had some income.

We had track meetings at school where I was one of the ticket sellers. We got out of classes for things like that. If we had transportation we could go to see them participate at other schools. I remember one time I drove the car to Farson with Trilla and Betty. We were wanting a snack, and I said I would buy as there was an old gas station nearby. I don't remember what Betty and I got, but Trilla chose those marshmallow top cookies. They were white or pink and had coconut sprinkled over the top. The marshmallow top was then frosted to a large round vanilla wafer. After having a few bites, she pulled the marshmallow top off from the wafer, and as she did, she pulled out long worms.

I also remember driving to Sigourney once and how silly we acted. Nowadays we probably would have gotten picked up. Trilla held out a sack of candy to some young girls walking down the sidewalk as we slowly drove by. I remember the girls saying, "Haven't you ever heard you are not supposed to take candy from strangers?" so, we said, "well, we will introduce ourselves ". How wild we were!

I rode my bicycle quite a bit and decided I needed a basket for the front of it. Aunt Erma and Uncle Frankie were going to Fairfield, and they said they would get it for me. They probably called me on the phone and told me when they purchased it. (we did use the phone for some things, but not much). So, I rode my bike over to their house. It was a three-mile ride, and it was a nice day. So, I gave them the money for it, and Uncle Bernie was sitting on his porch which was right across the street from Aunt Erma's. He said, "how are you going to get that thing home?" I hadn't thought that through. I guess I thought I would pedal with it under my arm. He said, "well come over here, and I'll put it on for you." It was one that had pieces to connected to the wheel. So, it took him quite a while. I was so thankful he did that for me.

We ordered our class rings in our junior year. The cost forty-five dollars. All that year I had grumbled to myself because when Pop got the baby chickens for the brooder, I took care of them daily. In fact, I remember saying to myself, "he hasn't taken care of these chickens once. I had raised them all the way from baby chicks to full grown hens. One day after school I told him I was getting a class ring and the cost. I had pulled out my savings (a small bank made out of a tree stump that had Yankton, S.D on one side and an engraved Indian head on the other) when I went to bed intending to pay for it. But when I went down for breakfast the next morning, there lay Forty-Five Dollars. Pop said, "Well, you have raised the chickens this year, and I think we made that much when we sold the fryers." Wow was I glad I only grumbled to myself. We wouldn't have dared disrespect our parents by complaining, except my conscience knew I did.

Lunch hours at school were always fun. We could eat lunch and then walk around the school yard...or go downtown. Trilla's Mom owned a restaurant for a time, and we would often go to her restaurant to have lunch. I think we could get a plate lunch for fifty cents. I washed tables for a while at school and got my lunches free. Lunches cost thirty-five cents. As long as I washed tables, Pop said he would still pay me the thirty-five cents. However, I didn't do that too long, as I missed hanging out with my friends. Washing tables were done after all the students had eaten and it wasn't long until the lunch hour was over and I had no free time.

Sometimes buses were overloaded, and we might have to wait until a bus returned from their route and take the second bus home. A classmate Linnie also had to ride the second bus route as I did, and we would walk downtown while waiting, and buy a double Popsicle. We would split it into two pieces and take turns buying. They were a nickel.

My senior year around Christmas time I was elected to buy our Coach's Christmas gift. I drove to Ottumwa which was about twenty- two miles away, where I had shopped many times. This particular time my dad said to me. " When you park, you had better take the key out of the ignition". We ALWAYS left the key in the ignition. couldn't imagine such a thing. And what was I to do with the key? We didn't have key-chains, and girls my age didn't carry a purse. Only billfolds were used. So, I put it in my coin section and worried the whole time I would lose it. We still didn't have to lock our car doors then. I bought what I thought was the perfect gift for the Coach. It was a clock that had a little fireplace with a flickering light. Story Book Dolls were popular that year. They were dolls about ten inches high and fashioned after Goldilocks, Little Red Riding Hood and others. Wanda and Bee bought me a bride and groom story book doll for Christmas. (Each of my daughter Debbie's children used those in their weddings for decorations) And that year Trilla gave me a similar doll with a hand crocheted dress and hat for a bridesmaid. I believe Betty gave me a scrapbook. I gave Betty and Trilla compacts. Autograph books were also popular. Carl gave me one and my friends wrote little rhymes in them. One was "apple pie without any cheese, is like a kiss without a squeeze". Wanda wrote, "May God be your comfort wherever you roam. Christianity your comfort and heaven your home".

When I was a junior, I was asked to usher for the Senior Baccalaureate. It was held at the Baptist Church that year in Ollie. I felt I needed a new outfit to do that. So, I got a new suit. It turned out for good, because the next year I wore it for my senior picture. It was checkered with off white background and purple stripes. I remember how proud I felt to be asked to be the usher.

Bee taught part of the year when she came back from Grand Rapids, but for some reason after teaching half a year, they told her she didn't have enough credits to teach. Remember she only had six weeks schooling yet had taught for two full years before. During that time a lady by the name of Mrs. Bell lived about three miles from us and was looking for someone to stay nights with her. She had a winter home in Des Moines, and her summer home was near us. Her husband had passed away, and she was afraid to stay alone nights. So, someone recommended Bee to stay with her which she did until she went back to Grand Rapids to attend Nursing School. She got paid a dollar fifty a night. When she left, she recommended me, and I got the job making ten dollars a week.

Mrs. Bell would come early spring and stay until fall. I would come home from school, do the chores, gather my school clothes and spend the night. If Pop didn't need the car, I drove over there and would return home in the morning, make Pops breakfast, do the dishes and catch the bus. If he needed the car, I would ride my bike and in the morning ride three fourths a mile to her neighbors; leave my bike in their yard and flag the school bus as it passed by. Sometimes that neighbor would invite me to wait in their house. I think they were lonely, elderly people and liked my chatter.

Mrs. Bell had a radio, so evenings we would listen to Rex Skelton and I would embroider, do school work or read. She was raised in West Branch, Iowa and her brothers were buddies with Herbert Hoover, one of our Presidents. She shared stories about him and her life as a Quaker. Her farm land connected to the cemetery where her husband was buried, and she would have me take flowers from her garden to the cemetery. It was a quarter of a mile, so I would walk there, and go in and play the piano at the chapel that stood on the grounds. I just had to be back before dark for sure. While I was delivering the flowers, I began to notice some tombstones that had Pop's half-sister and half-brother names on them. That was the first time I knew where they were buried.

Speaking of cemeteries, every May it seemed like most people would congregate at the cemetery with their "Pinnies". That's Iowa talk for Peonies. We would bring buckets filled with pinnies, and jugs of water and fruit jars. Our main family cemetery is in Packwood where we have many, many relatives buried. Without planning, people would arrive at basically the same time on Memorial Day, put their flowers out for their loved ones and visit, and visit and visit with others that had arrived. We were fortunate to have lilac bushes, peonies, and hollyhocks growing around our yard that we could bring. As a child, we learned how to make a "southern belle" with hollyhocks. We got a straight pin, and pinned a partially opened bud, to the open flower part which made the skirt, and the bud was the head.

One year after Carl and Vivian had married, they invited Pop and me to ride to Michigan for Thanksgiving. Rex had just built a new house, which we wanted to see. Gordon also built one just two houses down. Rex and Gordon had been in the service together and were very close as brothers. There was lots of snow driving there and being a country girl; I couldn't get over how beautiful the stores and streets looked with their Christmas lighting. I wanted to walk the streets after dark. So, Bee drove her car down the street for several blocks and parked it. It was apparently very, very, cold, so by the time we walked and got to her car and drove back to the house, my fingers were pretty much inoperable. I was embarrassed because I couldn't even get my boots off. Bee had to assist me. Explaining about boots. We had to wear rubber boots over our shoes rain or snow to school. They always left a chafed red ring around our legs. That is until a new fad came out with a bit of faux fur around the top of the boot. I guess Pop bought me some and I was so thrilled to have some new boots. When we exited the bus, if wearing boots, we went to the mud room to leave them there. After school when I went to get my boots, they were gone and an old pair of boots was left in its place. Boots that the backs were ripped from top to bottom. That's the only time I can think of that anyone ever took anything of mine. Pop suggested I bring those boots home and he would patch them. I shed tears over that thought and think I paid for a new pair myself.

The day we started back from Michigan was a snowy day. Our neighbors were doing our chores, but we needed to get back as that made them do double duty. We had chains on our car and could plow through the highway, but many were unprepared. So, at one point the roads became blocked with stopped cars, and it was night. There seemed to be some store that was lighted about quarter mile down the road, so Pop and Carl walked to it. They thought perhaps we could take shelter there. It happened to be a country tavern so when they walked back, Pop said we could tough it out. A tavern was no place for women. Early morning a plow came through and freed us.

My Aunt Erma always had and knew about the latest things it seemed. little lady for one thing when ball point pens came out, they drove to Ft. Madison Iowa where Schaeffer pens were made. There was only so many made per day and it was first come first served and cost fifty dollars apiece back. They left early of a morning to be the first in line and we watched with fascination as she showed us how they worked.

When they moved from the farm into Linby, she had a kitchen within a kitchen: a complete prep kitchen and cabinets. Her main kitchen looked even more spotless than her farm house ever did. She also had a mangle. That was a fancy type of iron that you could sit and iron all your flat pieces and the bodices of shirts. She had ways of keeping her house cool. In the early morning before the sun shone and while it was still cool, she would close all her windows and blinds. That made the house quite shady. In front of her hassock fan, set a twenty-five block of ice in a dish pan. That would blow cool air throughout the lower level. She also took down her winter curtains and replaced them with light airy ones in the summer and even had a summer bedspread. Her wall paper was always the latest print. If you ate a meal at her house, there would always be a choice of three or four kinds of desserts. Cookies, canned fruit, cakes, pies and always ice cream. And yet with all that she weighed less than eighty pounds.

Chapter Thirty

Winding Down

The fall before my senior year, Pop decided he and I should take a trip to South Dakota with our destination my brother Cecil's. I was excited about our trip, but I was also a little disappointed because he had planned the trip over the first day of school. That meant, I didn't get to pick my desk location. Nonetheless, we packed up and left. I think Pop probably realized that this might be the last trip as father and daughter and for the first time, my Dad said, "I think we had better lock the house." In all my seventeen years we had never locked a house. So, he found a skeleton key, and locked the house.

Our first stop was in Nashua, Iowa where we visited "The Little Brown Church" made popular because of a hymn written about it. We drove through Meckling, and Vermillion staying with friends and visiting places where we had lived. An almost tragic thing happened in Vermillion. As we were leaving town, there was a little girl of perhaps seven years old standing on the sidewalk. All of a sudden, she darted off the sidewalk and ran straight in to the side of our car. Pop honked, slammed on the brakes and jumped out of the car. The little girl was hopping on one foot and crying when her Mother came running out. Instead of checking if the child was OK, she started yelling at her and gave her a spanking. Pop kept asking if she was OK and her Mama said, "she's OK." But he left his address just in case. We were both so shook up we didn't say anything for miles.

Cecil and family lived in Vale, South Dakota. which was on the other side of Rapid City. They owned a General Merchandise Store there. As we traveled along we stopped to see the corn palace in Mitchell, and then Pop saw one of those wild animal zoos. He decided we should stop and see it. However, the wild animal part turned out to be mostly snakes. He paid for me to tour it, but I think I was through the back door before he saw one cage.

Then on to Vale. While we were there, it also happened to be Pops birthday. I had money, and so I went with Cecil over to his store, and we picked out a matching shirt and trousers that I had seen some classy people wear. It was a shiny gaberdine outfit. Cecil sold it to me for his cost, which made it even nicer. Pop liked it so much that he began to wear those type of clothes when he went to town, instead of his striped overalls. I didn't see much of Billy while I was there as he herded sheep. His ride honked around three in the morning and drove him about one hundred miles to the pasture land to herd the sheep. When he came home at night, he went right to bed. He would have been fifteen, so I was pretty impressed that he worked that hard as a young guy.

Once back home, we unlocked the door and never used the key again. I arrived at school a few days after it started...my last year. I could tell Pop was thinking of perhaps a way to keep me at home after graduation. He had me go with him to pick out a new washing machine. It was an electric Maytag, and we no longer had to kick start it. He purchased a few other things also which was interesting to me, since all the old stuff still worked.

Again, I don't know how I got this honor, but settling into my senior year, I was asked to be the editor of the yearbook. Many days, I got to go down to his office and work on the yearbook instead of study hall. People were in and out of the office all day as that's where the mimeograph machine was. The mimeograph had a purple gel-like substance that you laid the paper on to copy. If you got that ink on your clothes, it was pretty much permanent. On your hands. Might be there a couple of days. That had nothing to do with making the yearbook, but I wanted to tell you that's how we made copies then. I did most of the yearbook myself which I loved doing.

One of the things we had to do was sell ads for the Yearbook, to help pay for the expenses of making it. Nadine suggested that we go to Fairfield and see if we couldn't get some merchants there to buy ads. Nadine was a very quiet, intelligent girl who played on the basketball team, ended up being the class valedictorian and was well liked by the teachers. Anyway, we asked if we could skip school to sell ads the next day and Mr. Norris said ". Pop agreed I could take the car. When we got to school that morning, Mr. Norris evidently changed his mind. Nadine said, "look, let's go anyway. You have the car and we planned on it". We skipped school and did sell several ads. The trick was to get back to school before dismissal so we could get our school assignments for the next day. As we entered the gymnasium who should we meet up with.... but Mr. Norris. He said each of you turn in a 5,000-word page by tomorrow morning on the subject he named. Well, I was hard put to get that done. With chores, supper to make, dishes to do, school make up assignments, etc., it was a job. Not only that the encyclopedia that Bee owned didn't have much on that subject. So, I copied it almost word for word. Didn't want Pop to know I skipped school, and didn't want to be expelled for copying. Fortunately, none of that happened. I don't think God was pleased with me because I didn't sleep much that night.

We also had a Junior and Senior Play each year. I loved doing acting and learned several monologues that I presented at different schools and churches. One year the teacher read a preview of a play to us which sounded so fun. The problem was it involved two hospital beds, and she had no idea how we could come up with those. Well, reach way back when I was in 3rd grade, and I remembered the Packwood school where Carl attended had a hospital bed. Also, my Aunt Euma had one. Each of those places/people was contacted, and we were afforded the beds for that purpose only. And the play was hilarious. Of course, Aunt Euma made sure to attend that play. In fact, it was such a memorable play, years later someone mentioned it to my sister Wanda.

Our Junior Year and Senior Year we had something called the Junior/Senior banquet. If I remember right we had a special dinner at a hotel in Fairfield. It was to be a formal affair, but I didn't have a formal. Bee had a friend in Grand Rapids that was willing to mail me hers, but I didn't accept that kind gesture. You didn't have to wear a formal, but almost everyone did. Martha Roop rode on the same bus with me, and although we were not close as friends, she was the kind of person that seemed to look out for the underdog. She was the star basketball player and was well known. So, I was surprised when she said to me, "don't worry about wearing a formal." Just wear your church clothes, and I will do the same. I had gotten a blue polka dot skirt and a ruffled "see through blouse" for Easter, so I wore that. She and I were the only ones without a formal. Her kindness really melted my heart. I didn't go to the banquet my Senior year. Martha had already graduated, and I just excused myself.

As Seniors, we had the privilege of taking a "Senior Trip". It was decided our trip would be to the Mark Twain Caves in Hannibal, Mo. We needed to raise money for that event. The boys came up with the money-making idea to gleaning corn from the fields. I remember bringing a gunny sack full of corn several times to school to add to the mix. We dumped our stash on the corner of the school yard daily, making a huge mountain of corn. It was then sold, and the money divvied up for the trip. I also opted to not go on the senior trip. But at least I didn't have to go to school those days. I think there were two days allowed for the trip, but it may have just been one. Since I didn't go, my memory is not clear about that.

Another skip day was when we went to Ottumwa to get our senior pictures taken. I wanted a purple blouse to go with my suit, but since I was in between children's and adults size clothes, I couldn't find one. Someone told me I needed a jewel neckline for the suit, so I found a green blouse and Wanda loaned me her rhinestone necklace to wear with it. There were fourteen in our class and by the time we each had our "picture allotted time" we managed to be out of school the entire day.

One of our English teachers, Mrs. McClure, was perhaps the oldest teacher in our high school, and she didn't have very good control of the class. One day, one of the boys in the class picked up the loafer shoe of the girl in front of him and threw it out the window. So, the teacher told him to go downstairs and outside to get it. After a few minutes, he didn't return, so one of the other boys said, "I think I'd better go down and check on him. "and this repeated until all the boys had left the room. This happened on more than one occasion.

I can't say for sure if this happened the last year of school or not, but Halloween pranks included knocking outhouses over. That's just what kids did in those days. It was a great aggravation to one particular family who owned a restaurant there in Ollie. They lived upstairs over it and had a garage in the back. If you ate at their restaurant and wanted to use the outhouse, it was actually an outhouse inside their garage. I probably don't have all the details straight, but it seems to me, the proprietor sat in his car which he parked against the garage door inside the garage so that no one could get in. Someone had a gun and shot his gas tank. It kind of ruined his business. Pop felt sorry for him and we went there for lunch once. We were the only two there.

Now school life was winding down for us. Each year a baccalaureate was held at an alternating church in Ollie. Our year was to be in the Methodist church. The school board members that year happened to have two Catholic men on the board, and they suggested the service be held at the school. Sort of an interfaith service. For those not familiar with a baccalaureate, it is a religious service held on a Sunday night to charge the Seniors to live a godly life before starting on a new path.

Well, sad to say, the Protestants rose up with a petition, and a divided class met at the Methodist church for the baccalaureate. People signed petitions, and showed up for support. My Aunt Euma was always a supporter of my school things when I was a participant. We told her that the Protestants were meeting at the church, but she and Uncle Carl got mixed up and went to the school. (The faculty met at the school with I think four of the students). She said there were only about twenty people there, while the Methodist church was so packed that people stood outside.

The next day at school, Mr. Ewart, the Superintendent, addressed the class and apologized for the disunity. I think that ended that. There were no Catholic schools in the area, so that's why the Catholic Students attended the Public School. The public school did honor them by having fish on Friday's, which was the custom for Catholics.

Graduation announcements were sent out, and excitement mounted. We were measured for our caps and gowns a few weeks before so that they would arrive at just the right time. Norman was the one to measure us and fill out the forms. Each person had to give his height and weight. When he came to me, Norman said, "what do you weigh, about a hundred pounds?" I was so thrilled he thought I weighed that much, I said, "about". In reality, I weighed seventy-nine pounds. The Seniors finished school two weeks before the other classes as the last two weeks were always designated for final exams. At this point, you either were passing or failing. No exams were needed. Before those last two weeks, the yearbooks arrived. I was really anxious to see the finished product. I had lots of compliments and one very pointed complaint.

Back then you didn't have to look for jobs. You were sought out according to your integrity and familiarity. So, before the last day of school, I had two job offers. Bee had promised me that she was coming to get me, as soon as I received my diploma. But since the mail was slow and we didn't discuss those things on the phone, I accepted one of the jobs just in case things didn't work out. However, true to her word, Bee showed up along with several of the relatives, neighbors and friends to see me graduate. Rex's and Gordon's sent my graduation gift with Bee which was a large blue suitcase. That was a good thing as I had none. While we were in our final days at school, I think each of us talked about what we were going to do. Since I had said I was going to Michigan, my classmate Nadine had told others she was going with me. However, she had never talked with me about it, so I was quite surprised. One day, I caught up with her and asked her if she indeed had said that. Her answer was "yes". Soooo that was the plan.

Bee had already rented a new house for us to live in at Hastings, Michigan where she was working at the Pennock Hospital as a nurse. She asked one of our relatives that had a cattle truck if he would move our furniture. So, we loaded the maroon colored couch and chair and her bedroom suite and headed for Michigan. Nadine was there at the designated time, and we started off. Pop had a word of prayer with us and headed to the barn head down, with his milk buckets. Even today it brings tears to my eyes when I think of how alone he must have felt. Bee left the bottle gas cook stove for him...but now the parlor was empty of furniture as well as of people.

Yes, I left home, but Pop's teachings never left me. Today I am a Christian because of his training, and for that I am so grateful. Some of you may think I had a hard life, an easy life, an interesting life, or a fun filled life. I had all of the above. There is a verse in the Bible from the Message Translation. It says, "No test or temptation that comes your way is beyond the course of what others have had to face. All you need to remember is that God will never let you down; he'll never let you be pushed past your limit; he'll always be there to help you come through it.

I began my story with, "When I was a child, I talked like a child, I thought like a child, I reasoned like a child". And now I will complete the rest of the scripture, "But when I became a man (adult), I put the ways of childhood behind me."

Made in the USA
Monee, IL
21 February 2020

22023208R00106